Russell Margerison writes ⟨...⟩ world of the air gunner, sitti⟨...⟩ Europe, wrapped in severa⟨...⟩ destructive beauty of the sc⟨...⟩ out for enemy fighters and t⟨...⟩ the chance.

After many raids Margerison's plane was shot down. Weeks on the run with the Belgian underground were followed by many months of captivity in Germany. He describes the events of January 1945 when for eighteen days nearly 1500 prisoners were marched through blizzards to another camp, surviving on an inch of soup a day. A few months later, the prisoners' new camp was "liberated" by the Russians, but the author's adventures were not yet over. When Russell Margerison came home to Lancashire, he was still six months short of his twenty-first birthday.

This second edition includes a sequel telling of his return, fifty-nine years after he was shot down, to visit the Belgians who risked everything to help him.

Margerison was born to a very poor Lancashire family and is the only survivor of six children, four of them dying before he was born. He was always happy at school but was more interested in sport than academic subjects.

He volunteered at the age of seventeen and was accepted into the air force when he reached the minimum age of eighteen in 1943. Around two years after the end of the war he married Bette Coldwell from Huddersfield, the girlfriend of Frank Moody who unfortunately perished when Russell's aircraft was shot down.

In civilian life, he served an apprenticeship as a compositor with the then *Northern Daily Telegraph* in Blackburn and spent most of his working life in printing.

Russell Margerison

Boys at War

Northway
publications

Published by Northway Publications
39 Tytherton Road, London N19 4PZ, UK.
www.northwaybooks.com

The publishers acknowledge with thanks the kind permission of
Michael Malone for the use of the original typesetting. Cover by
Raven Design. Cover photo by Charles E. Brown, courtesy of
the RAF Museum, London.

A CIP record for this book is available from the British Library

First published in 1986 by Ross Anderson Publications

This edition published 2005

ISBN 0 9537040 8 4

Printed in the UK by CPI Bookmarque, Croydon, CR0 4TD

Acknowledgements

To Richard Reeves for the use of his diaries, Gilbert McElroy for various information provided from Canada, Albert Bracegirdle, a Manchester-based ex-PoW colleague, for allowing me access to his most comprehensive diaries, the Public Records Office for their invaluable history of 625 squadron, Kelstern, and to my wife Bette for plodding on for hours on her typewriter whilst attempting to decipher my scribble, and for her constructive comments and encouragement.

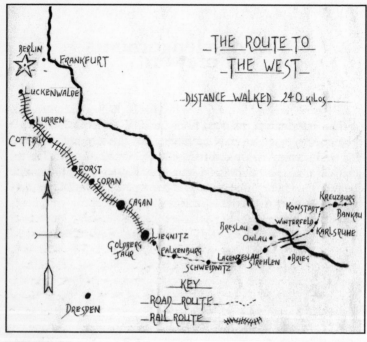

Sketch by the author of his journey as a prisoner of the Germans in the winter of 1944-45

Foreword

The experienced, mature, film and T.V. heroes, flying their
bombers through Hell and high water, whilst their gunners blasted
the German night fighters out of the sky, play no part in this factual
story of an 18-year-old's experiences, after performing the simple
task of volunteering for aircrew with the R.A.F. in early 1943, and
eventually becoming an Air Gunner.

As a youngster running and playing in the cobbled streets of
Blackburn, Lancashire, and living in one of the thousands of
rented "two-up" and "two-down" houses, which all looked alike
from within and without, and where we all shopped at the little
corner shop on "tick" ("Will you please put me dad's woodbines
in't back a book, Mr. Hardman please, 'cause me dad doesn't want
me mam to know about 'em"), I was far more interested in sport
and games than in my Secondary Modern education.

A viewpoint almost encouraged by my father, who on seeing me
preparing one evening to tackle some homework (a unique occasion
indeed), carefully picked it up, studiously screwed it into a ball,
and, with perfect aim neatly threw it into the glowing fire. "You're
at school from 9 o'clock until 4 o'clock, after that the time's your
own. Don't ever bring any more homework here." And so saying
he thus guaranteed that I would never become a bank manager –
thank God!

I did, however, after thoroughly enjoying a happy, but
uninspired childhood, possess a very strong urge to fly, and the
outbreak of war ensured that later on I would get the chance I
dreamed of. Much, I may say, to the understandable consternation
of my father, who had not only lost his wife but also six of his seven

children, I being the only remaining child. He, quite correctly, was far more interested in me making a success of the apprentice compositor's job I had fortunately managed to get on the local newspaper.

I got my way – hence the book.

Whilst it is written in the first person, I am really trying to tell the Bomber Command aircrew story, for in no way do I claim that my experiences were unique. I do, however, claim that the book is accurate. The times, names, dates, places etc are correct. But if in my researching I have slipped up on a fact, then I apologise in advance.

The laughing, boisterous, joking, but determined young men from all parts of the then Commonwealth, of whom Bomber Command aircrews were constituted, left a long and lasting impression on me, and each and everyone have their own stories to tell. Most, unfortunately, will forever remain untold. That is one reason why I wrote mine.

My four sons are the second reason. They have not the least idea of what war is all about. Amazingly their combined history lessons never touched on the Great War, let alone World War 2. If we are to prevent other wars, surely it is necessary for the younger generation to be aware of what it means. And, as I see it, if I write it then they will read it – I hope!

The story takes us briefly through training and Gunnery School in South Wales, lingers a little longer on the Operational Training Unit Stations, deals at length with certain bombing raids, climaxing with the almost inevitable shooting down, and on through the Belgian underground movement. PoW camp follows with the appalling forced march from Upper Silesia to central Germany given prominence (a story seemingly ignored by military historians); eventual release by – and skirmishes with – the Russians, before returning home a little wiser than when I left, some two-and-a-half years' earlier.

Should the reader hold strong views against mass bombing of cities and therefore populations, I could but strongly sympathise and agree. But in the 1940's we believed we were doing a good job in wreaking revenge on an enemy who had meted out the bombing on so many defended and undefended cities. So please forgive us – after all we were only boys, and please remember 55,573 of those Bomber Command boys died.

To my four sons,

COLIN, STEPHEN, RUSSELL and DALE.

Chapter One

The sun shone from a cloudless sky bathing the airfield at Stormy Down, South Wales, in its pleasant warmth. It was 11 a.m. on July 7, 1943, and I was striding out across the grass, my thoughts fully in accord with the weather, anxious to be the first of three trainees to climb aboard the Avro Anson aircraft which stood invitingly awaiting us. I had thought of little else but flying since the early days of the war and had spent hours gazing upwards each time an aircraft had trailed across the sky, enviously wishing I was in it.

At the ripe old age of eighteen years and eight months I had completed my basic training with the R.A.F. as an air-gunner and this was the first time I had been near an aircraft, let alone flown in one, so for the occasion I dressed in full flying kit complete with outer flying suit with its fur collar, fur-lined flying boots, helmet, glasses – the lot. Boy did I look the part!

As expected I reached the twin-engined machine first, totally oblivious of the wry smiles worn by the pilot and instructor accompanying the three of us, and climbed aboard. A strong sickly mixture of glycol, petrol and warm oil replaced the clean air I had recently been breathing. The temperature would have wilted tomato plants and as I paddled with difficulty through an inch-deep pool of sticky, slippery oil my visions of what the inside of a wartime aircraft looked like wilted accordingly. Sweating freely I sat on the baking hot seat, next to where the pilot sat, surrounded by perspex windows which stretched halfway down the length of the fuselage.

The other four members of the flight took their positions as the pilot, Flight Sergeant Crawford, settled down alongside me, dressed in shirt sleeve order with sleeves rolled up, tie loosened, shirt neck open and his oxygen mask, which contained his intercom, hanging loosely by the side of his carefree young face. The port engine fired into life, quickly followed by its companion, and in unison they roared as the plane vibrated in protest. We taxied across the bumpy field, turned around, halted as the pilot revved up to a cacophonous ear-shattering scream, then slowly and laboriously began moving forward, quickly gaining speed as we bounced along the rough grass till the field fell away and we were up into the bright blue with the sun beating mercilessly through the perspex.

On becoming airborne the pilot pointed to a wheel housed by the side of his seat making it obvious he wished me to turn it. This I did and found it to be no simple task. In fact it was particularly hard work, which was not surprising for I was winding up the under-carriage, and under-carriages are heavy objects to wind up! To hear the eventual "clocking" noise as the wheels finally locked up was a relief indeed, for sweat was now pouring from me.

As Stormy Down lay close to the coast it took us only a matter of minutes to reach the Bristol Channel, where shooting practice would be carried out, the object of the flight being for each gunner in turn to fire 200 rounds of ammunition at a white drogue being towed by a single-engined Martinet. Each 200 rounds was tipped with a different colour and on hitting the drogue – if one should be so lucky – a small coloured circle would be made as the bullet passed through, thus indicating each individual's number of hits.

At a height of some 5,000 ft., with the Anson rising and sinking at irregular intervals, the instructor called the first gunner to the mid-upper turret for him to try his luck. He quickly rattled off his 200 rounds and in the process filled the fuselage with cordite fumes, which when mixed with the glycol, petrol and warm oil produced the most nauseating stench – which did nothing to help my stomach, my sweating, nor my headache, which had developed during the wheel-turning episode. The second boy in the turret succeeded only in worsening the situation.

By this time I was feeling none too happy and it was with some reluctance that I left my seat to try my hand at this shooting lark. After struggling for some time to lever my slight frame up into the turret and huddled in a crouched position whilst I fiddled round my backside in order to locate the catch which allowed the seat to fall into position, I found myself sat in the smallest, smoke-filled sauna one ever saw. My head stuck up in the perspex dome like an electric light bulb in an upturned goldfish bowl. The fur collar, receiving the full attention of the sun's magnified rays, grew hotter and hotter till sweat literally dripped from the end of my nose and I found I had no room whatever for manoeuvring my foot, let alone my body.

"Commence firing in your own time," came the instructor's command as I tried to find my bearings. To my utter discomfort I discovered that when the hand grips were twisted towards oneself the guns elevated and down went the seat, twist them away, down went the guns and up went the seat. A see-saw no less. This combination of see-saw movement, the up and down motion of the plane, the stench and the heat, had the disastrous effect of turning me green. No longer was I interested in the Martinet, the drogue, or the Bristol Channel, for I never saw any of them. I simply squeezed the triggers of the two guns in order to get the whole performance over with as quickly as possible. As I did so the whole turret vibrated and shuddered, the deafening noise drowned the heavy drone of the engines and cordite fumes invaded my nostrils till I could barely breathe. It was a bedraggled, disillusioned young airman who eventually half fell out of the turret to be violently sick in that pool of oil, thus adding a further obnoxious smell to the already polluted atmosphere.

With me hanging on grimly to the framed structure of the fuselage, staring with sightless watering eyes at the floor and fervently wishing I had volunteered for work in the accounts section, we bumpily landed back at Stormy Down. An old Leading Aircraftman (he must have been all of 22) with a greasy, crumpled hat balanced precariously on his head, opened the door, took one sniff and said unsympathetically:

"Half a crown or clean it up yourself." I paid up.

Staggering back towards the billet involved passing the notice board on which I vaguely read: Flying 14.30 hours LAC Margerison. "You must be bloody joking," I said out loud. "If this is flying you can keep it." We had been airborne for just forty minutes.

With the aid of anti-sickness pills from the M.O., dressed in shirt sleeve order and making sure I was the last one in the plane, I managed to stagger through the next flight in the afternoon with my enthusiasm more than somewhat dimmed.

The Saturday found me stranded in Porthcawl at night, having missed the last bus back to camp, and in view of the fact that we had to be back by 22.30 hours or face a firing squad or something equally disastrous, I set off walking at a fast pace hoping to thumb a lift on the little-used road. I was eventually successful, the driver being no less than an old Army captain. He was a friendly sort and conversation flowed easily until, quite unexpectedly, he brought up the subject of girls. At the mention of the word sex his whole character changed for he slowed the vehicle to five miles per hour, slid as close to me as controlling the car would allow and his free hand began caressing the inside of my thigh whilst he made all kinds of improper suggestions. I felt like a young girl on her first date must feel when trying to repress the ardour of a passionate, experienced male. I gave the door of the car an almighty kick whilst depressing the handle and out I rolled onto the grass verge wishing he had not held the rank of captain.

It was, of course, well after the allotted hour when I finally arrived back at camp, thus bringing about my first charge in my short forces' career, the next fortnight's spare time being spent scrubbing floors, much to the amusement of my colleagues.

As the days went by I began looking forward to the hour-long flights, no longer noticing the smells which had at first seemed so repulsive. The whole course took on a brighter aspect and it was a delighted group of youngsters who, on August 6, 1943, paraded for the last time at Stormy Down to have their Air Gunner brevets pinned to their chests and sergeant's stripes on their arms.

* * *

The previous months had passed at such a pace I had barely had time to catch my breath.

Volunteering for Air Crew on my eighteenth birthday November, 1942, I had duly been asked to report to Padgate, still as a civilian, for the purpose of appearing before an Aircrew Selection Board. This proved to be an interesting two days for I was spun around in a chair then asked to walk along a narrow white line without wobbling off course, blow into a tube and hold the mercury up on the red line for two minutes on what looked like a great big thermometer, pegged to a chair by the back of my collar so that I could not strain forward then asked to draw what I could see on a very dimly – lit screen – all taking place in a pitch black room, and perform a hundred and one other tests all designed to decide whether or not His Majesty's Royal Air Force wished me to fly or not.

After written tests the two days culminated in my appearing in front of the selection board itself. Dry-mouthed I walked into a large room at the end of which, sat on a raised platform, was a row of old R.A.F. officers with enough decorations on their chests to cover a snooker table. I had heard from other would-be fliers that a silly question usually ended the interview, such as reported by one of the lads, "What would you do if you were on sentry duty on the fringe of a wood and were attacked by a submarine?"

"I would throw my cap at it sir," came the quick reply. He was accepted for training as Air Crew.

I had been so overawed with these high-ranking officers and concentrating so hard on the silly question I had not yet received, I barely answered a question correctly.

"How would you react if you saw a large bomb dropping directly towards you?" That was the one I was waiting for.

"Hope it was one of ours, sir."

"You have been selected for training as an Air Gunner, do you accept that?" the spokesman asked me.

"Yes sir."

"Are you aware of what you are volunteering for?"

"Yes sir."

"Very well then we shall call you up in a few weeks' time. Dismiss." I was overjoyed.

On May 10, 1943, I had reported to St. John's Wood, London, close to Lord's Cricket Ground and billeted almost directly opposite to Regents Park.

About eight of us had found ourselves on the top floor of quite a high building. On every landing of the stairs leading upwards a notice read: "In the event of the air raid siren sounding all personnel must proceed to the cellars immediately."

"If they think I'm trailing down to the cellar when there's an air raid they have another think coming," was one of the more delicately phrased objections to the notice, voiced by a number of the occupants of our room. We had, in fact, still not settled down for our first night when the sirens wailed their warning of an impending raid. This only added to the ribald comments till we could have done nothing for laughing.

An almighty bang drowned our laughter, the building shook from cellar to attic and the glass panes rattled in their sockets.

"What the . . ." Bang, another unbelievable explosion followed by a third.

The whole building had shaken and shuddered as we raced down the stairs three at a time, finally ending up huddled together in the cellar along with all the other resident trainees.

Not a bomb was dropped on London that night. The din had been made by three 4.9 anti-aircraft guns which were sited on a hillock at the rear of our mews.

The very rude welcome to the R.A.F. had not been improved by the following day when roughly six needles were put in both arms simultaneously, causing the young chap who had been put in charge of us, because he was an ex-sergeant of the Air Training Corps, to flake out whilst telling us "You must keep the arms moving chaps. You must keep the . . ." and out he had gone, sprawled on the grass of Regents Park.

"You require thirteen fillings young man," the dentist smilingly informed me, on the third day.

"Thirteen?" I had queried incredulously. "I thought they were O.K."

"They will ache when flying high. Thirteen it is."

Maybe it was just as well that I had spent only two weeks in London before being posted to an Initial Training Wing at Bridlington.

All wartime aircrew remember their period at I.T.W. with varying sentiments. It was a very intensive six-week course.

With our white flashes in our caps, which signified trainee aircrew to the initiated, we had covered the length and breadth of Bridlington from classroom to classroom at the regulation marching speed of 140 paces per minute. The various classes were planned as far apart as possible.

We had "run a mile, walked a mile" for twelve miles or so always ending up running along the pier and jumping straight into the sea. The cries of "But I can't swim corporal," made by the non-swimmers amongst us being completely ignored by the corporals in charge. However a small boat had lain in wait just in case.

Dripping wet we regularly formed up in threes outside of our terraced house billets to be told, "Outside for inspection in two minutes. Dismiss!" Those that had been late back outside were put on a charge and those that made it on time were also put on a charge for being "improperly dressed." Laces not tied or shirt lap flapping in the breeze, etc.

It was the typical forces no-win situation and sooner, rather than later, our evenings were spent polishing already highly-polished floors, dusting spotless sergeants' quarters or working in the cook-house.

We had fallen asleep at lectures and wrestled with upturned dinghies in the local swimming pool, learned our aircraft recognition and ignored, as best we could, the running in gas masks, particularly the folding of the gas capes into a roughly four-inch diameter roll.

The large, circular, yellow dinghy, we were told, was capable of holding seven men sitting with their feet pointing to the centre, and was automatically released from the housing in the wing, when the aircraft hit the water. Were they trying to tell us something? Taken into the dinghy was a surprising amount of equipment – providing one had the time – such as a small transmitter, operated by turning a handle on the top, emergency rations, a yellow block to trail in the water to give off a yellow dye, a knife which was so shaped that it would cut everything but the dinghy – it was even impossible to puncture the rubber floor – and a number of other items.

We learned to volunteer for nothing but to turn up early for meals in case there were seconds.

With our tea laced with bromide to such an extent it was unrecognisable as tea, so much excercise, and so many charges, we had neither the time, nor the will, for girl friends.

And so it was, that within three months of joining up, I was passing out as a Sergeant Air Gunner, having missed out of the curriculum a complete eight-week course. Not to say, I hasten to add, because of any special skill on my part. The answer was simple. The R.A.F. was running short of Air Gunners.

* * *

Whitchurch was an attractive village lying amidst the cultivated flats of Shropshire and it was to this pleasant, peaceful spot that we gunners had been posted after our first seven-day leave. A leave incidentally, in which I had considerable difficulty in convincing relations and friends that I was now a fully fledged sergeant. They just would not believe it was because I was brilliant! Perhaps I had better explain that all aircrew held the rank of sergeant or higher, apart from the very early days of the war.

From an individual's point of view Whitchurch was an Operational Training Unit (O.T.U.) and here pilots, navigators, wireless operators, bomb-aimers and gunners came together. The idea was that as trainees went through a set course of various training methods they met up with other air crew types and formed themselves into crews, thus giving a free choice to each individual as to whom he would eventually fly with. It was a sound method which worked well.

The flying part of our training at Whitchurch was carried out in twin-engined Whitleys. They were old, slow, cumbersome aircraft, but strong and stable, all pilots agreeing they were easy to land, possibly due to their nose-down attitude in flight. For us gunners they were a different kettle of fish entirely from the Ansons, as it was the tail turret in which we flew and one had to crawl on all-fours down a long, dark tunnel to reach it. After swinging into the turret it was necessary to close two sliding doors behind you thus completely cutting yourself off from the rest of the crew. There was also more of a sense of movement in the tail particularly when practising evasive action. We were introduced to night flying here and these flights often developed into long, cold, uncomfortable affairs. Due to the absence of a mid-upper turret, one of the gunners had to sit on the fuselage floor for half the flight, unable to see outside, with no duties to perform and slowly but surely freezing to death.

I was in class one day when the chief instructor walked in, separated us into two equal groups, and said: "You half rear gunners, the other half mid-uppers." It was as simple as that: I was destined to become a mid-upper gunner. The decision pleased me for I always considered one had a better view up on top and we no longer had those see-saw seats to contend with. Now I knew, it was possible to start looking round for someone with whom to fly. Sergeant Sawyer, a pilot, approached me a number of times but for some inexplicable reason I always put him off with some lame excuse, finally giving him an outright "No." It was as well I did for within two weeks he and his new-found crew crashed whilst taking part in a cross-country flight, all six being killed.

After being at Whitchurch just three weeks I met up with a crew short only of a mid-upper gunner and assessments on both sides were obvious. I considered it quite important to choose the right group and whilst we were chatting my thoughts were more on the individuals than the actual conversation. Was the tall, ginger-headed, ginger-moustached, pilot Fred Wade, the disciplinarian he looked? Was the smaller Canadian gunner, who was built and looked incredibly like Edward G. Robinson, going by the name of Gilbert McElroy, as tough as he appeared? And surely the wireless operator, six foot two, broad-shouldered, big-nosed, Richard Reeves, couldn't be as big a bluffer, con-man, drinker and smoker and as likeable a rascal as Cyril Leverett, the tall, thin, smiling navigator from Lancashire, said he was. Then Taffy, the bomb-aimer, said: "Being a Lancastrian Russ you might as well join us, at least we'll have one who can understand Leverett's accent. I'm buggered if we can." And so it was. I was part of a crew.

Little did I realise when being introduced just what Gib (Gilbert McElroy), Dick Reeves and I were to experience over the next eighteen months. Had I have known I would probably have opted out there and then. Dick and myself were destined to get to know each other like the best of brothers.

For some months we spent a most enjoyable time together. Dick, Gib, Lev and myself became inseparable in spite, or because, of our different accents. Gib was, as I first suspected, a no-nonsense Canadian. If you were his friend, fine, if not then watch out.

Dick, the wireless operator, who hailed from Tilbury, was a constant source of amusement. His expressive face could melt the hardest of hearts and he would persist to the point of boredom should he desire to take a certain course, usually against the wishes of his superiors, and he never failed to get his way. He was not, however, the apple of the wireless instructor's eye at Whitchurch, for time and time again he was admonished for his untidy logs and try as he would a tidy log was quite beyond him. Invariably it was ruined before take-off, for when the engines of the Whitley were primed a stream of petrol would arc through the air, saturate his log, and thus turn the ink into one huge blot, this being accompanied by a few choice phrases.

"I'll type my log out for that bugger one of these days," he said before take-off one afternoon. "I'll show him."

"If you had it printed you'd burn it with your cigarettes," I retorted.

The navigator, 25-year-old Lev from Nelson, Lancs, was prone to air sickness but had the happy knack of being able to recover immediately after being sick. One hour after take-off he had performed his ritual in the Elsan toilet and on his way back to the navigator's table stopped to ask Dick for a Q.D.M. (a request for a course to steer to reach a certain point). In order to converse above the roar of the engines he lifted one side of Dick's helmet and bawled in his ear. Dick could think of nothing but Lev's horrible sickly breath pervading his nostrils, and sickly lips pressed close to his face, until eventually, for the one and only time, he was sick – all over his hereunto clean log.

I never did see the inside of the local at Whitchurch, thanks to Gib and Dick, for prior to my having joined them Dick had begun tutoring Gib in the serious art of drinking at "The Raven", and this particular evening they had rounded off by riding their bikes round the kitchens of this establishment scattering kitchenware in all directions as they did so. For some reason the landlord, being a touchy sort, did not appreciate their manoeuvres and barred them for evermore. "That goes for your crew as well," said he.

My turn for a little light revenge for a previous episode came on the 22nd August, when we were scheduled to fly a night "bullseye". A "bullseye" was a training flight for both air and ground as it was the searchlight crews' job to try and cone us whilst over a particular area and our job to evade. As the crew stood chatting by the aircraft a smiling-faced, immaculate (even in flying clothes), Fred Wade, approached us, accompanied by an equally military-looking Army captain. Knowing of my little escapade at Stormy Down Fred turned to me.

"Russ," he said with his slight Welsh accent, "the captain is flying with us tonight in order to study the effectiveness of his searchlight battery from the air. Give him all the gen regarding parachute drill, etc."

The captain with his shiny boots, neatly pressed uniform and blancoed puttees, visibly winced at the thought of this fresh-faced, hatless young lad, dressed in oil-stained flying suit and scuffed flying boots, giving him any sort of instruction. It was my most friendly voice which asked him had he ever flown before and most hateful thoughts which rejoiced when he said "No."

Dearly wishing it was the captain from Stormy Down I began, "Should an emergency arise and baling out becomes necessary, wait for the skipper's order to abandon aircraft. Get the parachute from its stow near your seat, hold it firmly at the sides and smartly engage the two square metal brackets onto the hooks of your harness. Don't panic, make your way to the escape hatch in the nose, sit on the edge of it and roll out. Count three, then pull the chrome handle. Don't forget to inflate your Mae West on the way down by pulling the small handle housed in same in case you land in water. Land relaxed or you could break a leg."

As I went on to inform him of the dinghy drill in case we came down in the sea, I was aware of sniggers coming from the crew. The fact that we would not be over the sea was incidental. I managed to frighten myself with the elucidating details I gave him and when he eventually climbed aboard distinct ripples appeared on his forehead.

We took off at 22.00 hours with the captain comfortably settled next to the pilot. Or was he? Maybe he, like me before him, found the smell of wartime aircraft pretty unpalatable. Dick wound out his trailing aerial and against regulations found some pleasant music for us to listen to over the intercom as we set course. It took about thirty minutes of rising and falling on this very bleak night before the captain made his first visit to the Elsan. By the time the searchlights began to appear an hour later he was permanently seated on the freezing cold floor by it. The Whitley was thrown into steep diving turns by Fred in response to the instructions from the turret as the probing searchlights swung towards us, and the captain grimly held on to the Elsan, his bottom sometimes not touching the floor as we dived, then flattening very hard against it as we climbed. The seven hour trip must have seemed interminable to the man. On coming in to land Gib called from the tail turret:

"Dick, what about your . . ."

He never finished the sentence, for Dick moaned, "Christ, my trailing aerial."

Snap it went, and another aerial was lost to the R.A.F., making his fourth at Whitchurch and providing the wireless instructor with yet more ammunition to fire at him on the morrow.

We all felt sorry for the wreck of a captain who was wheeled off to sick quarters on landing, for never had I seen a man so ill from air-sickness, and all for nothing, for he had not even seen a searchlight. It left me feeling a heel. Revenge was not sweet.

To bring the crew up to full strength (seven) we still required a Flight Engineer to enable us to begin training on four-engined aircraft. We had been informed the Conversion Unit would be Blyton in Lincolnshire where we would be flying Halifaxes and later, Lancasters.

Accordingly we were duly allotted Frank Moody, from Huddersfield, a tall, slim, sharp-featured lad of nineteen. He proved easy-going and fitted in well with the rest of us in spite of the disadvantage of being a latecomer to the crew.

There was, however, a snag. Taffy, the bomb-aimer, apart from being a bit of a loner, could be rather argumentative and as a consequence crew rumblings began before we left Whitchurch. A happy crew was a successful crew was our belief.

Chapter Two

By October, 1943, the date of our arrival at Blyton, the bombing of Germany was reaching its zenith and the main item on the B.B.C. news three or four times a week was about these raids.

Morale was high and an air of expectancy hung over the whole country. Talk of a Second Front was rife. The Americans were pouring troops and equipment into Britain and there for all to see stood unguarded tanks, lining the streets in numerous towns, whilst the sight of crated aircraft stacked two high in the middle of the dual carriageways was not an unusual one. Landing craft and small ships cluttered every inlet on the East and South coasts and amongst us youngsters there was an overwhelming desire to be part of it.

The flying at Blyton was thoroughly enjoyable with each member of the crew having ample opportunity to practise his particular trade on these larger aircraft. Cross-country day and night flights, fighter affiliaton and bombing practice, at which Taffy excelled, filled our days.

The fighter affiliation was undoubtedly the biggest eye-opener we had met with so far and gave some indication as to what we were letting ourselves in for. Our next station would be an operational squadron.

The gunners' main role was to keep a sharp look-out for fighter aircraft and if attacked, to advise the pilot when to take evasive action in the fervent hope the fighter would overshoot you. "Corkscrewing" was the most effective way of providing a difficult-to-hit target. It involved throwing the aircraft into a steep dive towards the attacking fighter or searchlight, then pulling sharply up in the opposite direction – in other words twisting through the sky like a corkscrew.

We would rendezvous with a fighter at a pre-selected spot and he would then proceed to make mock attacks on us from all quarters. Our very first effort at this was with a Spitfire.

He came tearing in at us from a layer of structureless grey cloud at what seemed to me an unbelievable speed. The fighter was growing bigger by the second as I sat looking through my ring and bead illuminated sight waiting to give the order "Corkscrew starboard, go." He slid across my sights at an alarming pace and before I knew where I was his wingspan was filling my view. I screamed the order, concluding with "Go, go, go," and down roared the Halifax at the craziest of angles. The Spitfire appeared to be standing on its wingtip, but we had not lost him, for within seconds all I could see was a huge spinner and the flashing of his propellor as it came so close I could have hit him with a sponge. He flashed past us, giving a cheery wave as he did so, whilst I wiped the perspiration from my forehead.

"The stupid bastard," I said over the intercom. "Gib, how about that? You O.K."

"O.K.? For Christ's sake, I thought I was going to end up as French fries."

That became daily routine and the man that did not duck during this suicidal practice, on his first occasion at least, was a better man than I.

At this stage of our training it would be fair to say that the crews became a little cocky. Billets were rarely cleaned, hats were often not worn, coloured scarves predominated and a general lack of discipline appertained, much to our satisfaction, but not so for a few of the ground staff officers who were intensely annoyed, none more so than a ginger-headed Flight Lieutenant who tried all he could think of to instil some form of discipline into this rabble. He even went to the extent of having all crews on the square for "foot-bashing" – a thing totally unheard of. Unfortunately for him this developed into a farce as in twos and threes the lads simply drifted off with their officer companions and he was left with six or seven conscientious types and a red face.

The attraction at Blyton for the crews was quite unique. Across the drome, well inside the boundary fence, lay an old farmhouse in which lived two elderly ladies. Each day they baked pies of every variety and literally filled a massive white wood table with them.

Coffee was kept on the boil on two hobs over an open fire, the floor space being occupied by rocking chairs. No charge was made but a plate was provided if one should wish to pay. Before pay day little money found its way onto the plate but overall they did well for we were a generous lot when money was plentiful. The contest between this attraction and "square-bashing" was quite unequal and grateful thanks to these ladies are long overdue.

The Flight Lieutenant did, however, get his chance eventually. During a spell when flying was out of the question due to prolonged ground mist, Lev and myself nipped off the station intending to spend a few days at home. Unfortunately Special Constables picked us up in the Manchester Y.M.C.A. late at night and immediately despatched us back to Blyton. The ginger-headed wingless wonder smiled his delight the following morning and put us straight on a charge. We were duly marched through the Air Officer Commanding's door, our hats knocked off by the Station Warrant Officer as we entered, to be faced with no less than an Air Commodore. The Meeting lasted approximately two minutes. He said:

"I credited aircrew with more common sense. Have you no more wit than to go into a large Y.M.C.A. in the centre of Manchester at midnight without passes? Next time you do it, for Christ's sake pick a small country station where there are no S.P.s and use your bloody heads. Admonished!"

He was, needless to say, a pilot. That was the end of Ginger's attempt at discipline and he faded very much into the background, keeping a low profile during the rest of our stay.

When the ground mist lifted we moved on to the much talked about Lancaster and found to our delight that it was everything that was said and more. More manoeuvreable than the Halifax, faster, and from my point of view with excellent vision from the turret. The whole routine of "circuits and bumps," fighter affiliation, cross-country's and bombing practices was again carried out till we had just one week to go before moving out. Then it happened.

Friday, November 5, 1943, after completing a four and a half hour night cross-country in Lancaster ED 326, found us coming in to land on the long runway at Blyton. The approach by Fred was excellent and we were nicely lined up with the runway. As we were settling, the Lanc just fell out of the sky, falling some fifty or so feet. Someone shouted "power off," then we hit the tarmac of the perimeter track with an almighty crash, the whole machine juddering and shuddering violently. My sling-type seat snapped as my head tried to force its way through my shoulder blades, but instinctively I managed to get my elbows onto the ammunition canisters, which were housed at either side of the turret, before we shot back up as fast as we had fallen, to some thirty feet. Now completely out of control the Lanc hit again with sickening force, bouncing back up just as fast. Three times she bounced until finally the aircraft remained on the tarmac, careering madly along on her belly with the wheels up through the wings. The sparks were so intense that I was convinced she was burning and I jumped down into the fuselage falling flat on my face. The grating and screeching drowned all other noises. She eventually came to a jerky, silent halt, bringing about a tremendous feeling of relief.

ED 326 was no more. It lay at the end of the runway a mangled wreck. All that could break seemed to have done so. But she was not burning and six of us vacated in record time.

"Taffy, where's Taffy," someone asked.

Three of us dashed back inside to find Taffy still in the nose. He had removed the escape hatch but was so shocked to find tarmac just three inches below him that he could not move.

By pure luck no-one was seriously injured but a look round the young ashen faces in the M.O. room a little later told its own story, some were more affected than others and a crash of such severity would not be easily forgotten. In fact it was the beginning of the end for this crew as we knew it.

Shock treatment was administered by Sgt. Bill Hawson, N.C.O. i/c sick quarters. Bill, as he later informed me, was in charge from September '43 to September '44, in which period he attended no fewer than 120 crashes from Blyton, many of them fatal. Such were the casualties that a racket developed with the supply of coffins to the station which also involved charges for laying out the dead. The individual responsible was eventually rumbled by Bill and made to pay back to the R.A.F. a considerable sum of money. Just how mercenary can one get?

"Just one of those things," Gib was saying in the Mess the following day.

"But surely someone must have slipped up. Do you think Frank shut off power too early? How the hell did he end up sprawled over my table?" Lev interjected. "After all, landing and taking off is a joint effort of pilot and engineer."

Dick and I remained silent. We had all been reluctant to discuss it with Fred and Frank and there had been a distinct reticence on their part to give an explanation.

Finally I said, "Let's just forget it. Their confidence has taken a beating and it won't help if we stir it up. The chances of it happening again are nil. How many have we known where it's happened twice? None."

The matter rested at that. I was soon proved wrong.

Over the next four days we flew three apprehensive check flights with perfection and this brought us to the end of the course. The C.O. posted us to 166 Squadron, Kirmington, Lincolnshire. The big time had arrived! We were going on operations.

Exactly seven days after the crash, Friday, November 12, to be precise, we were landing at Kirmington after completing our first night familiarisation flight from that station when a copybook of the first crash was achieved. It was identical except that this time, as we scraped madly down the runway, a crash-tender was actually speeding alongside with its search-light on us, giving me an even more frightening sensation that the whole thing was about to explode. The Lanc eventually slewed round to face the way we had come, another crumpled mess containing seven shaking men.

Fred was the last out. He was a changed man. His face was wrinkled where wrinkles had never appeared before. The totally shattered pilot with a worried, yet vacant expression, came slowly towards the group of us and quietly muttered, "What a careless bugger I am."

No-one spoke. It was obvious to all this was the end for Fred Wade.

It was with mixed feelings that goodbyes were said the following day. Fred had been both friend and gentleman to us all. We had had the utmost confidence in him up to eight days ago. Now all that had gone. The sorry farewells were genuine but necessary.

Although the number of crashes on the training stations were high, it will forever be a mystery to me why the figures were not a great deal higher. The training was of a very high standard but, in a war situation, youngsters were thrown in at the deep end in every form of military life, and pilots were no exception. We, who did not actually handle the aircraft, could get away with making mistakes. Not so the pilot. Within weeks of leaving twin-engined aircraft they were given four-engined monsters to fly, and fly them in appalling weather conditions which would have grounded civil aeroplanes just three years' earlier.

We were all novices at the flying game and no-one involved considered it a disgrace for the pilot to have a "prang" or two. In fact it was treated as something of a joke, providing it was not too serious, and that was purely the luck of the draw.

Within a few days of our losing Fred, Lev went down with appendicitis. We never flew with him again.

A depressed and depleted crew went on leave. Two members down and not an operation done. The big time had not arrived!

Chapter Three

It was to be the 20th January before we flew again from our new station, Lindholme, near Doncaster, the intervening period being occupied by numerous trips into Doncaster, mainly spent in Silvio's Cafe followed by the Green Dragon, a lively pub in the High Street.

Lindholme itself was a very busy conversion unit and we felt very much outside of it all. A pilot and navigator would have to be found, but where on a drome specialising on crews converting from Halifaxes to Lancasters? At varying times we were asked to have a chat with a few spare pilots in accordance with the R.A.F.'s policy of free choice, but none met with our approval. One Flight Lieutenant from Coastal Command actually expected to be called "Sir" even when flying. His chances were nil.

Eventually, by pure accident, we met 1st Lt. Max Dowden of the U.S.A.A.F. who had joined the R.C.A.F. before America entered the war. He was a tall, rangy, craggy-faced man from Santa Cruz, California. We chattered at length with this Yank as he lay sprawled on his bunk eyeing the five of us, a cigarette dangling from his long fingers. We were immediately impressed with him even if he was an "old man" of twenty-eight years.

"So us guys are going to crack it together, eh? Welcome aboard. Meet my room-mate Dave Weepers," Max said, sweeping his arm to the doorway where a young chap had just entered.

The navigator's brevet and the word Canada on his shoulder told its own story.

"Oh no. Bloody hell. Don't tell me we've going to have another Canadian with us," Dick said delicately. "We've enough with this mad bugger," nodding at Gib.

Handsome Dave smiled slowly, lifted his hand which was holding his officer's hat and waved it at Dick.

"You don't deserve me you big bastard, but they've sent me over here to show you Limeys the way around."

We were a crew once more.

Our Conversion Unit training began all over again, with the first flights in Halifaxes going well. Our new skipper experienced no difficulty whatever and was soon flying solo.

The night of February 21, whilst starting humorously, brought the downfall of another member of our crew.

We took off for a cross-country from Lindholme, slowly climbing to 18,000 feet. Dick, busy taking loop bearings and such like, was feeding both navigator and pilot with the necessary information and whilst doing so became engrossed in Dave's charts, which were illuminated by a small circular light. All he could see was a series of meaningless little squiggles. Thinking to himself this was a funny way these Canadians had of navigating, he moved up front, climbing over the bulkhead as he went and squeezing to the back of Frank, who sat illuminated with the ghostly green glow of a hundred-and-one dials, leaned over to Max and shouted in his ear:

"We've got a right silly bugger here. We're supposed to be flying a precise course and Dave's drawing cartoons on his charts."

"Keep your eye on him Dick," said the skipper, nonplussed.

On his way back he found the squiggles had developed into long sprawling lines and circles covering the whole of the charts, and as he watched the drawings became more pronounced until Dave's pencil shot off the table and he slumped over unconscious. All purely a slight slip on the part of our faithful wireless operator, for whilst passing Dave the slips of paper he had contrived unwittingly to disconnect Dave's oxygen supply. Great guffaws of laughter filled the aircraft when he announced over the intercom what had happened.

Things were soon restored to normal – if one can describe normal as being at 18,000 feet in a bitterly cold aircraft, on a pitch black night and hopelessly lost. Dick now found himself working like a Trojan getting Q.D.M.s and fixes in order to discover our whereabouts.

An ominous crack, like the sound of a rifle firing, coincided with the port inboard engine bursting into flame. Fire streaked over the wing, hugging it as if afraid to leave. Taffy jettisoned the escape hatch and donned his parachute.

"Feather inboard port engine," drawled Max as he put the aircraft into a dive.

Thankfully the engine extinguished itself during the dive and no harm was done apart from the cold draught caused by the removal of the escape hatch. We returned to base by the shortest possible route and landed on three engines.

This was Taffy's last flight with us. Rightly or wrongly he had got rid of the escape hatch in readiness for baling out, but the rest of us held the view that he ought to have done nothing without specific orders from the pilot. Panic in the air could not be tolerated, seven lives were at stake, not to mention the aircraft, and by now we had been thoroughly brain-washed into never panicking no matter what the circumstances. Truth to tell it was the opportunity we had been waiting for. Taffy himself joined another crew with which, I believe, he was more content.

Within days Taffy was replaced as bomb-aimer by yet another Canadian, Arthur Brickenden, who before joining up was at medical school in Toronto. One American, three Canadians and three English lads became our final crew.

Our nights in Doncaster carried on much as before but with all seven of us now. Max soon proved he could handle the drinking situation and on occasions would get quite merry but on the whole he was careful not to overdo it, as were Dave and "Brick" the new bomb-aimer. Dull moments, however, did not exist, as the Canadian Army sergeant who felt Dick urinating down his leg one night whilst engaged in conversation with myself and Gib in the toilet of "The Green Dragon" would vouch for. Apparently wetting down someone's leg is not the normal function in Canada and the sergeant was very, very displeased.

He chased open-flies Dick halfway round Doncaster without catching the long-legged brute.

During this mêlée Gib went missing and search as we would no trace could we find. In desperation Max and I called at the local police station and sure enough there he was, sat in the corner of a cell down the stairs wearing anything but a worried expression. I handed him a bag of fish and chips through the bars, saying:

"At least they've got you in your rightful place McElroy. These lads'll keep you quiet. What you bin doin' anyway?"

"Piss off Margerison while I eat these," was all the thanks I got.

21

Apparently he had been calling a barmaid an "old bag", and she had reported him to the police. Not getting much change out of him the police had put him there to cool off. Max went into a long-winded rubbishy explanation as to how in Canada the words "old bag" meant something totally different from over here and finally he was let out in time for us all to catch the last bus back to camp.

* * *

"Brick's" first trip with us on a night cross-country was an initiation not of the best order and our roughest so far.

We had dog-legged round a route from Lindholme to Worksop–Barmouth – Thame – Winchester – Taunton – Bury St. Edmunds – back to base, at a height of 20,000 feet, the last fifty miles or so being flown on the white-topped hilly crest of some filthy-looking cumulo-nimbus cloud. Not a break in the great masses could be found, leaving us no alternative but to come down through it. This we had experienced before, as all fliers do sooner or later, but not so "Brick". On descending, the Halifax was enveloped in dirty grey balls of cotton wool, the threshing propellors succeeding only in stirring up the swirling mass. Vision was nil. The feeling was one of driving in the thickest possible fog at 200 m.p.h. not even seeing the white line and not knowing where the road bends.

Ice began to pile up on all leading edges, including the windscreen and the back of my domed turret. The speed ice builds up at has to be seen to be believed; one can watch it piling up a half inch or so at a time. Within minutes inches of ice had moulded itself to the aircraft and as it did so the plane became more and more unstable, the aerodynamics being severely affected.

A bumpy descent was getting worse by the minute when an ear-splitting crack accompanied by a brilliant, blinding flash, illuminated the compact area in which we were flying. Down went the aircraft at that sort of angle which renders any physical movement impossible and the engines screamed.

My first thoughts convinced me that we had exploded in mid-air and could I have moved I would most certainly have clipped on my 'chute and jumped, but realisation that we were in fact still in one piece – even if at an abnormally steep angle – brought home the fact that we had been struck by lightning.

I sat there tight-lipped and helpless, the blood rushing to my head, not even conscious of my feet touching anything solid, hoping sincerely that at least Dave had been right when he had told

22

Max before coming down that no high ground existed in the vicinity.

Lights suddenly twinkled in the distance as we broke out of cloud at an alarming speed, then came the expected crack-cracking as the ice flew off the aircraft in large chunks. Simultaneously Max heaved the great machine out of its headlong rush for the ground and we levelled out at some 200 feet, whilst globules of water streamed round my turret from the melting ice.

The welcoming lights of Lindholme never looked better. The Halifax had done us proud and had stood up well to the hardest buffeting we had experienced. On examination the only damage suffered was the loss of the trailing aerial which had been cut off where it entered the aircraft. Max had been temporarily blinded by the flash, and had become completely disorientated.

Throughout the whole episode not one word had been spoken. We had at last achieved the essential – discipline in the air. Discipline on the ground was purely incidental.

The initials L.M.F. were well known in aircrew circles and periodically cropped up in conversation. It was a distasteful subject for it stood for "lack of moral fibre". As will always happen in wartime some men (or should I say boys, for that is what we were) crack, and can go on no farther. When this happened the boy in question was sent to the Isle of Sheppey, reduced to the rank of AC2 and treated shabbily by men who had never set foot in an aircraft. This never ceased to annoy us and at no time did I ever hear one word of reproach against the "guilty" person for we were only too well aware that it could happen to any of us. It lies purely in the mental make-up of an individual and one never knows how he will react to a given set of circumstances until tested. Flying was a peculiar job, as indeed were many jobs in the forces. One day a flight would be so thoroughly enjoyable one wanted to do it for ever, the next could be so frightening you never wanted to see another plane.

L.M.F. could work very unfairly when in fact the man lacked anything but moral fibre. Such was the case at Lindholme one afternoon when a Lanc taxied into the back of another, whilst on the perimeter track, slicing through the rear turret and stopping a few feet short of the mid-upper turret, which was housed well to the rear in the Lancaster. The nineteen-year-old mid-upper gunner, whom I knew well, sat there petrified, staring speechless at this huge monster, so close to his face, which had just gobbled up his best pal.

He eventually climbed out, walked slowly over to the flights section, ignoring everyone around, threw his helmet on the gunnery leader's table and said simply:

"I shall never climb into an aircraft again."

That boy was posted immediately L.M.F. in accordance with the rules of the R.A.F. The Air Ministry were sticking rigidly to their view that all aircrew were volunteers and knew what they had volunteered to do.

It was with some trepidation, on the part of the remaining four of us who had been involved in the crashes, that we once again climbed into a Lancaster. Four long months had passed since those eventful seven days.

"Now watch it Max," Frank earnestly pleaded. "As soon as the wheels touch, stick forward or she'll bounce like a tennis ball."

Gib, lending strength to Frank's request, commented, "Yeah, and once she bounces there's no holding her. We don't want scattering all over the runway again."

Dick and I added our chippings leaving Max in no doubt as to how we felt.

He could have turned on us and asked who were we to tell him how to land a plane. A man who was flying as a bush pilot before hostilities started and had an envious number of flying hours in when he joined us. He could have pointed out it was we who were the novices, as indeed applied to most of the instructors, for he had had more time in the air than they.

But no, with a knowing, understanding smile, born of experience, this lovable, fractionally boastful, Yank said, "What kind of landing do you guys want – two or three point? And for every bounce over six inches there's a pound per man."

Needless to say we got not one penny piece. For the first few landings Frank, Dick, Gib and myself sat in crash positions in the fuselage, pasty-faced and quiet. Each of us had his own memories of the unpleasant few minutes when life itself had been in the balance. One by one we drifted to our various positions as Max landed and took off again and again with perfection. It was a great relief for all of us. We were back home!

Within two weeks our training at Lindholme was complete and our long awaited posting to squadron arrived.

Chapter Four

Some eighteen miles inland from the seaside resort of Mablethorpe, on the East coast of England, off the Louth to Market Rasen road, the tiny village of Kelstern is to be found. A stranger, driving along the countless country lanes in the area, could be forgiven for passing through it without a second glance, but the more observant may notice, a mile outside the village, a small memorial stone, often carrying a spray of flowers, standing on the corner of a T junction. It reads simply:

625 Squadron, Royal Air Force, October 1943 – April 1945

"We Avenge"

A more peaceful spot than this plateau, surrounded on all sides by gently rolling plains as far as the eye can see, cannot be found in the length and breadth of this old country.

It was not so on March 11th, 1944 when the crew of 1st Lt. Max Dowden arrived to begin their tour of operations, for they found the bustling, purposeful aerodrome, lying as it did in the very heart of "bomber country", a hive of activity.

The whole atmosphere of this operational squadron was totally different from that on training stations. The ground staff were noticeably friendlier and more helpful, getting to know the smaller number of crews presented no problem, morale was unbelievably high and the aircraft a delight in both cleanliness and maintenance. It was soon obvious that efficiency was the key word – it was also soon obvious that it needed to be!

We flew four familiarisation flights in order to become accustomed to the airfield and its surrounding landmarks – of which there were precious few – and found to our amazement that the outer circle lights formed three links in a chain. Kelstern was in the centre, Binbrook, a large Australian squadron, on one side and Ludford Magna – often known as "Mudford Magna" for the drome was forever a sea of mud, on the other, the lights actually overlapping. "One Group" Bomber Command's 'dromes were to be found in every direction in this part of Lincolnshire.

625 Squadron was a comparatively small one consisting of some twenty-two Lancasters, all of which were never operational at the same time, two or three invariably being in the huge hangars for repairs or maintenance. A total of 25 pilots and 153 other aircrew made up the flying strength.

Four days after arrival the seven of us stood by the perimeter track in the fading light of a dull, chilly evening as nineteen Lancs rolled slowly along, line astern, like a battle fleet of the Navy on manoeuvres. But this was no manoeuvre. Their bellies heavy with bombs, these huge proud monsters were about to take off to drop their loads on Stuttgart. Their noisy but impressive march-past included "A Apple", with its great big letter "A" commencing the word "Avenger" which tapered down the whole length of the fuselage. "T Tommy" was similarly painted with the name "Trespasser", and "S Sugar" with a huge, nude, curvaceous blonde, her panties embarrassingly around her ankles, carrying the words "We drop them by night".

Slowly the leader turned onto the runway, up went the green flare, fired from the chequered caravan at the beginning of the runway and off she trundled with a roar which drowned the noise of the engines of her waiting companions. It slowly grew smaller as it gathered speed, eventually staggering into the air at the far end, struggling with the tremendous weight to defy the laws of gravity.

When all aircraft had become airborne Max turned to us, "Well you guys, sure as hell it'll be our turn on the next one. Feel ready for it?"

"Ready or not it's too late to turn back now, that's for sure," I answered.

Dick, who had been bitterly disappointed to leave 166 Squadron so quickly, particularly when he realised they had done thirteen Berlin raids in a row, said, "I wish to hell I was with them now. I want some ops in my log book. I'll tell you boys if we are not on the next I'll blow my top."

"You'll be scared stiff when you get over there Reeves, so don't be in such a goddarn hurry," Dave declared.

"Rubbish," Dick spat out, "don't you forget I was in Tilbury during the blitz and saw what those bastards were doing and I swore then if I got half a chance I'd get some of my own back."

Some of us could not help but chuckle at Dick's patriotism. He came out with so much at different times it was difficult to take him seriously. But on this occasion he was deadly serious. The noise of a hundred or so Lancs milling overhead, struggling to gain height before setting course, stirred him to greater efforts to convince us of his sincerity.

"I'll tell you now, and let God be my judge, if I'm lucky enough to get through this tour of 30 ops, I'll immediately volunteer for another tour," he went on.

"You'll sure as hell be flying on your own," chipped in Brick, "if we get through thirty I'll get drunk and jump the next ship back to Canada. We'll have done our whack."

"Personally," I commented, "I'll reserve judgment. We haven't a clue what it's like yet. We're not goin' on a picnic you know."

Max concluded the conversation as we strolled back to our Nissen hut. He put his hand on Dick's shoulder affectionately and said, "I'll say one thing for you guys, you're sure approaching this in the right spirit and I'm pleased to be flying with you bunch. If only you could all speak goddarn English."

The following morning we discovered that Flt. Sgt. D. J. Gigger, Sgt. F. O. Hodgkins, Canadian Flt. Sgt. J. P. Bulger and crews had failed to return. Talk of us doing thirty raids dimmed with the news for one need not be a mathematician to realise that with losses like that six ops would wipe out the whole squadron. We were also aware that, since the foundation of the squadron at Kelstern, in October 1943, not one crew had completed the magical figure of thirty.

Chapter Five

Max was correct. The notice board read: Dowden operations. At 10 o'clock on a cold, but fine morning, the first of the crews who were scheduled to fly that night jumped on the waiting crew buses ready to take them to their particular aircraft, which were sited around the drome on their tarmac dispersal points, for the purpose of ground testing them.

Being "sprogs" we were amongst them, anxious to see the machine which would take us there and back safely, wherever "there" might be. We had been allotted Z 5009 for the raid and on arriving alongside her quickly noticed line after line of small bombs and mines, painted in miniature below the pilot's position, indicating she was a veteran. A comforting thought indeed. Why we walked slowly round the plane, as if we had not seen a Lancaster before, examining every part minutely, I know not. However we did. The interior received the same treatment, till eventually we got down to the purpose of our visit.

The trailers carrying the bombs arrived as we climbed out, so we stayed around at a discreet distance and watched the "cookie," a 4,000 pound bomb, being winched up and secured into the huge bomb bays, followed by eight 500 pounders and, lastly, large canister after canister of incendiaries. Nothing more could be done till early tea at 16.15 hours, as we were not allowed to leave camp on an operational day, so the afternoon was spent by Dick and myself playing shoot pontoon in the Mess with P/O Roscoe's crew whilst Gib, Frank and Brick wrote letters – something at which I was very lax, much to my parents' annoyance.

At 17.00 hours the door to the large Nissen hut, which served as the briefing room, was unlocked, and in trooped all the crews to sit themselves down on the long forms provided, facing a large blank blind above a platform. When everyone was settled, in walked the C.O., followed by the leaders of each section, the meteorological officer, the Adjutant and a few more unspecified officers. As a mark of respect to his rank as Wing Commander, everyone stood.

"Sit down chaps," the smart, 28-year-old C.O. said smilingly to us youngsters.

A glance around the room would have sent an Army Sergeant Major rushing for his tranquillisers, for battle-dress buttons remained unfastened, hats were treated as an unnecessary encumbrance and therefore left in the billet by many, scarves of every colour were draped around numerous necks, and some even wore plimsolls on their feet.

The whole situation suited my temperament ideally, Bull not being my strong point.

A haze of cigarette smoke floated ceilingwards as the C.O. raised the blind, revealing a huge wall map of Europe. From Kelstern stretched a red ribbon giving us the route we would take, finally turning at Frankfurt for the start of our return journey. The Intelligence Officer spoke:

"There you are chaps, Frankfurt. A heavily industrialised city in the heart of Germany which has been badly neglected by us these past few months. We aim to remedy that tonight. It contains railway marshalling yards and is a vital communication centre. 846 aircraft will be bombing-seventeen of these being provided by 625. You will bomb on the markers laid down by the Pathfinders and the Master Bomber will inform you which colour to go for when approaching the target. New crews in particular watch out for the dummy fires they may light away from the target area."

He droned on giving us the relevant details and was followed by the various leaders, each adding information regarding the night's operation. "Watch these three areas on the route particularly," the little Gunnery Leader was saying, pointing with his stick at three blue circles which lay close to our route. "Bazi, Ida and Otto are Luftwaffe fighter beacons around which the Wild Boar night fighters will be operating. Frankfurt is heavily defended by anti-aircraft guns so watch out for those searchlights you gunners."

"That's all, any questions?" asked the C.O. No one spoke. "In that case then off you go. Have a good flight and give them hell."

A normal under-the-breath comment from the crews might have

been "Whilst I have a drink in the Mess." But this could not justifiably be said, for all the leaders, including the C.O., flew on operations from time to time – and in fairness it was not the easier ones (if there was such a thing) they chose. It had, in fact, become necessary for H.Q. to bring in a rule disallowing the leaders from flying in the same aircraft, for only a few short months ago a Lanc had been shot down carrying nothing but Section Leaders, thus leaving the squadron in difficulties till replacements arrived.

The business of dressing for us gunners was a long and arduous one, often necessitating the help of a crew member and so, after handing in our personal valuables and leaving nothing but our dog-tags with which to identify us and receiving in exchange a small escape pack, we dressed first.

I donned my ladies' silk stockings, woolly knee-caps, fleecy long coms with full-length sleeves and high neck, shirt and trousers. I put on my normal socks and long woolly white socks. Next came a thick white sweater and battle dress top, followed by an electrically-heated full-length suit, then my kapok-filled yellow outer suit. My electrically-heated slippers went on, completed by fur-lined flying boots. On the hands we wore white silk gloves, followed by electrically-heated long black gloves, topped by leather gauntlets. I then strapped on my parachute harness as tightly as possible and finally tied on, with its tapes, a Mae West. Anti-freeze ointment was then spread on our faces. This was particularly essential for the rear gunners as the perspex had been cut away from the front of the turrets to allow for better vision and frostbite was a real danger.

Thus dressed, and carrying our 'chutes and helmets, Gib and I waddled out to the waiting crew bus in which sat the rest of our crew and Roscoe's crew. We each took a "wakey-wakey" pill to keep us awake.

As we bounced roughly onto the perimeter track I turned to Roscoe's tail gunner:

"In case you get the chop tonight Porky, where do you keep your money, then I'll know where to look tomorrow morning? After all you took enough off us this afternoon at cards."

"You can piss off you Lancashire Get. Touch anything of mine and I'll come back and haunt you," he good-humouredly replied.

Roscoe, a squat, broad-faced individual piped up, "If you get anything out of that bastard, dead or alive, you'll have done better than any of us. We can get nothing out of him."

"Just keep your eyes open boy," Dick chipped in, "I'll screw every halfpenny out of him next time I get him on the card table."

The light-hearted conversation was rudely interrupted by the Waaf driver hitting the brake pedal so hard it threw us all into a bunch at the front of the van.

"Z – Zebra" she called sweetly.

"She'd make a good pilot," laughed Gib as we climbed out onto the tarmac.

"See you guys later; have a good trip," Max called out after the retreating crew-bus.

It was also their first trip.

We climbed into our Lancaster for the night, to give a final test to engines, wireless, navigational equipment, turrets, etc. and finding these satisfactory Max switched off. The time had come which all aircrew dreaded, the three-quarters of an hour or so wait before take-off. We lounged about, talked to the ground crew, joked and forcibly laughed and got through approximately ten nervous urinations each round the back of the dispersal Nissen hut. All subjects were discussed apart from the operation itself and the ground crew never asked where we were bound. The airfield was deathly quiet.

At long last Max said, "Come on fellas, the time has arrived," and in we climbed, but instead of going to our usual positions the crew hung around the back door until the last man entered and it was closed. We quite automatically shook hands all round. "Good luck, see you in the morning." Then we climbed to our respective positions. The peaceful evening was shattered by Lanc after Lanc starting up their four Rolls Royce Merlin engines and seventeen of us slowly taxied onto the perimeter track with thumbs up from the ground crews.

It was 19.15 hours on the 18th March, 1944, with Z Zebra at the end of the runway revving up for all she was worth then slowly moving forward up the uphill part of the runway at Kelstern, gathering speed as we passed the watch tower, which was lined by a goodly collection of officers and Waafs all giving the encouraging thumbs up sign. To the very end of the runway we raced, Max heaving her off at the very last moment. Up she went, then down she sank dangerously low. Up again with her load of 1,800 gallons of 100 octane aviation fuel and 12,000 lbs of bombs she staggered. Out to sea we flew under a veil of whitish cloud which gave the evening sky a milky appearance, and back again, slowly climbing as

31

we flew.

This performance was repeated for an hour till a height of 20,000 feet was reached. During this period of climbing I plugged in my electrically-heated suit and engaged the fitting for the oxygen supply, which initially produced a sweetish smell in my oxygen mask, my intercom having been plugged in before take-off. The sky was full of tiny black flies performing the same ritual as the night closed in.

As we set course I could still discern many aircraft above and below, in the front and to the rear; their number would soon swell into a stream of bombers stretching across the sky for some 65 miles, all heading for Frankfurt and timed to pass over the city in a thirty-minute period in an attempt to completely saturate the defences. I switched on the ring and bead reflector sight and put the guns on "Fire". Without even thinking I muttered, "The grace of our Lord and Saviour Jesus Christ, the love of God and the fellowship of the Holy Spirit be with us now and forever more, Amen." Since the age of ten never had I uttered that simple prayer nor had I attended Church, and I clearly remember thinking how unfair it was to turn to God only when feeling some need of this kind.

It was soon impossible to see any other planes and a feeling of being very much on our own encompassed me. I switched on my intercom. "If there's supposed to be 846 kites on this raid where's t'other 845?" I asked of no-one in particular.

"Quiet Russ!" Max retorted.

A vibrating of the Lanc, as if travelling on a bumpy road, assured me we were not on our own for this was caused by the slipstream of another aircraft in front.

There I sat in the small compact turret where all available space had been utilised and all pretence of comfort discarded, the ammunition cans by the side of my legs allowing no room whatever for fidgeting, and all I could do now was to settle into as comfortable a position as possible, with hands on the motor-bike type twist grips and fingers between finger guard and triggers, like John Wayne at his best, staring into blackness and hoping nothing remotely like the blurry shadow of a fighter would cross my vision. All was silent, if one could overlook the roar of the engines, which, incredibly, was entirely possible providing they did not change their note.

After an uneventful flight across the Channel we crossed the enemy coast, altering course according to the route. A little light flak was going up in the distance, too far away to be of any significance. Below us the ground was suddenly illuminated by a great white splash of twinkling stars as someone jettisoned their incendiaries, possibly to gain the 23,000 feet at which we were now flying.

Brick began the thankless task of pushing bundles of strips of silver paper known as "window" out of the chute in an attempt to confuse ground radar. The Lutfwaffe night fighters by now, unfortunately, carried radar equipment which rendered "window" virtually useless. Dick periodically broadcast the strength of the wind back to base. Dave, as usual for navigators, was forever busy with his charts. The art of navigation – and it is an art – forever mystified me, and consequently I admired them. Frank was sat alongside Max checking and rechecking the masses of illuminated dials which told him just how the engines were performing.

One of my feet was cold, the other too hot and I dearly wished it was possible to switch them. I made a mental note to have my suit checked.

A few searchlights appeared on the port beam and it surprised me to see just how wide the beams were at our height, particularly when the tops of them flattened out against a patch of cloud spreading an irridescent glow too close for my liking. A stream of brilliant white snowballs left the ground in an almost leisurely manner, becoming larger and larger as they headed straight for us. I was frightened, yet fascinated, and was about to call the skipper when the white balls, now much larger than footballs, shot off at a tangent at an alarming speed and disappeared into oblivion way, way below. Another mental note, forget those little white chains in future. A further batch of incendiaries split open the darkness below, bringing home what had been stressed at briefing.

"Don't jettison the incendiaries. All you are doing is to light up your route for the Luftwaffe. They'll be round you like wasps round a jam pot," the Bombing Leader had lectured.

As if to accentuate his words three flares appeared above and to starboard, hanging in the sky in a straight line like three great chandeliers in a banqueting hall. It seemed as if I could hear him saying, "I told you so." My eyes bulged out of their sockets as I leaned as far forward as possible in an effort to spot the tell-tale shadow of the fighter or fighters which had dropped them. Two silvery bombers were flying directly down the centre of the

33

banqueting hall. The rest of the sky might well have been a huge blackboard.

The third flare took its last breath, finally spluttering out and shrouding us once again in our black cloak. But the damage had been done, for a short perforation of white dashes ending at a little red glow like the tip of the element in a gas lighter told its own story. The glow grew into a vicious red ball and it slowly but irretrievably headed earthwards.

Max broke the silence, "How long to the target, Dave?"

Back came Dave's unhurried, pleasing Canadian drawl, "Thirty minutes Max boy, we're slap on course. Change coming up."

Eight vivid red hot exhausts, not more than twenty feet up, swept over us. I instinctively ducked as the huge black beast momentarily wiped the stars from the blackboard. The aircraft had turned too early and was thus flying across the stream and within seconds a red and white searing streak announced the crash, forming itself into a gigantic pin wheel with showers of coloured sparks flying off it as it spun. The pin wheel's centre was so brightly intense it hurt my eyes and I was thankful it lasted only for seconds before extinguishing itself. Two more would never reach Frankfurt.

A sharpish bank, followed by a levelling off, brought Z Zebra in direct line with the target, the last leg of our route before heading homewards. After some fifteen minutes flying I rotated my turret to face forward and so enable me a glance of what lay ahead. I could not believe what I saw.

It was quite light, with hundreds of probing beams searching the sky for a victim, but what staggered me most was the flak. The sky in front was one mass of bursting shells, never-ending flashes covering the whole of Frankfurt. This display of pyrotechnics appeared to me to render quite impossible any attempt to fly through such a ring of metal without being hit. On our run into this virtual daylight all the bombers we had not seen now attended for roll call and scores of them were sweeping across the city. To my utter amazement, not 200 yards away, its Luftwaffe markings clearly visible, flew a JU88 night fighter, with its unmistakable twin engines protruding beyond the nose, and its large single tailfin etched on the fires below.

"JU88, port side down. See it Russ," came Gib's urgent voice.

"Got it Gib," I answered, swinging my ring and bead sight just in front of the enemy's nose.

The fighter was flying a parallel course and never wavered.

Then followed an unbelievable "shall we or shan't we" discussion. We were only too well aware that our .303s were as "pop" guns compared to his lethal cannon. One hint of tracer from us and he would react violently and quickly. He obviously had not seen us against the darker sky, but I frankly could not understand why, for it was no longer really dark.

"Let sleeping dogs lie," was my closing comment. "We'll watch to see if he makes a move."

With my head touching the perspex on the port side I watched as he slid underneath us, his red hot exhausts glowing like a car's rear lights and the dials in the cockpit glowing an eerie turquoise. Whipping my head over to the starboard side I heaved a sigh of relief as he appeared and carried on drifting away, totally oblivious of the fact that he had stopped my heart from beating for a full two minutes.

"Bomb doors open," called Brick.

Wherever I looked it was a matter of seconds before a searing flash appeared, followed by a greyish irregular-shaped ball of smoke, completely destroying what remained of my night vision. The Lanc shuddered time and again, rising and falling as she relentlessly ploughed on her buffeted way. To describe it as turbulent would be the understatement of the year and yet I could hear nothing of those exploding shells. However the smell of cordite was strong in spite of my tightly-fitting oxygen mask.

Before take-off Dave had said he was going to have a good look at the target for just that once "and then I'll never look at another." He stuck to that statement and the fact that he was indulging in viewing the scene was confirmed by a strong Canadian "Jeeesus Christ", before Brick chanted:

"Left, left, steady, steady."

Up went the port wing alarmingly as a shell exploded below it.

"Blast it," shouted Brick. "Hold the bloody thing steady. Left, left. Beautiful. Hold it. Bombs gone."

The Lanc lifted appreciably as the load and she parted company. We flew straight and level for one minute to allow the camera, housed in the bomb bay, to take its photographs, then, "Bomb doors closed, nose down and home James," he called.

Looking down on the target was not recommended, for the glare destroyed one's night vision, and the danger of being bounced by a night fighter was very real on the way out. But who could resist such a temptation? From four miles up I could clearly see the streets and buildings, many of which were burning fiercely. Huge blotches of red and green markers stained the area, mingling with the angry red and yellow flashes of exploding bombs. Bright white oblongs made the incendiaries easily discernible, some turning crimson like a summer evening's sunset on a silvery sea, and, surpassing all in brightness, the vivid one-tenth of a second brilliant white streaks as photo-flash after photo-flash burst, allowing each aircraft's camera to take its automatic film. A fantastic, awe-inspiring, frightening scene and yet, in a strange way, beautiful beyond description.

A nearby Halifax Mark 3 with its four big radial engines brought me back to reality. It reared up till it was standing on its tail, as if having received an uppercut from Popeye, and as quickly fell. I could see no visible signs of damage, nor was it burning; it simply got itself in a vertical position and dropped out of the sky to join the holocaust below. I remember thinking in a detached sort of way that no-one would get out of that one, but I surprised myself by discovering that watching these aircraft going down left me unmoved. So long as it wasn't us, what the hell, and it wasn't going to happen to us so why worry?

With considerable relief we flew out of the false daylight into the haven of darkness only to find ourselves alongside a burning Lanc which incredibly was flying straight and level. Max banked away from the aircraft but it followed, as if wanting company. Inexplicably, each time we banked, she banked. I found myself wishing it would go down for by now the crew must have baled out, but I was conveniently overlooking the fact that seriously wounded may be aboard, unable to vacate. Eventually the Lanc's nose dropped and it curved a long lazy path downwards, reluctant to the last to meet its doom, after having remained aloft for a well-nigh impossible length of time in that condition.

A reasonably good journey home followed, my time being spent staring, staring and staring into the inky blackness, looking for the slightest sign of those unseen fighters, all thoughts of one foot hot and the other cold having long since been forgotten.

Crossing the North Sea I began thinking of the night's events and my previous flying over the last eight months. How time had flown. It seemed a lifetime since I had first climbed into the Anson. It had developed into great fun shooting coloured tipped bullets at the drogues, trying to shoot them away, which incidentally I finally managed (much to the annoyance of the instructor) and later shooting smoke floats out of the water as we flashed past at low level. Surely this must have been every boy's dream of excitement. But now it was different. It gave me a strange feeling when I realised someone had been shooting at me trying to hurt – no – trying to kill me; it was so easy when the bullets had been zipping away but they were now coming towards me, a different kettle of fish entirely. The fun and games were over.

Ahead lay the welcome static crossed searchlights of Mablethorpe. Between these we flew, now fast losing height.

"Hello Peek Frean. Hello Peek Frean. Z Zebra." Max's voice broke the silence which had seemed interminable.

"Z Zebra," came the Waaf controller's pleasant, but brief reply, "Join circuit 2,500. Out."

"Z Zebra joining circuit 2,500. Out." Max confirmed.

Other Lancs, now with navigation lights switched on, were circling the drome, stepped up 500 feet between each, all anxious to get their wheels on terra firma. As one landed so the airborne aircraft were brought down 500 feet. Eventually the skipper called:

"Z Zebra downwind," indicating the initial stage of landing. We were flying parallel to the runway lights, invitingly stretching out like two strings of beads on this clear, early morning. A long steady turn brought us in line with the runway.

"Funnels," called Max as the long tapering lights appeared on either side.

"Z Zebra pancake," returned the Waaf.

"Z Zebra pancaking," and in we went for Max to make his usual featherbed landing. The flight had lasted five hours and fifty minutes.

It was with a feeling of elation and achievement that we taxied into dispersal, guided by a torch-carrying corporal.

"Where've you been? Had a good trip?" greeted us as we climbed down the ladder. The ground crew on squadron being just as keen as we were, their enthusiasm and concern were obvious.

I had no time to answer him. My ready-to-burst bladder had been protesting for the last hour and with watery eyes I was tearing at my zip and fiddling inside the bulk of clothes to find the necessary instrument with which to relieve myself. The fact that the Waaf's driver's headlights on the crew bus were shining on me mattered not.

The packed, smoke-filled crew room carried an atmosphere of

joviality as tense, pent-up feelings were released. Everyone was trying to speak at once. Porky, Cosgrove's plump Yorkshire rear gunner, came over to me, his outer flying suit already discarded.

"How'd it go Russ? Good trip?"

"Yeah, reasonable. A lot of flak. How the hell have you managed to get back so early?"

"We don't mess about like these Yanks you know," he retorted. "As for the flak, you're right. I never expected as much."

All the Section Officers, including the C.O., engaged themselves in chatting with crews whilst the Padre handed out generous helpings of rum. Gib and I discussed the JU88 we had seen and came to the conclusion we had done the right thing in not firing and giving away our position. I felt a little guilty as I concluded:

"Our job's to drop bombs and get back in one piece, not one of playing heroics with night fighters."

"Listen boy," said Gib with his arm round my shoulder, "I'm not looking for any posthumous D.F.M.'s. Let's forget it, but we'll sure as hell never get another chance like that." We didn't.

Debriefing, carried out by the Intelligence Officer in a side room, lasted but a few minutes for each crew. The navigator had to log such things as aircraft seen to be going down by the crew members and these the Officer would ask about.

"In your opinion was it a successful raid?"

"Any special happenings or sightings?"

"Was the weather as forecast?"

These and other relevant questions being dealt with we made our way to the Mess, in which awaited us very welcome real egg and bacon, steaming hot tea, bread, butter and jam, and after a delicious, but very noisy, meal, we retired to our billet, full, tired, and completely whacked, rolling in our bunks for sleep to overcome us almost immediately.

Chapter Six

"And he stood there for over an hour trying to convince the ticket collector that his platform ticket had been bought there in Doncaster and he hadn't travelled from Tilbury with it. The hard-faced devil had his kitbag and gas mask with him. Sure enough the ticket collector gave it up in disgust and let him through."

Gib, Brick and myself were sprawled comfortably in the easy chairs of the Sergeants' Mess the morning after the raid on Frankfurt, listening to Frank. The topic was Dick, whom we had left fast asleep in the billet.

"The best ever," I recalled, "was when I took him home to Blackburn. We got two platform tickets at Gainsborough and caught the train to Manchester. As usual it was packed with servicemen and we had to climb onto the roof racks. It was a corridor train and I went to the toilet towards the rear. I could hear the inspector shouting 'Tickets please,' so I strolled back into our compartment and said to Dick, 'What we goin' to do now, bright boy? Inspector's coming for tickets.' "

" 'Oh they're a bloody nuisance,' Dick said as he climbed down and left the compartment. We only had two bob between us. Within minutes he came back and handed me a ticket, keeping one for himself."

" 'Where the hell have you got them from?' I queried."

" 'I just went down towards the front of the train shouting, "tickets please" outside of every occupied toilet. "Slide it under the door, please." ' "

Gib's loud guffaw could be heard all over the Mess, "Jees, that big gahoot would twist his own grandmother."

So saying in walked the man in question. "Come on you idle sods, let's get down to prayers."

"Prayers" was the name given to an every morning meeting of the crews down at the crew room, a large Nissen hut which housed a few of the Section Leaders, dressing rooms and a general room which was empty apart from notices and P.O. Prune cartoons lining the walls. The photographs of the previous night's raid were pinned up along with the C.O.'s comments, such as: "Where the hell were you Blackshaw?" or "It was Frankfurt we were bombing, Smithies!" A delighted Brick read ours: "Well done Dowden, smack on the aiming point."

"God, there'll be no holding him now," laughed Frank.

The official Air Ministry report of the raid was that it had been extremely successful. Bomber Command lost 22 and we at 625 one, F/O I.E. McMaster failing to return.

We bombed Frankfurt again on March 22, Berlin on the 24th and Essen on the 26th, all in Lancaster PED940 – which incredibly had survived over one hundred operations. We were destined to end that run of P. Peter's. Things were moving at a fast pace in Bomber Command – but so were the losses.

At this stage superstition crept in with a capital "S". Before an operation one began to notice the lads performing all manner of strange things and, though it was camouflaged by jokes and laughs, virtually everyone developed a little quirk of their own. Gib, for instance, always stamped both palms of his hands on the ground prior to take-off; Dave never flew on operations without his officer's hat resting on his navigation table; Frank always carried his uncle's First World War medal and had hanging in the cabin a fluffy little rabbit; and I was known to completely undress and start the task all over again because I had not put on my left sock first! To simply change the socks round would not have sufficed at all. It really amounted to remembering something we had done on our first operation and making sure it was repeated on each subsequent raid.

The Berlin raid turned out to be our worst so far. Due to 100-mile-per-hour cross winds the main force was blown all over the sky, completely disintegrating the stream of bombers. This gave the Luftwaffe night fighters a far easier job, for isolated aircraft could be picked up on their radar sets and with frightening regularity tell-tale tracer marks punctuated the sky, invariably ending in fire, and down would go another bomber.

We got through to Berlin unmolested by fighters, but having had to contend with some very heavy flak in the form of box barrages. This however, whilst being more alarming, was preferable to the deadly and very active night fighters. It was whilst flying through a curtain of flak that Gib and I got a good close look at a "scarecrow" and, as these caused considerable interest back at base, we took careful note of it.

A mammoth explosion on the starboard beam blew us violently sideways, like a dried leaf on a windy day, and there in the cloudy night sky hung a huge colourful lantern, from the centre of which dripped vivid reds, greens, blues and yellows. Oily black smoke rose from the irregular mass. It was so close I felt I could have leaned over and touched it. This was a "scarecrow." I was convinced, contrary to what was believed at base about these things being fired from the ground in order to simulate an aircraft exploding, that in fact it had been dropped from above like some sort of aerial "land" mine, for it certainly was not falling. Max steadied the Lanc and we left the spectrum dripping its colours as if being squeezed by some unseen hand. If the intention was to scare the crews the Germans had succeeded with one of us anyway.

On the bombing run I rotated my turret on the beam and out of the corner of my eye saw Dick in the astro-dome jabbing his finger upwards in an attempt to catch my attention. "Bomb doors open" said Brick as a Lanc, some eighty feet up and directly above us, opened its huge belly. I stared in horror at the 4,000 lb "cookie" and 500 pounders which hung, clearly visible, in its bomb bays. We waited with bated breat as the two aircraft moved in unison, as if connected, unable to do a thing at this vital stage in the operation.

"Bombs gone," shouted the bomb-aimer.

God knows where the other bombs fell, for I only had eyes for the big one, as I sat there dry-lipped watching that "cookie" from above slide between our wing and tail. Completely disregarding the very low temperature, sweat had formed on my brow and I watched it freeze on the back of my glove when I wiped it off, the rest of the crew being blissfully unaware of the event. Dick grimaced and disappeared from view, no doubt getting back to his "fishpond" radar screen, used to search underneath for the fighter sneaking up from below.

The return journey was difficult for Dave as he slogged away in an attempt to keep us on course, constant alterations of which he kept giving to Max. We eventually found ourselves flying North of

41

the Ruhr in a quiet sky well off course, but at least away from "Happy Valley," as the Ruhr was known, where many unfortunates were succumbing to a pounding from the ground.

"Pass me the can Frank," Max requested over the intercom.

"Just one minute Skip, Dave's using it," Frank returned.

Brick chipped in, "Jees, I'm tired of emptying your guys' piss down this chute. It's full of icicles now."

It was at this point that my aching bladder burst and I soaked myself, enjoying every second of it.

I had tried using the Elsan toilet at the back of the aircraft in the past. It entailed unplugging my intercom and electric suit, disconnecting from the oxygen, unclipping my seat and groping with my foot for the single foot-rest. Then in the fuselage, connecting to an emergency bottle of oxygen in total darkness, removing three pairs of gloves, making sure no cold metal was touched with bare fingers, for they would surely stick and tear the skin, unzipping two flying suits and unbuttoning my trousers, then searching for my Old Man, which by this time had completely disappeared into its shell. Repeat the whole performance with freezing hands. And in view of the fact that leaving the turret on operations was an unhealthy procedure I had long since decided the effort just was not worth it. I was by no means on my own in this matter – most gunners came to the same conclusion.

A lone pale blue searchlight suddenly encompassed us in its brilliance – one second darkness, the next blinded – and pale blue meant only one thing – radar controlled.

"Dive port," Gib shouted but before he had got it out, Max, foreseeing the danger, sent her screaming down in a curving dive. The searchlight followed, then stopped dead, and we raced into darkness. Another Lanc, up and to starboard, glistened silver like a length of tinsel in a fairy light's gleam. There was a searing flash and down it spiralled – a blow torch no less. Just one shell had been fired and the whole episode took about twenty-five seconds.

Relieved to be out of it all we flew across the North Sea calling up "Peak Frean," our base call sign before we hit friendly shores, for it had now developed into a race as to who would get back first, and never yet had we beaten Cosgrove and his crew. The earlier the call was received – the earlier an aircraft joined the circuit. We were the third to touch down – Cosgrove the first, after having been airborne 6 hours 45 minutes.

"I'll get down before that Limey one of these nights," vowed

Max. His forecast dramatically came true a few weeks later.

It was no surprise to learn that this raid had been a disaster. Seventy-three bombers had been lost – the heaviest loss of the war on a Berlin raid – and 625 squadron had lost three out of the seventeen despatched. A bad night all round.

It was on this raid incidentally that one of the most amazing escapes of the war took place. Nicholas Stephen Alkemade was in his Lancaster's rear turret as they flew over Westphalia on the return flight. Flying at 19,000 feet, Nicholas's Lanc lurched violently, followed by a series of jolting thuds. Two cannon shells smashed into his turret showering fragments of perspex in the air. One piece drove into his right leg. He saw the attacking fighter, a JU88, and opened up, but screaming he fell backwards as a blast of flames scorched his face and hands. His oxygen mask melted on his face. The skipper ordered them to bale out. As Nicholas opened his turret doors the intense heat in the fuselage made him close them, but not before he had glimpsed his burning parachute.

He now had two choices, jump, reasonably sure of a quick death, or stay and be roasted alive. Nicholas turned the turret on the beam and rolled out backwards. His flying boot became jammed between control pillar and the turret's side and he badly twisted his knee before freeing himself. He fell some three and a half miles. Three hours later he opened his eyes. By a billion-to-one-chance his fall had been cushioned first by tree branches and then by a deep drift of snow.

The Germans did not believe his story but found he had a twisted right knee, splinters in his thigh, a badly bruised back, a deep head wound and first degree burns on face and hands.

Luftwaffe officers then interrogated him and a search party found the crashed Lancaster. Charred remains of Alkemade's parachute were found on the floor of the fuselage. Further searching found the snowdrift with a four-foot deep depression. On April 25th 1944 he was presented with a certificate by the P.O.W. Camp Commandant, which reads:

"It has been investigated and corroborated by the German authorities that the claim made by Flight Sergeant Alkemade is true in all respects, namely that he made a descent from 19,000 ft. without a parachute and made a safe landing without injury, the parachute having been on fire in the aircraft. He landed in deep snow amongst fir trees."

Chapter Seven

On March 27th all crews met in the crew room in order to meet our new Squadron Commander, D. D. Haig. He was a smart chap, of some 28 years, and as he sported a D.S.O. and D.F.C. had obviously seen more than his fair share of operations. He gave us a brief and jocular introductory chat rather than a speech – thereby favourably impressing us – and ending by saying:

"That's all for now chaps apart from one item of good news I have to impart. Sergeant N. D. Brown, Flight Engineer, who was reported missing on 27/28 January, has evaded capture by the enemy and is now back in England. He is the first man from this squadron to have done so since its formation."

A cheer went up from all present, mainly because good news of missing crews was always welcome and encouraging. It seemed as if we clung to the very misleading belief that men always baled out and never got killed.

"That calls for a celebration," said Dick. "We haven't been out for a bit."

"Okay, Okay," drawled Max, "we'll all go. But take it easy. We're not on training station now."

A few crews gathered together in a pub in Louth that evening for a not too riotous time, but during which Max had to take more than a reasonable amount of leg-pulling, being the only American present. He always took it in good part and gave back as much as he got and more, but after a few beers he was never slow in telling them how good he was.

A Flying Officer, by the name of Nicholls, said:

"I'll tell you what Dowden. I'll bet you £1 you can't fly round the water tower at Kelstern with one wing lower than the top of it."

"Any more takers," said Max looking round the room. "It's gotta be worth my while."

Every pilot in the room put £1 on the table.

"You're on," he accepted giving us a broad smile.

"Not so fast. Not so fast," chipped in Frank. "Don't forget we'll be with you – or are you going on your own? That tower is only about 30 feet up and you're going to bank round it for six quid. I'm . . ."

Max waved into thin air, "Relax Frank boy. I'll piss it."

A beautiful morning found us down at "prayers" the following day and as no ops were scheduled we had been allocated P Peter for bombing and "Y" practice. "Y" was the code letter given to the latest navigational aid, known to us as "H2S". It consisted of a scanner housed in a large bulb under the fuselage and gave the navigator an image on a screen, some eight inches in diameter, of the coastline or built up area by means of a series of blips from the rotating scanner.

These daylight flights undoubtedly proved the most enjoyable of all our flying for one need not dress in cumbersome flying suits and more than a little larking about took place whilst listening to the popular music of the day. As we became airborne on this particular morning Max put the Lanc into a climbing turn and came tearing back over the buildings of the 'drome. A goodly number of aircrew had gathered outside the Sergeants' Mess – which lay some two hundred yards from the metal framed water tower – in order to watch the performance. We flashed past them, down went the long slim wing for the aircraft to turn tightly round the tower. The main thing I saw was Gib's and Dick's heads in the astrodome with noses touching. It all happened so quickly no-one had time to complain.

"That'll have gotten them guys talkin'," piped up Max when we had got a little more distance between us and the ground, "they won't be as anxious to lose their money next time."

"You'll lose your bloody head if you ever try that again, Dowden," I laughed.

We flew on low, making sure that any washing hung on the lines by the hard-working farmers' wives ended on the ground, much to their consternation and our amusement. The skipper then spotted some pylons in the distance and made straight for them. As the lines became clear he lined up with the lowest part of the sag and sank lower and lower.

"You aren't going under those cables, Skip, are you?" exclaimed Brick anxiously.

"We're not taking you for any more beers," Dick added, "You've gone bloody mad."

As we neared the cables it became obvious we would well-nigh have had to touch the grass to get the huge tailfins below the cables, and at the last moment, much to our relief, Max lifted the nose, allowing the machine to sweep over them. We gained height and flew on over the patchwork quilt of Lincolnshire with its little villages nestling peacefully in the gently rolling landscape, each complete with its attractive little old church, their spires pointing a little accusingly at us for disturbing the peace. A less warlike scene would be hard to find.

Whilst on this exercise we came across an American Flying Fortress, which also seemed in the mood for play, and an absorbing half hour was spent trying to get on each other's tail. On a couple of occasions Max managed to out-turn the Fort and as a consequence had to accept our criticisms of "these bloody rubbishy American Forts", which they were certainly not. On completing our bombing with tiny practice bombs over a range specially provided for that purpose we returned to base. Max called up "Peak Frean" and received an immediate reply from the C.O. himself:

"I trust you are higher now Dowden than when you left this airfield?"

"Yes sir, I am," replied a subdued Max.

"Report to my office immediately you land," the Wing Commander snapped.

"You're going to get your balls chewed off," sang Gib from the tail. "You'll be sorry." He always had a habit of singing the words when pulling someone's leg.

"Better wear your slacks over your arm when you go in Max, you never know your luck," I suggested.

"Belt up you bums," came back the skipper, "I've still got my £6 to come. I'll talk to him real nice and put on my best 'American accent.' "

"It'll take more than your accent to get you out of this," chipped in Dick, "You'd be better off talking like Jean Harlow."

Ist Lt. Max Dowden duly reported to the C.O. as bade. "God," he said, when he came out, "I've just gotten my arse kicked from California and back. If ever I do that again I'll get posted out of here so fast my arse won't touch the ground. This Haig ain't gonna stand

46

for no nonsense, that's for sure. Still I suppose he's right. If I get away with it, everybody will be at it, and somebody's sure to hit the tower. Come on, let's have a drink."

It was, as can be imagined, a most unusual life we were leading – totally unreal. A life of contrasts. One evening would be spent having a few beers in Louth, at the camp cinema, or playing cards in the Mess, and the very next would find us over a target with all hell let loose wondering if we were going to get back in one piece or not. Yet, whilst losses of crews and aircraft were heavy, morale was at a premium and, inexplicably, one found oneself wanting to go on another raid as soon as possible. Strangely, operations rarely came up in conversation. When one was done, it was done, and that was that. On the training stations however, should we be broke, a quick "recce" round the pubs to find some "sprog" Yanks was always recommended and then we would talk all night about raids we had never done.

"My God Gib that 109 went up with a wallop when you hit, didn't it?" Dick would say in a voice just loud enough to be heard.

"Quiet Dick. Quiet, not here," falsely embarrassed, Gib would protest. A plethora of free drinks would begin to flow as sure as night follows day, with this type of subdued conversation, and weird and wonderful embellishments would follow thick and fast for the benefit of the Americans' ears, at a time when we had not even seen a 109.

* * *

From the Luftwaffe's point of view, this period of night bombing belonged to them. They had undoubtedly got the upper hand, mainly due to three things.

Firstly, the ME110, whilst not a fast machine, had proved itself to be a very capable night fighter, its twin engines giving it a good operational range – vital for the territory which had to be covered. The machine had recently been fitted with the new secret SN-2 radar, which rendered our "window" dropping virtually useless, and picking up the bombers had consequently become a far easier task for the German pilots.

Secondly, the 110 had been fitted with two upward-firing 30-centimetre cannons, mounted in the roof, set to fire almost vertically upwards and slightly forwards. The orthodox night fighter attack came from behind, but the fitting of "schräge Musik" ("slanting music") as the Germans coded it, enabled the fighter to stealthily climb and fly directly underneath the bomber without being spotted. So successful had this method of attack proved for the Luftwaffe that a number of their pilots had been lost due to the resultant explosion of the target when hit, and as a consequence, due to the ME110 being a very stable gun platform, the pilots actually began aiming at a particular spot – the engines – leaving the bomb bays well alone. A few explosive shells in these was all that was needed.

Little wonder the Luftwaffe had nicknamed the 110 "The Destroyer".

And thirdly, they had developed an uncanny knack of ascertaining where a particular raid would be. On this they had a few pointers. The German listening posts situated on the enemy coastline were capable of detecting the switching on of radios and the H2S navigational equipment on the British airfields during the morning tests taking part on each squadron on operation days. They therefore knew a raid would take place that night – but where? It required only the odd agent in England to watch an airfield through field glasses to decide whether a raid would be of deep penetration or otherwise. Should each Lanc, for instance, take a bowser and a "bit" of petrol, (2,100 gallons), the flight would be a long one. Alternatively, should the bowser move on to another aircraft to empty the remainder of its contents – the flight would be of shorter duration. The bomb-loads could also be watched as they were winched in. Full bomb-loads meant a comparatively short flight, a smaller bomb-load a long one. The rest was a guessing game most of the time, but this knowledge did enable the Luftwaffe to switch their night-fighter force around long before a raid took place.

Such was the scene on March 30, 1944 as we raced down the runway in faithful PED940 on our way to bomb Nuremburg, blissfully unaware, as indeed was the whole of Bomber Command, of these recent innovations – and the impending disaster.

Whistles of derision had gone up at briefing when the huge wall map had been uncovered showing the ribbons leading to Nuremburg, for a long straight leg of some 350 miles was unusually long without a turn and passed perilously close to the fighter beacons Ida and Otto. In view of the fact that this was our longest trip to date – we would be airborne for eight hours – this route was not to our liking. But worst of all a bright moonlight night was forecast.

The main force turned onto this long leg over Charleroi, Belgium, with the half moon clearly showing up the condensation trails of each bomber. It all made a very impressive sight, but one I would rather not have seen, for if I could see dozens and dozens of aircraft, so could the enemy. Within half an hour the half-expected fighters were amongst us; their arrival being announced by a blossoming reddish glow on our port side as the first bomber fell in the Aachen area.

By the time another fifteen minutes had passed string after string of flares, dropped by the Hun, illuminated our course and the uneven battle started in earnest. Red and green tracer criss-crossed the sky as Max tried desperately to gain more height. An explosion on the port side down showered hundreds of flaming fragments across the sky.

"Halifax going down, port side, Dave," I said.

"Got it Russ," replied the navigator.

"Lanc falling to the rear," came Gib from the tail.

No sooner had he got the words out than I watched mesmerised as a Lanc's wing folded at right angles to the aircraft like a drop-leaf table and it just toppled over and over, quickly disappearing from my view. An excrescent flush of orange flame from another Lanc soon enveloped the whole plane and it skidded out of sight below us.

"Another Lanc . . ."

"Let's just forget it Gib," I interrupted. The whole thing was so demoralising it seemed pointless making it worse.

"Guess you're right, Russ," came the answer.

It was like flying down an endless well-lit stretch of motorway. I knew now how the merchant sailors must have felt on the Russian convoys as the U-boats picked them off one by one.

Along with jettisoned bombs, particularly incendiaries, burning aircraft marked our course, and, with prickly beads of sweat on my forehead, I realised we were now illuminated from above and below.

A banner of red and yellow flame streaked in front of us, then completely broke in two. I tried turning away from this madness to search the darker part of the sky but it seemed that no matter where I looked an aircraft was falling. Watching a bomber going down had not previously disturbed me unduly but this was ridiculous. Apart from becoming jittery I found myself becoming emotionally disturbed.

A huge flash introduced a scarecrow in our midst with its black oily smoke and dripping colours. Thank God it was not till after the war that we learned that no such a thing as scarecrows existed, they were in fact bombers receiving a direct hit on their bomb bays.

Burning petrol spewed out of a Halifax and its whole tail unit disappeared, the nose went down and the last I saw of it the machine was going down vertically.

On and on went the carnage and I would estimate that Gib and I saw some 15 bombers go down. Some floated down from side to side like a leaf falling from a tree in Autumn, some flew straight and level for half a minute or so, even though the flames looked huge in comparison to the size of the plane, some just toppled out of the sky, whilst others screamed straight down as though in a hurry. Anyone unfamiliar with this kind of warfare could be excused for not believing the incredible fact that through the whole of this action no-one in our aircraft saw a fighter plane.

At long long last, after the most frightening two-and-a-half hours of my life, we made a 45 degree turn for the run over Nuremburg. Cloud had moved in and covered the whole of the city, rendering normal ground marking impossible. Emergency wanganui marking had been used by the pathfinders and two widely separated clusters of flares hung in the sky, suspended over translucent cloud, made so by the searchlights below.

It was eerie over the target, unlike any we had met. Flak was spasmodic and inaccurate and the few bombers I could see below us, like spiders on a white backcloth, looked totally uninterested and uninteresting. No fires could we see, but what was more important, we couldn't see any fighter activity either.

"Jees, all this way and nothing definite to aim at," grumbled Brick, "Where the hell shall I . . . Oh to hell with it. Bombs gone. Let's get to hell out of here."

Brick's disgust showed.

A couple of turns, the last one being south of Stuttgart, brought us onto the long leg to France, but by now the moon had settled and we were in familiar darkness under a canopy of stars. The sweat had now subsided but my eyes ached with searching. For the twentieth time I tried to rub off a smear of dirt on my turret which had made me whip round in its direction so many times thinking it was a fighter that I felt like knocking a hole in the perspex to get rid of it, and I vowed I would clean my own turret in future. My thoughts began to wander. Just what had gone wrong?

"Corkscrew port, go go!" screamed Gib.

Down we plummeted into the familiar corkscrew and with a renewed awareness of danger I stared and stared for a glimpse of the fighter Gib had seen, but alas in vain. Was the Canadian rear gunner imagining things? We resumed course straight and level. He's probably jittery like me after tonight's episode. God, he's there. A small black shadow of a single-engined fighter was sliding onto us from the starboard up.

"Corkscrew starboard, go, go," I found myself shouting as I rotated the turret in his direction. With commendable rapidity the skipper flung the huge machine down again and the blur disappeared from view.

"We're being stalked by this one," called out Max. "Dick, up in the astro-dome. Everyone eyes peeled."

"I've been there for the last five minutes, Skip," replied Dick.

Five minutes of straight flying in the darkness without a sighting relaxed the tension. There was no flak and no sign of combat.

"Starboard go," Gib and I bawled in unison as vicious-looking white tracer gashed the sky feet above us and careered off at an acute right angle in the distance. And still no clear sight of the offending fighter.

"Okay, guys, that's it," Max determinedly declared, "I'm gonna corkscrew for the next hour."

A seemingly ridiculous statement, for this manoeuvre was a particularly tiring one for the pilot. However, as usual, he did precisely that, and as a consequence no further trouble was experienced from the persistent German.

Fifteen minutes from Dieppe and once again, thankfully on a level course, Max called:

"Our fuel tanks are dangerously low. It's fifty-fifty whether we can make it over the sea or not. Gib do we have a go or bale out?"

"Have a go, Skipper," replied Gib without hesitation.

"Russ?"

"Try it," I replied.

He put the question to the six of us and it was unanimously decided to try and make England.

We steadily lost height as we flew towards just a hint of lighter sky. The first signs of dawn. As we neared Selsey Bill Max began the emergency call:

"Hello Darkie, Hello Darkie."

Within minutes we received a response giving us a course to fly to

51

the nearest available drome, Silverstone.

Flying at 1,000 feet and thankful to at least be over Mother Earth, we approached the airfield, but much to our disgust, in reply for permission to land, we were given a definite "No", and another course to fly, to the American Fortress drome at Bovington. (Unbeknown to us at the time a Lanc had crashed on the runway at Silverstone).

As dawn was breaking our position was fast becoming intolerable and whilst Max began to steer us on the new course it was obvious we could keep airborne no longer with safety.

"All tanks are now reading empty. Take up crash positions. I'm gonna take this baby in." Max's cool American drawl was very reassuring but all I could see from 500 feet in the grey dawn was trees, trees and more trees.

The five of us huddled in the fuselage, our backs against bulkheads facing rearwards, feet braced on anything solid and hands clasped round the backs of our necks, pulling our heads down hard. The familiar arresting of speed as the flaps were lowered, and the changing note of the engines, were all expected, but the "clocking" of the undercarriage as it locked down was definitely not. A crash-landing was invariably carried out with wheels up.

I hated sitting inside the aircraft, unable to see out, and trying to imagine what Max and Frank were attempting to do. If this was to be the end I at least wanted to see it and I all but climbed back into the turret, but commonsense prevailed at the realisation that if it broke its back on landing it would surely go at the weakest point – the mid-upper turret.

Driven white we anxiously awaited the horrible vibrations and rattlings which would be the very least we could expect. No-one said a word, though some of the tension was eased by the mere fact of pulling hard on the neck. Max banked steeply.

The touch-down was unbelievably immaculate and someone gasped, probably me. A rising and falling sensation set up the expected violent vibrations but the rumbling noise assured us our wheels were still on the ground. The vibrations, to our amazement, ceased, and I might have been back at Stormy Down landing in the Anson, it was certainly no worse than that. To everyone's relief the Lanc came to a standstill and we lifted our heads, smiling in disbelief. The engines idled to a halt and nobody moved as we drank in the peace and quiet, gathered our thoughts, and silently congratulated ourselves on surviving our third crash. Life was beautiful.

We climbed out of P Peter at exactly 5.55 a.m. on a grey, but fine morning, to find ourselves in a field, some fifty yards or so from a road. The last out was Max, already enjoying a well-earned cigarette.

"Well that was a bloody good effort," said Dave as he moved forward and shook his hand. We all concurred, shaking his hand in turn.

Max smiled, "I don't know about a good effort. I couldn't find a goddarn field, never mind a drome. Frank spotted this one at the last minute. We didn't even have time to decide whether or not it was level."

We had, in fact, touched down in a small field in Little Chalfont, Buckinghamshire, where we had run parallel to the A404 Amersham to Watford road, some thirty yards from the backs of the houses there, ploughed through a small hedge and crossed Stony Lane, climbed up a banking and passed through some small trees, Max having chosen the widest gap. Unfortunately the gap had not been wide enough to cope with the 102 foot wing span and consequently half of the port wing was left neatly wrapped around the largest of the trees. A pig pen had been demolished and a small hole had appeared in my turret. But there, at Great House Farm, part of The Duke of Bedford's estate, PED 940 stood proudly, having completed the last of her operations, still undefeated. She would now have to be dismantled and removed piecemeal.

The first man on the scene was a member of the Home Guard waving a rifle, and dressed in a nightshirt which was betopped by a greatcoat. He was quickly followed by streams of villagers coming up the field accompanied by the village policeman, all in some form of night attire.

The villagers welcomed us as long lost heroes and gazed at the Lanc with intense interest. The bobby took charge of things mainly, I think, because he was anxious to get inside the aircraft and have a look around. He was eventually successful. Max, giving way, afforded him a conducted tour.

"Better have the guns and bomb sight out," Max requested. "We don't want any mishaps now." He omitted to mention that a canister of incendiaries still hung in the bomb bays. This equipment, along with navigational charts, parachutes, Mae Wests, outer flying suits, helmets and electric flying suits was piled onto the grass, by which time the Home Guard had organised a guard of two men, complete with rifles.

"I thought I was breathing my last when I was awakened by this almighty roar and my windows were rattling like mad," said one of the Home Guard men. "I'm glad you're alive, mind you," he added.

We gratefully accepted breakfast from a few of the locals, after which Max went to the police station to report to Kelstern by phone and contact Bovington for transport to that station. The Yanks, as usual, were most obliging, promptly despatching a vehicle for our collection. After a morning's rest they provided us an excellent lunch in the Officers' Mess and transported us, along with our equipment, to King's Cross Station, London.

Unfortunately no train was running to our destination till 5 o'clock. We therefore commandeered a large luggage trolly and commenced loading guns, etc. onto it, much to the amazement of the railway porters. In the process people constantly came over to us.

"God bless you boys."

"You're doing a great job."

"Let me shake your hand."

It all became terribly embarrassing. No busier place existed than King's Cross Station at 1 o'clock in the afternoon.

"I'm getting out of this lot," said Dave, always a quiet modest type. "I'm going to the cinema out of the way."

"Okay, let's go," I said, and, turning to a bewildered porter, "Look after this lot will you. We'll be back at 4.30."

As we walked to the bottom of the station approach the newspaper poster boards read "96 down", and the vendor was shouting "R.A.F. tragedy" as he sold his papers like hot cakes. "Good God," exclaimed Dick incredulously, "I knew it was bad, but 96 . . ."

Max, Dave and myself went to a nearby cinema where we got in free, for we had no English money, and promptly dropped off to sleep. The other four spent the afternoon drinking free beer. On meeting up later to catch our train all four were three sheets to the wind.

Gib unfortunately had to spend a few days in hospital back at base due to a frostbitten face, contracted in spite of the anti-freezing ointment we smeared on our faces. The missing perspex panel was no joke for the tail gunners.

It is now history to say that this Nuremburg raid was the heaviest loss Bomber Command suffered throughout the war. Apart from losing 96, the final figure was more like 110, for many crashed in England, and little damage had been done to Nuremburg. The Luftwaffe christened it "The night of the long knives". I strongly recommend anyone interested to read Martin Middlebrook's book "The Nuremburg Raid", as this is, in my opinion, the finest and most comprehensive book on a particular raid ever written.

Back at 625 Squadron, the score-sheet for March, our first month of operations, read thus:

March 1 – Ten to Stuttgart. Nine successful. One aborted.

March 15 – Nineteen to Suttgart. Sixteen returned. Flt. Sgt. D. J. GIGGER, Sgt. F.C. HODGINS, and Flt. Sgt. J. P. BULGER and crews missing.

March 18 – Seventeen to Frankfurt. Sixteen returned. F/O McMASTER and crew missing.

March 22 – Seventeen to Frankfurt. All returned.

March 24 – Seventeen to Berlin. Fourteen returned. Flt. Sgt. R. D. W. JAMIESON, W/O J. D. OWEN, F/O (A/F/L) N. A. W. CLARK and crews missing.

March 26 – Fourteen to Essen. All returned.

March 30 – Thirteen to Nuremburg. Twelve returned. F/O (A/S/L) T. M. NICHOLLS and crew missing.

In seven operations the squadron had averaged the despatch of fifteen aircraft per raid at a cost of eight crews – half of our flying personnel. We had completed five. Thirty seemed a terribly long way off.

Chapter Eight

A ten-day lull followed the disastrous Nuremburg raid whilst Bomber Command licked its wounds and built up its strength. New faces appeared on the squadron along with new aircraft, and Ludford Magna, our neighbour squadron, needed them badly, having lost a staggering seven aircraft on the raid.

The lull provided us a welcome relief from what had been a hectic initiation into operational flying and we took full advantage of the respite. It was during this period that a "Wings for Victory" week was held in Mablethorpe and a number of crews were detailed to march through the streets of the resort along with a Waaf and ATC contingency, headed by a R.A.F. band.

Acting Squadron Leader R. W. H. Gray reluctantly accepted charge of the parade, knowing full well that marching was not our strong point. He assembled the crews in a dingy back alley on the outskirts of town and in a not too confident voice said:

"Now come on chaps, don't muck about, get yourselves in threes. We'll have to put some short of show on, after all we are leading the march past."

With humorous, unprintable replies raining on him from all directions, cigarettes were "docked," hands removed from pockets, and ties roughly straightened as we shuffled into some semblance of order ready to march out to meet up with the rest of the parade.

The sea-front at Mablethorpe was lined on both sides with a goodly number of people, including many soldiers, who no doubt would be justifiably critical of our half-hearted attempt at marching, especially when the Waafs were putting up a very smart show behind us. However all went well up to the saluting base, but as soon as that had been passed the lads began to duck out of the ranks thick and fast and in no time at all Sqd. Ldr. Gray was left alone, ahead of a great gap, marching smartly behind the band. Pity really, for he was a good sort.

The crews congregated in a large smoke-filled pub just off the sea front, after this marching fiasco, much preferring a pint to reverting back to our Initial Training Wing days with all the marching that that had entailed.

"Well Russ, what's your feelings now of ops?" asked Max unexpectedly, for it was the first time we had mentioned them specifically.

"Pretty much as I expected I suppose. Probably more side issues than I thought." It was a conversation I did not really want.

"One thing that suprises me is that we never fire our guns on operations," I continued. "We just do not see the fighters clear enough. As soon as we see a blur one of us screams 'corkscrew' and we've lost him, thank God. It's eyes we need, not guns."

"I doubt if any gunner on the whole squadron has fired a bullet in anger during our time here," enjoined Max. "The fighters sure don't hang around if we are alert enough."

"Yeah, there's a few things cropped up that were never mentioned on the training stations. It's like everything else, you've got to do it before you realise what it's all about," said Frank, drawing on his cigarette.

Serious chats of this nature were just not part of our life-style and I tried to change to something more light-hearted.

"Should be getting some leave soon. Ten days every six weeks whilst on squadron. Only a fortnight or so to go."

Max, looking more serious than I had ever seen him, persisted.

"If we get hit I'll ride the baby down."

"And me," rejoined Frank.

"What the hell are you on about," I exploded. "I've never heard anything as silly in my life. If you can get out, then get out – it's as simple as that. There's no way you're goin' to live by riding it down. Anyway, who says we're goin' to get the chop? We're doin' thirty, that's it."

Losing my temper was a rarity, but I could feel my temperature rising. I just could not comprehend their line of thought.

"Oh gee, Russ, come on," said Max placatingly. "Don't get so uptight. It's sure enough a simple statement. I'll go down with it."

57

"And I'll be with you, but like Russ says, I think we'll do thirty," Frank stated.

"And you're thinking of getting engaged to Betty on your next leave and marrying within three months? Yet you're talking like that. Frank, it just doesn't make sense. I wish I'd never sat with you buggers, you're in a miserable mood," said I.

"I don't feel in the least miserable Russ. I've told you what I'll do, and I'm sticking to it. Come on, let's have a stroll outside." Max was emphatic.

I ended a conversation which I failed to understand, but which I eventually had cause to remember, by saying, "You're both crackers."

It was a far more cheerful evening a few days later when Gib, Dick and I went into Louth for a few beers and a game of darts. The drinking had been curtailed somewhat at Kelstern by virtue of the fact that we had been busy and Max had requested us to ease up whilst on squadron. However the inevitable happened, it got a little boisterous, more and more ale was consumed and the end of the evening found me steering two well-under-the-weather lads back to the last bus.

"Why don't you goddarn Limeys build your roads straight like we do in Canada?" grumbled Gib half-consciously as the bus wound its way along twisting country lanes.

It was pure misfortune that found Max and Dave strolling back to their billets as the bus arrived at the drome and spilled out its contents.

"What are you two bastards doing in that state? You're drunk," Max bellowed, spotting his two wayward crew members.

As he spoke Gib slowly sank to the ground and lay torpid by the side of the road.

Dick, drawing himself up to his full height, stood swaying in front of Max. "Drunk," he said, "we're not drunk."

"Not drunk!" Max spat out incredulously. "Not drunk, look at my gunner, he's unconscious. Pissed as a newt."

"Well we are drunk," Dick answered graciously, "but not with drinking beer. We are drunk with the ecstasy of the evening."

At this, Max could not suppress a grin, which slowly spread from ear to ear. "Dick get to your billet for Christ's sake. And take that bloody Canadian with you," pointing to the prostrate Gib, all pretence of authority having been vanquished by Dick's eloquence.

58

We attacked an ammunition dump situated at Aulnoye, France, on the 10th April, flying in a brand new Lanc, Y LM513, which had been allocated to us after the loss of P Peter, and carrying a record bomb-load of 14,000 lbs of high explosives. It was the only raid we carried out in which we saw nothing of the enemy, no searchlights, no flak and no fighters, the only thing of note happening on the run up to the target. Someone planted their load smack on the ammo dump and the resulting mammoth explosion seemed to lift the whole earth. Smoke mushroomed upwards and at 8,000 feet it was like flying in thick fog. Unable to see the target Brick dropped our bombs "in the vicinity". Incredibly – 625 lost one crew, that of Flt. Sgt. W. J. GREENE.

I had a further grandstand view of this explosion two nights later, for we had been sent on our expected ten-day leave complete with pay and the £1 per day generously given to all operational aircrew by Lord Nuffield, and thanks to the Pathe Pictorial cameraman saw it on the newsreel at a local cinema.

It was on this leave that, for the first time, I realised it was far harder to stay at home waiting for news than ever it was doing the job. I was the last remaining child of seven in our family, five of them having died before I was born, and having lost my mother at the age of fourteen my father had married again. He was a likeable, funny rough diamond, and having "roughed" it most of his life, took things as they came. But it was patently obvious when I arrived home that he was intensely worried. What little hair he possessed had turned a few shades lighter and the easy smile and jokes had been replaced with a seriousness foreign to him. A huge map of Europe, pinned on the wall, evidenced the fact that he was actually plotting and keeping a list of every raid in which he thought I had taken part. I felt sorry for him – it had never even entered my head. So much for selfish youth. I vowed to write more regularly in the future.

On returning from leave we were immediately faced with a Cologne raid. Some 379 aircraft attacked the city on April 20th. Whilst the flak was, as usual over the Ruhr, extremely heavy, the raid was remarkably successful from the R.A.F.'s point of view and I could still see the orange glow of the fires as we approached the English coast.

The race was on to get down first but once again Cosgrove pipped us in contacting base.

"Just how the hell does that guy do it?" drawled a puzzled Max, for it had now become a personal thing, much to our amusement.

On this beautifully clear night we were flying downwind at some 400 feet, parallel to the welcoming lane of runway lights as S Sugar, containing Cosgrove's jubilant crew, banked slightly in the funnel lights on her landing approach. With wheels and flaps down she was almost there, then to my utter amazement a pair of navigation lights appeared directly behind Sugar.

I pointlessly shouted into my switched-off intercom, "Look out, look . . ."

My involuntary warning was never finished, for streams of cannon shells were being pumped into the Lanc from a terrifyingly close range. Red and white sparks danced along the fuselage, the machine shuddered violently, like a dog which had just emerged from water, and in she went, with feeble flames never having the chance to envelop her. No explosion occurred. It was all over in seconds. Frighteningly final.

"Intruders, intruders," screamed the Waaf controller as all lights were doused, but not before I saw what I believed to be a twin-engined JU88, with its undercarriage moving upwards, tearing above the Kelstern runway.

Nothing could be more disconcerting for a crew about to land, after a tiring trip, than to find oneself once again in darkness – the friendly lights having disappeared leaving a void of inky blankness in which lurked a night fighter. But this was as nothing compared to the loss of P/O J. P. Cosgrove and crew so dramatically. He would never be first again. It was a terrible personal loss of our friends. Had they just been missing it would have been acceptable, but to see them perish without a chance forever left its mark.

After a lapse of five minutes, which we spent orbiting the drome, all lights reappeared and in went Y Yorker for a normal landing, carrying a very quiet and subdued crew. To us at the time it all seemed so unfair. If a crew had managed to cope with the hell over enemy territory surely they should be left to enjoy the haven of England. We compared it with a chap being machine-gunned in mid-air whilst falling by parachute. But this was war and our Mosquitoes were performing the same type of operations successfully over the German airfields. This was undoubtedly the most demoralising experience of our career.

The following morning we learned that the aircraft buried itself deeply in the ground and the bodies had had to be dug out. P/O Cosgrove had been decapitated and Porky in the tail had been hit by no fewer than 32 cannon shells. The only consolation was that the whole crew had perished instantaneously. Flt./Sgt. D. Y. Bishop and crew also failed to return from this mission.

In the afternoon we were ordered to fly to an aerodrome which was used mainly for emergencies in order to pick up a 625 squadron crew which had forced-landed there. The name of the 'drome eludes me but it was a visit we could have well done without making. Wrecked aircraft littered the whole field. Pieces dangled from them, turrets of some had simply been shot off. Other aircraft were peppered with holes of various sizes – some large enough for a man to walk through. Some appeared to have no undercarriages at all. How many of them ever got home was nothing short of a miracle. I had no desire to know the casualty rate on this emergency landing strip – and these machines were never counted as "Missing".

It is a mystery to me to this day what kept the morale so high. We had long since realised that our .303 guns "building up a cone of almost impenetrable fire some 30 foot in diameter at 400 yards," as was driven home to us on training stations, was a completely useless piece of information – whether true or not. The fact was we rarely saw a fighter and the chances of shooting at one were almost non-existent. In any event the fighter's 30mm or 20mm cannon left us on a hiding to nothing whatever the circumstances. It was almost a time for celebrating when a fighter was reported shot down. However, in spite of the odds stacked against us, morale remained unimpaired.

Bomber Command's activities increased ever more during this period. Every raid, H.Q. asked for a maximum effort and consequently by the end of April we had successfully bombed Düsseldorf, Karlsruhe, Essen, Friedrichshafen and Maintenon, the last-mentioned giving cause for celebration, for Flt./Lt. Middlemiss, on returning from Maintenon, completed thirty operations, the first crew to do so since the formation of the squadron on October 1st, 1943.

There had been little time of late for entertainment of any kind and the whole squadron joined in this binge, few remaining sober by the evening's end. To all concerned, the fact that a crew had actually managed to complete a tour was indeed encouragement.

"Well, if they can do it so can we," Max said as he downed a pint in fine style. "Do you realise we are one of the oldest crews here now?"

"We'll do it Max," rejoined Gib, "and if D-Day starts soon they'll sure as hell get easier."

Dick entered the conversation by saying, "Another five weeks at this rate should see us through, but I still wish we had gone on the pathfinders when we had the chance."

This was a reference to us having been offered the opportunity of joining PFF (The Pathfinders' Force marked the actual aiming point, with coloured markers, on which the main force would bomb) a couple of weeks earlier but by vote we had declined the offer.

"But don't forget," said Max, "we would have had to do 45 then – not thirty-and the USAAF have already told me that I shall have to do an immediate tour on Fortresses when I go on to an American station."

"What do you want to go with the Yanks for?" I asked. "Why not stay with the R.A.F. and if it comes to a second tour we'll crew up again."

"Too late for that Russ," he answered, a little ruefully, "I'm now officially only on loan to the R.A.F. I'll go to an American drome as soon as we're finished here."

"Anyway let's finish this one then we'll see," chipped in Frank. "The war may be over soon and none of this will apply."

As it turned out it was all wishful thinking, for fate had decided otherwise.

Of the raids in April, the Friedrichshafen one was by far the most outstanding.

Seventeen of us took off at 21.35 hours on the 27th, on a cloudless but bitterly cold night, for the longest trip we ever made, and by the time we reached the French coast both the tail and mid-upper turrets were frozen solid, along with our intercoms, rendering speech from the turrets impossible. This was the third time we had had frozen microphones on ops, despite the smearing of the provided cream on the diaphragms, and I could but come to the conclusion that the American throat intercom was a better idea. Our only method now of giving instructions to Max was by pressing a small button which lit a little bulb. Each crew member possessed the same fitting near at hand. One press meant corkscrew port, two presses starboard. We ought really to have aborted and returned to base but once airborne nothing short of an engine dropping out of the wing would induce the skipper to do that.

Apart from the usual flak, which varied in intensity, the long outward flight was normal. The weather was all too clear, but fortunately the fighters were conspicuous by their absence.

The target was anything but normal, for it presented a picture unsurpassed in beauty by anything I have ever seen.

The bombing run took us on a direct course towards the snow-capped peaks of the Alps, clearly visible beyond the target area. Continual shell flashes and puffs of light-coloured smoke flashed by, great menacing beams slowly swayed backwards and forwards and those peculiar bright white lights left the ground, gaining brightness as they came upwards, only to race off harmlessly below. But all of this was surpassed by the target far below. The reds, yellows and oranges of the fires intermingled with the greens and vivid reds of the markers. Dummy fires and paler coloured markers, lit by the Germans, burned on our port side. Blue and purple hues issued from a particularly large burning mass.

I was looking down on a full artist's palette, the view interrupted only by periodical vivid searing white streaks of the photo-flashes. Shimmering Lake Constance, lying as it does alongside Friedrichshafen, reflected the whole scene as accurately as a mirror and in turn transformed the snow-topped mountains into colourful candelabra majestically overlooking the whole panoramic spectrum. Orangy red flames were dancing on the peaks. So incredibly beautiful was the scene that the most frightening part of any operation – that of flying over the hell of a target – was for the one and only time completely obliterated from my thoughts. The perpetual puffs of greyish smoke were merely a nuisance, for they occasionally blotted out part of the picture. Even the odd burning aircraft – always an eye-catcher – could not deter me from looking below. I was mesmerised and realised that never again would I see a sight remotely like it.

Ironical that the dropping of bombs on civilians – the most diabolically devilish thing conjured up by man to date – should create such beauty.

Against all neutrality laws, we were routed over the Alps into Switzerland, where a sharp turn to starboard allowed us to fly over Swiss territory until we hit the Besançon region of France, thus avoiding the defences over Germany for our return journey. It was a good plan with which we crews had no argument – but it was not too successful, for extremely accurate anti-aircraft fire from the Swiss had no fewer than three bombers going down in flames within a few minutes of our being over their territory and we were only too thankful to end our trespassing and get back over France.

It was as we were crossing the English Channel that the skipper said:

"Gib, are you rotating your turret from side to side?"

"I'd have one hell of a job doing that Skip," laughed Gib, "It's still frozen solid. I haven't moved for the last seven hours or so."

"Oh gee, I'd forgotten that you devils were frozen up but this goddarn aircraft is as unstable as a mule. I can't get it trimmed right," moaned Max. "Brick, check the bomb bays," he said as an afterthought.

Two minutes later Brick was screaming in the intercom, "For Christ's sake open the bomb doors Skip, the 4,000 pounder's rolling from side to side in the bays."

"Bugger me!" swore Max. "No wonder I can't get the bloody trim right. Bomb doors open."

So saying, up rose Y Yorker, relieved to be rid of the weight but not half as relieved as her crew.

"Next time Brick," said Max sternly, "make damn sure they're all gone before asking me to close the doors. That thing could have gone up at any time."

The thought of it made me sweat. We landed safely after a nine hours, ten minute, trip.

Two things of note happened on this raid.

One pilot from 625, and I regret his name escapes me, found his Lanc on its back after a shell exploded under a wing, but he had the presence of mind to keep it moving and consequently righted the aircraft. A fine example of quick-thinking even under the shock of an explosion. Just imagine actually rolling a 18-ton aircraft!

Another Lanc ditched successfully on colourful Lake Constance, five of the crew taking to their dinghy and paddling to the shores of Switzerland, where they spent the rest of the war in extreme comfort, as did all crews who managed to get to this country. The other two crewmen baled out.

Chapter Nine

By the 15th May only a few of what we considered the "old crews" remained. I can only recall W/O C. L. Mims, another American flying with the RAF, P/o D. M. Blackmore, S/L J. R. Canham and ourselves, but there may have been others. We had spent a hectic two weeks completing five more raids and had had little time for anything but flying but it was now our turn to say goodbye.

On the 21st May twenty Lancasters lined up on the Kelstern perimeter track scheduled to bomb Duisburg in the Ruhr Valley. Our dispersal point, being close to the runway in use, put us first in line.

"Max," called Dave, as the huge shadowy outlines of aircraft stood stationary at the back of us with engines ticking over. "I've forgotten my bloody hat. I'll have to go back for it."

"Too late, Dave, sorry, we'll be getting a green for take-off any minute now," answered Max.

"Jees Max, I'm sorry but I have to insist," wailed Dave.

A green flare curled over the runway giving an eerie glow to the immediate surroundings and Y Yorker began to trundle forward slowly. We all felt sorry for our Canadian navigator – a hat was nothing, but superstition had become openly acknowledged amonst us and nothing was allowed to interfere with it – nor was it any longer laughed at.

Dave fell hopelessly silent.

A huge explosion ahead of us turned the dusk into momentary daylight as we raced down the runway, and on becoming airborne we flew over a mass of burning aircraft. An Australian crew from

Binbrook had not managed the take-off and had gone in with full bomb-load aboard. I extended my little prayer, for never had we experienced such an ominous start to an operation.

The usual light-fingered welcome was received as we crossed the enemy coast at 20,000 feet, but it was not until we were approaching our final turn to starboard, which would take us over Duisburg, that things started to go wrong.

"I've seen a number of them turning Dave," called Max. "When are we due?"

"Two more minutes yet on this heading. If there are some turning now they are too early," answered Dave.

I sat there wondering how on earth Max could see them for I certainly could not see a thing – it was pitch black.

"I'm certain they've turned Dave," insisted Max.

"In that case you'd better make the turn," succumbed Dave.

It was not long, however, before it was obvious that the navigator had been correct, for over to port Duisburg was taking a pounding from the heavies. We had missed the target for the first time. What was more to the point we were now ahead of the bomber stream. There was now no alternative but to drop our load on a parallel course to Duisburg, probably killing a few cows in the process, then follow the course through, making the necessary turns accordingly. Anything other than this would have entailed flying across the stream – a suicidal practice.

The return flight found us boxed in with some extremely heavy and accurately predicted flak, which violently rocked us from one side to the other, filling the aircraft with cordite fumes. The yellow flashes were blinding and no matter which way we turned the flak was there. The most peaceful moment of my life was experienced when the bursting shells abruptly ceased.

At 1.20 a.m. the skipper asked the navigator, "How long before we hit the coast?"

Dave replied, "Twenty-eight minutes, Max."

We sailed along quite peacefully at 23,000 feet for eighteen minutes – then, in no uncertain fashion, "got the chop."

There was a sudden heavy rattle of cannon which I distinctly heard above the roar of the engines and vicious sparkling white tracer was whipping either side and through us, disappearing to the rear. The Lanc appeared to stop dead, as if to gasp for breath, then lurched on like a drunken man. Both port engines were ablaze and flames spewed back over the port tail-plane and fin. The firing lasted for no more than two seconds. It was more than enough. Down went the nose of the aircraft, the engines screaming in agony, and my head felt as if it was going to burst with the pressure.

"Pull the bugger out, pull the bugger out," someone shouted, and in reply the aircraft slowly adopted an attitude at which it was possible to move.

"Feather port engines," Max ordered, then immediately, "Abandon aircraft. Abandon aircraft."

I sat unbelievingly, watching little curls of metal rolling off the huge oval tailfin revealing the framework underneath, shocked at the suddenness and speed at which events were moving.

Off came my gloves and I uncoupled my oxygen supply and electrically-heated suit, then vacated the turret in record time. The whole fuselage, from the armour-plated bulkhead door to the mid-upper turret, was an inferno. Flames licked at my parachute, which lay on the floor, for I had always had difficulty in putting it in its proper stow.

I grabbed it, grasped the material handles and with a sharp tug tried to engage the two metal brackets onto the hooks of my harness. I failed. Gib, wearing his chute, opened the back door, turned, gave me thumbs up and disappeared from sight.

Smoke and lack of oxygen were making breathing difficult as I tried once again to clip on the chute. I failed again, leaned against the fuselage side and said aloud, "Well, this is it."

The heat was intense and I moved nearer the door. Ammunition was exploding. I was gaping at flames outside, which I could see through the holes made by the cannon shells. "What the hell am I doing?" screamed my fogged brain and in sheer desperation I banged on the chute. It stayed. I rushed to the door and something tore off part of my helmet which I was mistakenly still wearing. Owing to the slipstream, it was difficult to kneel on the step but as I poked out my head I was whipped away with a fierce icy cold wind, my arms clutching the parachute.

I wrote a few days later that the whole episode lasted two minutes.

It felt as if I was travelling a thousand miles an hour in a sitting position. When I pulled hard on the metal handle there was a flapping noise and I was brought to a dead stop in mid-air. By now the oxygen situation was playing tricks, for whilst I realised I was safely out, I was in fact going upwards instead of down.

Strangely this realisation did not concern me one iota.

67

What did concern me, however, was the noise of the fighter, coming closer and closer, and as his engine or engines became a deafening roar I tried to curl myself into a little ball. Thankfully the noise faded, but the night was so black I never saw him.

It was indeed a grim sight watching Y Yorker curl ever downwards, streaming flame as she went. I had seen many go down but this was different. This was our aircraft and some of my mates could well be inside it. The Lanc hit the ground to leave a circle of fire and I turned my head away.

"Please Lord," I prayed, "let all my friends be safe – and please, somehow let my parents know that I am safe. Amen."

Floating down after that was almost pleasant, but bitterly cold. Dampness encompassed me and it was like entering a warm pool of water as I passed through a layer of cloud. On looking down into the inky blackness and deciding there was a long way to go yet, I relaxed totally, but with a surprising bump I landed immediately, rolling on the ground. Twisting the release catch, then hitting it, caused my harness to fall off, and there I lay unhurt, in total darkness, with my knees in the air.

The only lesson we had ever received on parachute jumping was an instructor saying: "Don't forget to land relaxed should you have to bale out." By chance I had done just that.

I prayed again for my parents.

"What now Russ, what now?" I asked myself aloud.

★ ★ ★

During the whole period from when the shooting started I never felt in the slightest way scared, nor had I had any qualms in jumping from the aircraft, for it had all happened with amazing speed and it had been a relief to vacate the blazing Lanc.

Now that it was all over I felt really frightened and most of all so helpless. I believed I was in a cornfield but was unaware if it was in Holland or Belgium. My brain simply refused to function and consequently I could not think what to do. The night was warm, but so dark and still. I lay on my back, exactly where I had landed, afraid to make the slightest noise, for I knew not whether the Germans were two yards or two miles away.

The drone of the bombers returning home restored a little confidence. Standing up I towed the chute from off the corn into the hollow made by landing, as the last of the aircraft faded into the distance. Deathly quiet reigned and again the feeling of helplessness crept over me. Sleep, I decided, was the only answer. I therefore pressed the little chrome lever on my Mae West so as to inflate it for a pillow. The noise of the inrushing air, sounding as if a train was letting off steam, startled me and I hopelessly tried to stifle it. Wrapped in the 'chute and curled in a ball, I managed an extremely restless sleep.

Dawn was never more welcome and as it became lighter I ventured to stand up to ascertain my whereabouts. I had landed in the middle of a cornfield, the corn being so high it was possible to stand up without being seen. Seven farms of varying sizes lay within sight, the nearest being seven or eight hundred yards away. There was no sign of life.

My chute and harness came under inspection and I found to my amazement that my earphones, oxygen mask and intercom wire had wrapped around two cords of the 'chute.

It was too late to reprimand myself for not having discarded the helmet. Had the flex wrapped itself round all the cords the 'chute would have candled. Not inflating the Mae West on descent had been another mistake, for I might have landed in a lake or river. However, as fate had decided, I was in fact in the ideal hiding place, which gave me time to think. I could not have chosen a better spot had I have been afforded the opportunity to do so.

Chapter Ten

Dressed in battledress and wearing flying boots, armed with my escape pack, six pieces of silk, and a length of cord, I waited until mid-afternoon on a gloriously warm day before I made my move, having rolled up in the chute my extraneous clothing along with the parachute harness.

The farmer and his wife at the nearest farm had been in and out of the farm continually and my observation had convinced me no-one else was present. I therefore walked, without hesitation, straight up to the farmer, who stood by the doorway. He was a chap of about fifty, with the typical ruddy weather-lined face of a farmer, but as he stood frozen to the spot watching me emerge from his cornfield like something from outer space, he went paler and paler. He was more frightened than I.

"I am an English flier, R.A.F.," said I as matter-of-factly as I could, "Have you a drink of water and something to eat?" making a drinking action as I spoke.

He never moved but looked at me very warily and then gave a shout which brought his wife to the door. She drew her breath in sharply and screwed up her face. A brief conversation followed between the two of them and, as one, both disappeared inside, closing the door.

"Good grief. I've had better receptions from the Station Warrant Officer after being late back off leave than that," I thought to myself.

The door opened, a cup of liquid was thrust into my hand and the door slammed to again, all in one movement. I emptied the cup in one. It was vile. A gritty, brown, lukewarm substance. I was to drink gallons of the stuff later. This was Ersatz coffee.

In view of the fact that up to joining the R.A.F. I had never been farther afield than Blackpool and Southport and my linguistic qualifications were non-existent, it was perfectly plain the language barrier was going to be difficult to overcome. To me, at that time, I was in a far-off land amongst people of whom I knew nothing. Deciding help was not forthcoming I set off through the fields on what appeared to be a hopeless journey in a direction which would take me away from the coast, as per instructions from our intelligence officers during lectures on evasion, aided by compass and maps from the small escape kit. We were well supplied with tiny compasses which took many forms – the base of my collar stud, for instance, was a compass.

For about seven miles I walked, mainly along a narrow cobbled road. It was flat, open country, and it was possible to see in all directions for a considerable distance, which was very much to my advantage. Also advantageously there ran a ditch at either side of the road. During the walk I passed through a few small villages. Everyone I saw stared in amazement then smiled, nodded or waved, but no-one made an approach and I had quite decided not to make an approach myself unless invited to do so. I just waved back. On two occasions I jumped into the ditch at the sound of an approaching car engine. Four workmen digging a trench in a field beckoned me over and as it was in open country I felt nothing could be lost by going over to them. They took one look at my uniform and I was immediately treated like a long-lost brother, shaking my hand and hugging me, all smiles. Out came welcome sandwiches and drink. Sat on a mound of earth, with our feet dangling in the ditch, I learned by the means of sign language, drawings in the soil, and the maps from my escape kit, that I was close to the Dutch-Belgian border on the Belgium side, near to a place called Meir, and that I mustn't turn left at the next cross-roads for that way lay the Deutsch. I must keep straight on.

Thanking them profusely and shaking hands all round once again, I waved them farewell and continued my journey.

It had been very enjoyable walking. At least I was doing something, but flying boots are anything but walking boots and my feet were sweating and aching. I was short of a plan, but a plan needed assistance. Fortunately it was forthcoming at the next village.

"Boy, boy," said an elderly woman who was standing at the gate of a cottage on the outskirts of the village chatting to two other women.

I ignored her, keeping on walking.

"Boy, boy," she said insistently.

I turned and walked slowly back, the smile on my face becoming broader and broader, for the situation was not without its humour and it was perfectly obvious they knew I was British.

"Have they landed? Have they landed?" she asked excitedly in good English. "Are you part of the invasion force?"

"I've landed, love, but I'm sorry to disappoint you," I said, "I'm on my tod."

She looked at me quizzically.

"I'm by myself. I've been shot down," I explained.

At this her face fell solemn.

"When are they coming? We have waited so long," she questioned.

My hand went on her shoulder, for I suddenly felt sorry for her.

"You won't have to wait much longer. They will be coming very, very soon," I confidently predicted.

The rumbling of a cart over cobbles and clip, clop of hoofs, interrupted us, and as it came closer the lady spoke in Flemish to the man holding the reins. He drew to a halt, looked me over from head to toe, smiled, shook my hand and motioned me to get into the cart, which was laden with heavy logs. I lay hidden under the logs, unable to move, whilst we moved off on what turned out to be an extremely bumpy ride. One of the logs persistently bumped my head with every above-average dip in the road surface. After what seemed an endless journey we arrived at his farm. It was with considerable relief that I climbed down from the wood cart. We were in a small, cobbled, courtyard with farm buildings on three sides. A dust-hatted lady, her apron tending to emphasise her rotund appearance, stood at one of the doors. She gaped, silently, unable to believe what she was seeing, then, having gained her composure, directed a meaningless string of words towards the man. On receipt of his answer her expression changed, and along with two children, who had by now joined us, she came to me, shook my hand and smilingly led me indoors.

A large bowl of steaming porridge stood in the centre of a huge scrubbed white-top table and the five of us sat round it whilst the wife supplied each with a large dish and spoon, her clogs clattering on the flagged floor as she did so. Oblivious of the children's eyes, which never left my face, I tucked into the delicious porridge with gusto, but after only four or five spoonsful, I could eat no more. I felt terrible. They had been so helpful and friendly and yet I could not have eaten without being sick.

"I'm sorry," I spluttered, holding my stomach, "It really is good but for some reason I cannot eat."

The aftermath of the experience I had had in the early hours of the morning was setting in. I knew it, but how on earth was I to explain to them?

Explanations proved unnecessary. The older and wiser couple looked at each other understandingly and nodded. The wife came over to me and tugged at my sleeve. "Cum," she said. I followed her into a barn and up a rickety pair of ladders into a hay-loft. She put her hands together, smiled and rested her head on them, motioning sleep, then disappeared down the steps. I slept the sleep of the dead with mice as companions.

Someone was vigorously shaking me and I slowly opened my eyes, only to close them quickly, for a light was shining directly into them. The fourteen-year-old son was saying, "Cum, cum," as he shook, and I got the impression he had been trying to awaken me for some considerable time. Back in the house the farmer was waiting with some old clothes and a pair of Dutch clogs. I gave him in return my flying boots and sweater, putting the clothes provided over my uniform, and on being joined by another farmer we set off at 11 p.m., on foot, across the fields. No-one spoke. The outline of a farmhouse loomed up in the darkness and on reaching the door he waved me in first. With very mixed feelings I felt my way along a dark corridor towards a chink of light, wondering where on earth it was leading. I pushed on the door and it opened into a well-lit, smoke-filled room, containing seven or eight people.

"Russ. Oh Russ boy. I thought you'd had it."

I was being hugged and kissed by that big friendly Dick Reeves.

Never in my life have I been so delighted to see anyone, and of all people, Dick. We just clung to each other.

"I opened the bulkhead door and everything was on fire. I couldn't . . ." he was saying.

"What happened up front? Did they all . . .?" I interjected.

"I was broadcasting a wind, what . . ."

It was impossible. We were both excitedly talking at once, gabbling away like incoherent madmen, completely overjoyed at meeting up, and totally oblivious of all around us.

The Belgians in turn smiled their satisfaction. They had learned what they wanted to know – we knew each other and were obviously members of the same crew. Beer was put on the table and all toasted "Après La Guerre".

A neatly dressed young lady came over and handed us a list of instructions, printed in English, which we had to memorise. The instructions pointed out that a strict curfew was in force and that everyone had to be indoors by 10 p.m. We should be travelling at night, therefore silence was vital. At all times it was essential we obeyed our guides without question and these might be changed periodically. We were reminded that lives were at stake and they ended by wishing us a safe journey back to England. After reading them she took them away.

"Comprehend?" she said.

We nodded.

In turn Dick and I went round the room shaking hands and thanking each individual. Two women took us outside where awaited four cycles.

It was a heavy, overcast sky, and black as the ace of spades, for which we were very grateful. The women rode in front, I next, and Dick in the rear. I soon came to the conclusion that a decent road did not exist in Belgium for we kept continually to narrow dirt tracks which ran alongside cobbled roads or cart tracks. Dust, in places, was at least six inches deep, causing the wheels to dig in and act like brakes. Cycling in complete darkness, on strange heavy bikes, with wooden clogs on my feet, was not just difficult – it was well nigh impossible, but incredibly the women were making great speed which caused them continually to halt whilst we caught up. Silence had gone by the board for Dick and me as we struggled to keep up and we crashed along like a mechanised army. Our greatest difficulty was the brakes, for our only means of stopping these infernal machines was to stop pedalling and press hard with the feet.

For thirty minutes we rode as fast as possible until suddenly the women stopped abruptly. I just managed to skid to a halt. Then crash. Dick ploughed straight into me with a clatter which sounded loud enough to be heard in the centre of Berlin. Our guides melted into the darkness. We were all alone, not daring to breathe.

Minutes ticked by then out of the shadows three shapes materialised. They were three young men, and they conversed in low undertones with each other, solemnly shaking hands with the two of us.

Once again our cross-country started, this time with Dick and a guide up front and I with the other two, fifty yards to the rear.

This is one bike ride we will never forget. For five hours we rode, walked, pushed, climbed over walls and crossed fields and ditches. In some places we carried our cycles very quietly under the very noses of German sentries. To make matters worse an air raid started. The cold shimmering fingers of search-lights sprang up at irregular intervals, probing the night sky. Thundering crashes of anti-aircraft guns reverberated through the quiet of the countryside bringing into relief every bush and track. On our stomachs, dragging the bikes, riding like fiends, then walking quietly past a guarded spot, we progressed.

The leading guide stopped till we caught up.

"S.S. officer," he said, pointing at the shadow of a huge house ahead. "Shh," with finger to his lips.

We rode silently, line ahead, with myself at the rear. Completely forgetting the back-pedal braking system I decided to free-wheel past the house so as to make less noise. So doing I shot straight over the handlebars with such force that I flew into the ditch, the bike following with a noise like twenty galvanised dustbin lids being dropped onto concrete from a great height.

I was alone in the ditch, gasping for breath, fully expecting the worst as the flashes lit up the house. Nothing stirred. With heart pounding I gingerly remounted and pedalled off into the darkness in hot pursuit of the guides.

It was all so unreal – another world. Every moment I was tingling at the thought of a rifle shot. At each bridge and house I expected to be challenged, but our luck held until, after what seemed an eternity, we pulled into what appeared to be an orchard, and stood under the trees waiting.

A gentle crackling of the undergrowth sent my nerves jangling but the tension was relieved by the appearance of one of our guides, accompanied by a much older man. He beckoned us to follow. For ten minutes we struggled through a tangled mass of bushes and undergrowth, carrying and dragging the heavy bikes. Our new-found friend stopped and breathed into my ear in English, "Take precaution, Germans near." Within seconds we acquired the stealth of Indians, eventually coming into a large clearing. Standing on the far side of the clearing was a big daunting-looking house, its main outlines being clearly visible in the eerie gloom of the searchlights. We made a quick quiet dash across the clearing into the sanctuary of the house's shadow. With a faint click the front door opened and the five of us followed the older man inside.

Without making much noise we tiptoed across a very spacious room, which was unshuttered. In that brief moment I recalled a film I had seen, "Dangerous Moonlight", for the scene was identical. Searchlights fingering the sky, the crumping of heavy guns, causing a fine spray of dust to fall from the ceiling. All that was missing was Anton Walbrook playing the "Warsaw Concerto".

Entering a large room at the back of the house the older man struck a match and applied it to a lamp. The light was just sufficient to cast a gentle glow over a sparsely-furnished room with heavily-shuttered windows.

For the first time we could see the faces of our helpers and were surprised to find the three guides could be no more than fifteen or sixteen. The kindly-faced older man of medium build was probably in his fifties and, as we sat down wherever convenient for a well-earned rest, conversation flowed comparatively easily. The three youngsters, particularly, asked question after question, using the older man as interpreter. They wanted to know what Dick and I actually did in the aircraft; how many times had we bombed Germany; what was it like in England; when was the invasion expected; did we think we would win; had we plenty of food or were we starving like the Germans said; had we lots of tanks, guns and aeroplanes; did we still play a lot of football and who were the popular names.

Their thirst for information was unquenchable and it was perfectly obvious that they considered Britain the finest country in the world. We had been placed on a pedestal so high in their minds that it would have been impossible for any country to live up to the standard set. Our tired bodies and minds did the very best possible in satisfying their eagerness, with Dick giving them a full résumé of our sporting activities, which had tears of laughter rolling down their faces.

It was, however, a welcome relief when, from out of nowhere, a particularly attractive young lady appeared and lisped "Tea?" The older man, whom I had assumed was her father, spoke gently in Flemish to her and before long we were tucking into a large plate of ham and eggs complete with a steaming mug of tea. This extremely enjoyable meal broke up the party and the guides left, but not before shaking hands vigorously. It was a great feeling to be held in such high esteem.

"You will be back in England by 'flying machine' in two or three days' time, but now you must sleep," said the older man and so saying led us upstairs to a small bedroom which was empty, apart from a double bed. As dawn was breaking, Dick and I, tired and weary, climbed into it, wearing vests and underpants.

"Two or three days' time, I hope . . ." I never finished the sentence. We were both fast asleep.

It was impossible for me to know then that before the war was over we should be cuddling up together, night after night, just to survive.

Chapter Eleven

It was mid-afternoon the same day when a deafening noise brought us back to life.

"What the hell . . ." Dick blurted out only for his voice to be drowned before he could finish his sentence by the ominous crackling rat-tat-tatting of machine guns.

I rolled out of bed, hit the floor with a thud and rolled underneath in under a second – I would not have won the prize had it have been a race, for Dick was already there beating me by .2 of a second. With our hearts beating at some 350 beats to the minute we lay quite still, listening to the rattling guns and whine of bullets, till realisation dawned that no bullets were coming in our direction. The firing ceased. Silence reigned.

Somewhere in the lower regions of the house someone was moving about. At every noise up went the heartbeat. As one, we eased forward with tense white faces, listening for each movement, hoping we had been mistaken. A door opened and footsteps echoed clearly from the uncovered floor boards, the noise grew louder, then clump, clump, they were climbing the stairs. Did this mean capture? That's why the firing stopped. The Germans must have followed us here. All these thoughts ran through my mind as the footsteps halted outside the door. Slowly it opened and long black locks appeared as she said, "Cum, eat," and disappeared.

I looked at Dick, reminiscent of Laurel looking at Hardy, and sheepishly we got to our feet. The firing started again but by now our composure had returned somewhat. We therefore went over to the window and peeped through the cracks in the shutters. In amazement we stared at a ME109 fighter plane, no more than 200 yards away, its tail lifted off the ground, around which stood a number of Luftwaffe pilots awaiting their turn for firing practice.

"Would you believe it. We're on the edge of a bloody Luftwaffe station. No wonder he told us last night not to make any noise," I said, stating the obvious.

"What a place to hide us," Dick answered. "Frightened me to bleeding death."

"Never bothered me," I said, giving him a sly sort of look.

"Ee bah gum lad, tha will have thi little joke." Dick's efforts to imitate my accent were atrocious but always good for a laugh.

We dressed, and went downstairs, to find the table laid and the young lady of the previous evening ready to serve. Boiled eggs, bread, butter and tea, followed by a bowl of porridge, met fully with our approval. The young lady was more than a little shy now she was alone and approached us warily. I got to thinking we must have seemed a rough-looking pair with our prickly unwashed faces, and even Dick's attempts at humour met with obvious nervousness.

"Toneet cum," she said after clearing the table and washing the dishes, then disappeared from the house. All was silent, the firing having stopped.

Dick and I returned to the gloom of the bedroom, the only light coming from little rays of sunshine which squeezed their way through chinks in the shutters. Lying on the bed, we held our first conversation alone.

"Dick, what happened up front when we were hit? Did they all get out?" I asked.

"I really don't know Russ," Dick replied. "It's a good job they did pull it out of that first dive or none of us would have got out. I was tuned into the broadcasting station and they started transmitting bang on time, but no sooner had I put pencil to paper than the aircraft gave a terrific shudder. I switched over to I/C to hear Max saying, 'Feather the engines', then 'Abandon aircraft, abandon aircraft'. I opened the bulkhead door only to be met with a wall of flame, so I slammed it to, chop chop. Dave had gone when I passed his table with my chute on, so he must have baled out, but Max and Frank were struggling with the control column when I climbed into the bomb nose. Brick was sat on the edge of the escape hatch as if deciding whether or not to jump. The seconds were ticking by so I tapped him on the head and yelled at him to jump, but he looked up at me blankly. I bunched my fist and hit him in the

79

back and all but knocked him out of the aircraft and, of course, I followed. But I'll never forget looking back up and seeing the faces of Max and Frank, lit by the flames, which were licking their way around them. They were both staring straight ahead, their arms wrapped around the control column, pulling as hard as they could. Damn it, I hope they made it."

"Yes, I hope they did," I answered solemnly, "but somehow I have my doubts. I never mentioned it at the time but a few weeks ago they both told me that if we ever got hit they'd ride it down. I know it sounds stupid but they meant it. It's a good job they did pull it out of that first dive or none of us would have got out. Anyway, Gib made it, he went before me."

"Oh great," Dick was overjoyed. "Trust that bugger to manage it. I honestly thought you had both bought it. What hit us anyway?"

"It was a fighter of course. You probably heard his guns like I did," I replied, "but do you realise he hit us from the front? Port quarter up. The closing speed must have been 500 miles an hour. He must have picked us up on radar, got a quick glimpse and fired. It just had to be at close range, he only fired for a couple of seconds."

"From the front?" he exclaimed in a surprised voice. "I thought they told us we would never be attacked from the front, the closing speed was too fast at night."

"Yeah, I know. You'd better go back and tell those instructors they're talking through the back of their necks."

"If we get back I will," Dick said with feeling. "I'll also tell them how quick it is when it happens. One minute you're okay, and within five seconds you're a goner."

"Anyway, it's all water under the bridge mate. Point is, what are we going to do now?" I asked.

"I've been wondering that myself. It looks as if we have got with the underground," he said, "but they know precious little about us yet. They haven't even asked our names. But fair enough they have been very helpful and friendly and I certainly liked his comment last night about two or three days then back home by aircraft. How the hell are they going to manage that?"

"I'm sure I heard someone mention vaguely about Lysanders landing and bringing the lads back when they had deposited the spies over here," I recalled, "but at all the lectures they said head for the Pyrenees and try to get into Spain."

"We've a bloody long way to go to get there," the big lad answered, "and if it's anything like last night's journey we'll be knackered long before we arrive."

"You can say that again. Anyhow we're at least free. Let's play it by ear and see what these people come up with. What I'm bothered about is what are our parents thinking now. They'll have had the telegrams long since," I said.

"For God's sake, Russ, don't mention that. That's the worst part of it. I've deliberately been trying not to think about it. My old mum will be heartbroken," he answered sadly.

At the mention of home we both fell silent, each with our own thoughts. What a blow it must have been for them. I lay on the bed picturing them receiving that dreaded telegram and trying to visualise the look on their faces. It was a terribly depressing silence. Here we were, fit and well but without any means of letting them know at home.

"Come on, let's snap out of it," Dick broke the silence. "There's nothing we can do. Let's have a root around."

As luck would have it we came across two packs of playing cards and in the gloom passed away the dreary hours "gambling". By the time darkness fell Dick owed me £17.10s., and the cheeky so-and-so offered to pay me in French francs from his escape pack. I refused point blank.

It was with great relief that we heard the clicking of a key denote once again the arrival of our guardians.

(AUTHOR'S NOTE: It is not only difficult to continue this story but also unfair towards the people who aided Dick Reeves and myself without giving the reader their names and addresses. It must be realised, however, that it was not till we received letters after the war that we ourselves discovered the identity of these brave people.)

Whilst Emilie Vermeulin, a very attractive young lady, was understandably shy and retiring, her father Marcel was quite a humorous individual, possessing a dry wit which appealed to us, and it was not difficult to like the pair of them.

During the meal the four of us sat and chatted at length. They, deliberately I believe, asked no embarrassing questions but were full of interest in Britain and the likelihood of an early invasion. We were extremely sorry to receive the news from Marcel that the leader of our three guides of the previous day had been shot in the stomach on their return journey. However he was at present reposing comfortably in the local hospital. A diary which he had been carrying was fortunately found by Marcel near the spot where he had been shot; had that fallen into enemy hands the game could have been up for the lot of us.

Marcel and Emilie lived at Wit-Hofken, in Brecht, Belgium, and owned the house in which we were now staying. It had been put out of bounds to them in view of the fact that it stood by the training camp, hence its uninhabited appearance. Fortunately it was reasonably easy to approach the house through the orchard without being seen from the camp, but nevertheless it was a risky business for them.

A fund of stories came from the older man, during the telling of which it was not difficult to detect the hard times the Belgians had been having under German rule, but somehow he managed never to dwell on the unpleasant aspect. Typical of one of the stories he told us was one about some German officers who visited a café in Antwerp. Apparently on entering the café they were greeted with a great gust of singing by a number of Belgian students, seated around one of the tables, of a popular German song at the time, "We sail against England, We sail against England." The officers were elated and applauded accordingly as the students left the café on completion of their performance. The café settled down to normality only for the doors to suddenly swing open as each student tramped back to his seat soaking wet. The significance of their actions was missed by the Germans until the locals began to chuckle.

No-one was to blame for the fact that Dick and I spent five long dreary days in the gloom of this house, never once setting foot outside, for Marcel and his daughter kept us well fed and well hidden. What more could we want? The promises of "one night then England", which we received daily, had worn a little threadbare, and we soon came to the conclusion that it was being said in order to keep up our morale. It was not going to be as simple as that. During our stay a number of visitors came to see us – most we believed out of curiosity – but as neither group could speak the other's language nothing was achieved, if Marcel was not present, apart from a little relief from our boredom. We even came to watch for the Luftwaffe pilots at shooting practice each day, taking turns at peering through the cracks in the shutters.

On the fourth day, however, a man came to see us who spoke good English.

"I am an official of the 'White Brigade'," he announced, pumping our hands up and down, his face breaking into a smile momentarily and just as quickly wrinkling back into the frown which he had worn on entering.

He was a well-dressed chap, maybe forty-five years of age, and carried a certain amount of authority in his voice.

"It is necessary for me to ask you some questions in order to ascertain that you are definitely R.A.F. boys. You will appreciate that Germans dressed in R.A.F. uniform try to infiltrate into the underground from time to time and therefore we cannot be too careful. Your answers will be confirmed or otherwise by London so I hope you will think carefully before you answer," looking at each of us scruffy-looking individuals in turn.

A silence followed which I eventually broke by saying, "We understand the situation and the danger you are putting yourself in by helping us and are, of course, extremely grateful. However, you must also realise our position. We not only don't know who we are speaking to but we don't even know where we are. Officially we are allowed to give only name, rank and number. With respect, you yourself could be a German. We have no means of knowing otherwise."

He looked rather stern at this, then said, "Be that as it may, we cannot divulge our identity for obvious reasons and for us to help you further you must answer my questions. However, we are already ninety-five per cent convinced that you are genuine due to the way you received each other on meeting up, which incidentally, coincided with an aircraft crashing at Meir, a place only a few kilometres from where you were picked up."

"Okay," Dick chipped in, "Let's have the questions, but we don't promise to answer them all."

At this he placed a sheet of paper on the table, withdrew his pen and asked, "Name, rank, and service number."

We answered in turn, spelling out the names slowly.

"Type of aircraft?" without looking up.

I looked at Dick, shrugged my shoulders as if to say, "There's nothing to learn from that," and answered, "Lancaster."

"Your duties?"

"Wireless operator and gunner."

"Squadron?" he asked next.

"625," I answered.

"Where based?" he came back.

"Sorry," said Dick, "We cannot answer that one."

It was his turn to shrug. He asked a few more pointed questions which we either refused to answer or answered vaguely.

Realising the shutters had gone up and he was going to get nothing else he said, "Thank you. You will be pleased to know that tomorrow afternoon at one o'clock you will be moving into Antwerp. I wish you a safe journey back to England." And so saying he rose, shook hands and disappeared out of the door before we had time to speak further.

Chapter Twelve

The following morning, May 29th, Marcel, in his usual thoughtful manner, produced shaving equipment, of which we made excellent use in removing seven days of growth from our faces.

"At one o'clock," said Marcel during breakfast, "I want you to leave by the front door and go straight through the orchard. By a tree on the roadside you will find two cycles. Emilie, myself and a man you have already met will ride by. Follow us at a respectable distance. We will part company when we arrive in a small town. You must follow the third guide, who will take you by tram into Antwerp. Sit as far away from him as possible but always keep him in sight. He will get the tickets. Alight when he does. All clear?"

"Yes, fair enough, but if we should be asked for our papers what's the procedure?" I queried.

He looked at us, smiled and said, "Sorry boys, but if that happens at this stage you are on your own. There is nothing I can do about that. I will have to be going now. See you later."

"Before you go," said Dick, "We'd like to thank you and Emilie for all you have done. We understand you're taking a great risk hiding us. Let us at least pay you for the food we have eaten."

And so saying he produced the Belgian money from his escape kit.

Marcel looked hurt. "I would not dream of taking money from you boys. It's your efforts and the risking of your lives whilst bombing Germany that will eventually make Belgium free. The very least we can do is to help fliers who fall into our hands. I wish you a safe and speedy return home."

After handshakes all round and a few slaps on the back I handed Marcel one of my pieces of parachute on which I had written my name and address.

"Thanks, Marcel, hide it well and write to us after the war," I said.

"I will."

And at that we parted from our helpers.

A sparkling sun shone from an azure sky as Dick and I walked outside to once again join the land of the living, and as we made our way through the orchard it was with a sense of relief and elation, mingled with apprehension, for as yet we had met no Germans face to face and that would obviously be remedied soon.

The cycles were easily found and it was indeed a strange-looking pair we made awaiting our guides. Dick's large faded jacket hung on him like a sack in spite of his size, his trousers glistened with grease and the huge shoes on his feet looked like two invasion barges, whilst my half-masted drain-pipe trousers, adorned with many patches, hardly matched my 19th century jacket, for that is when they would have been in their prime. Completing the ensemble were a pair of well-worn slippers, tied on with white string, which I had decided would be an improvement over the Dutch clogs for cycling.

A staggeringly attractive Emilie appeared, followed by her father and the other man, making me think of much more pleasant things than our forthcoming ordeal. We followed, well behind, riding on the dirt track alongside the cobbled road. After ten minutes' riding, and having passed through a small village, it became apparent to us that no-one was taking the slightest bit of notice. This knowledge gave me all the confidence I needed and I began whistling, thoroughly enjoying the fresh air and exercise. If Dad could only see me now, I thought.

The scene changed abruptly as we rode into a small town. The place was heaving with humanity, most of which unfortunately, wore German uniforms. My heart missed a beat or two and the whistling petered out to allow me to draw a deep breath.

Our pace slowed dramatically, and we soon found ourselves edging past groups of people who had spilled onto the cobbled streets, and in one instance actually riding through a tram queue, brushing shoulders with a member of the Wehrmacht in the process. I have always preferred the countryside to towns and nothing that had happened over the past five minutes had made me change my mind!

It was with positive relief that we saw our third guide turn into an alleyway, by a café, and nod for us to follow, whilst Marcel and Emilie disappeared into the mêlée. Our bikes deposited in the alley, Dick and I followed the guide on foot out into the street, to eventually join a queue patiently waiting in the square. Immediately in front of us stood three haughty-looking Luftwaffe officers, one of whom wore the Iron Cross. Dick looked at me with an expression the like of which I had never seen before and was probably thinking the same as I was. There we stood, speechless, in this busy square, as German lorries of every description picked their way past dozens and dozens of cyclists and pedestrians, whilst two white-helmeted Belgian police tried in vain to control the chaos.

Dick left my side and strolled conspicuously – or so I thought – across the square to enter a urinal. With his head and shoulders looming large over the iron plate, and his massive shoes protruding below whilst he relieved himself, he almost gave me hysterics, for I could not help thinking to myself, "Trust Dick to want a toilet at a time like this." This single act, we both agreed later, did more to put us at ease than anything that had happened hereunto.

I was becoming interested in the horrible, guttural speech of the officers in front of us, when a further Iron Cross-adorned flier joined the others with a smart click of his heels and a Heil Hitler salute, which seemed totally out of place in this busy square. I had to grudgingly admit to myself they were extremely well turned out and looked particularly fit. I found myself staring at them in curiosity and it was just as well when, with a screech of brakes accompanied by rattles and bangs, the tram stopped alongside. The front tram was towing two other carriages, giving the appearance of a miniature train, but even so, each compartment was jammed solid, and only with considerable pushing and shouldering did we manage to get our feet onto the platform.

Off we went on one of the craziest juddering, clanging, jerky, noisiest rides of our lives, screeching to a halt at every other lamp standard, where people well-nigh fought a pitched battle to get on or off. I noticed that every German had a seat. Slowly, but surely, the tram made progress with a frustrated lady conductress attempting the impossible task of collecting everyone's fares. A task I might add which involved the female in question in a bit of Commando work, as she had to climb over two lots of railings and stride over the couplings, each trip she made between compartments. To start and stop the infernal machine she blew on a curved horn.

Dick and I eventually managed a seat inside, spotting our guide at the back as we sat down. As two sailors were sitting directly opposite we carried on a mock conversation with Ja, Ja's, and nodding of heads, which met with our requirements but really would have fooled nobody. By now we were oozing confidence but nonetheless the sooner the journey ended the better. Fortunately the fair damsel collecting the fares had not approached us and we sincerely hoped she would not.

A crash and a screech threw everyone forward and both Dick and myself found ourselves virtually in the laps of the enemy. The tram had hit a cart, and fruit and vegetables littered the road in front, along with splinters of wood which would have been ideal for fire-lighting. A much unwanted delay ensued during which one of the sailors touched Dick's arm to draw his attention. Dick chose to ignore this, but was awarded a stronger nudge for his efforts. The sailor was holding an unlighted cigarette and I nodded to Dick. Quick to catch on, he fumbled in his pocket, withdrew a box of matches and gave the naval man a light. They were English Swan Vestas matches. We looked at each other quizzically, expecting the worst, but the Germans were back into conversation oblivious of Dick's mistake.

After a three-quarters of an hour run we arrived in the centre of Antwerp without further incident. As we alighted a comical-looking little fat chap stepped forward and, in spite of the fact that there were literally hundreds of uniformed personnel in the immediate vicinity, shook hands with us and unconcernedly led us to a side street where awaited a small car. Driven by a hatless, speechless, pasty-faced individual, we were transported in grand style to a more residential district of Antwerp, stopping at the door of 29 Boomgard Straat. It was an interesting ten minute ride which afforded us the opportunity of seeing an occupied city in a leisurely manner. The most notable things were the vast array of uniforms we passed – I doubt if I could have identified ten per cent of them – and the lack of male teenagers.

The little plump man nimbly bounded the two steps up to the front door with Dick and myself immediately behind him, but before he could knock the door was opened wide by an unseen hand and we entered a large thickly-carpeted hall. The door clicked to and before I had even a chance to take stock of my surroundings, a pair of female arms encircled my neck and pulled me close, and I was soundly kissed on both cheeks. Heady perfume pervaded my nostrils making me think of anything but Germans and evasion. Dick received the same treatment.

She stood back, smiling broadly, displaying a gold tooth as she did so. I guessed her age to be thirty-three or upwards, a small woman of some five feet three inches, not desperately beautiful but with an attraction of her own, mainly stemming from her amused and excited eyes which sparkled through her spectacles as Lake Constance had in the flak flashes. The lady ushered us into a large, well-ventilated room, beckoning us to be seated at a round glass-topped table, whilst she herself glided her Marilyn Monroe figure across the room and sank into a luxurious armchair, still smiling.

"Hello Belgique," she said, struggling with the word "Hello."

"Thank you for our reception," I answered, smiling back at her.

"Ah-h-h-h-h," she sighed, "Engleeshmen."

"I must tell you," broke in the plump man in a strong foreign accent, "Madame has been waiting since yesterday for your arrival. She was so anxious to meet you. She thinks the English are doing a wonderful job and asks me to tell you that you have the freedom of the house during your stay and anything at all you may require please ask." So saying he waved his hand round the room.

It had already become apparent to Dick and me that we were surrounded by opulence. My eyes travelled from the chandelier to the mahogany glass-topped furniture, to the richly-carpeted floor. I had never seen anything like it, the room oozed wealth. War seemed a long, long way away, and we felt so terribly out of place dressed as we were. It just was not true, it could not be happening to us.

Our guide informed us we would spend only a few days here before departing by flying machine to England, but in the meantime clothes of a more suitable nature would be found and necessary papers for travel would be provided.

"This will entail taking your photographs," he said, drawing on a huge cigar, the smoke of which circled the room, thus giving an expensive aroma in keeping with the setting. "I will bring a photographer tomorrow and will call on you periodically to keep you informed of progress." And so saying he rose and bade us farewell with our thanks ringing in his ears, Madame accompanying him the door.

"How about this for a set-up?" Dick queried of me when were alone.

"I just can't believe it, Dick, it's fantastic, and what a welcome. Never in my wildest dreams would I associate this with the underground movement," I replied. "They seem to know what they're doing. I wonder if he will come back tomorrow with a photographer?"

"Well we will just . . ."

Dick was interrupted by Madame flouncing in followed by a maid, complete with white apron and hat, carrying a tray of sandwiches and cakes which she placed in the centre of the table. She left only to return in seconds with another tray of cups, saucers, coffee jug, etc. and no fewer than five brands of cigarettes. Obviously there had been much precogitation. It was unfortunate that the sandwiches contained raw bacon, with which Dick and I struggled smilingly, but not too successfully. In fact much of Dick's ended in a piece of his parachute, now being used as a hankerchief, craftily spit there at every convenient occasion throughout the meal. Inexplicably conversation never flagged, if gesticulating wildly and using all manner of signs can be described as conversation. The lady made a far better job of understanding our English than we did of her Flemish.

"Cum," she said, after the meal and proceeded to give us a conducted tour of the whole house, which left us gasping.

The building was a large three-storey one, complete with cellar, the latter having been developed as a games room with a bar billiards table, darts, table tennis, etc. On the ground floor was the beautifully furnished lounge we had first entered, a good-size workmanlike dining room and a well-equipped kitchen alongside. The first floor carried two bedrooms and a huge fully-tiled bathroom, exquisitely furnished with turquoise bath, toilet, washbasin and separate shower; two circular mirrors and an attractively tiled floor, completed the décor. But if the bathroom was eye-catching, Madame's boudoir was breathtaking.

It was, as indeed were all the rooms, spacious. The room, however, boasted a considerable array of expensive furniture. Against the far wall stood a massive wardrobe made from 1½ inch thick oak, as was all the furniture. Alongside the near wall a set of matching drawers carried beautifully carved figures which adorned the polished top. The bed filled the top end of the room, stretching down to the centre of the rich blue carpeted floor, and the semi-circular head and foot carried extension cupboards, their surfaces being covered with plate glass. A golden-coloured overlay covered the whole bed. Let in the wall, which ran parallel to the street, was a bay window in which stood the most beautiful dressing table I had ever seen, complete with carved figures, glass top and well-designed handles. The centre of the room was occupied by a round glass-topped oak table, a finely crocheted design lying beneath the glass. Small drawers and cupbards to the depth of six inches surrounded the table and were opened by unique glass handles. Silver stars of various sizes stood in relief from the pale green walls, and over the bed head, set in the wall, was a large painting of trees and lovebirds, with stars and moon in the background. All was tastefully lit with hidden coloured fluorescent lights.

I had seen comparable bedrooms only on the silver screen straight from Hollywood. As we left the room Madame indicated, with a wave and a point, that this was to be our room. We were speechless!

Three further attractive bedrooms on the second floor completed the interior.

Outside, a glass-covered sunken garden with various exotic plants and bushes, reminding one more of a conservatory than a garden, provided the only greenery, for at the back of the house were brick-built workshops which now stood empty and had obviously seen more active days.

* * *

After having a welcome hot shower Dick and I returned to the bedroom to find Madame busy laying out all manner of clothes for us. Unabashed she sat there as we chose and tried on various trousers and jackets, frowning her disapproval or smiling her satisfaction accordingly. Dick finally plumped for a blue serge lounge suit, which fitted his big frame to perfection, silver blue dress-shirt and a maroon coloured tie, tie pin included. I adorned myself in a brown suit and open-necked white shirt. Everything of an R.A.F. nature had now disappeared. We had been transformed into men-about-town.

"If they could only see us back at camp now," I said. "They'd all bale out."

Hermine Scheire, as Madame was called, seemed anxious to tell us about herself. It transpired that she was thirty-five years old and had been married twice. The first time was for five years, from which there were two children, Georges and Marie. The second was for six years, her present husband now regretably languishing, after considerable ill-treatment, in a concentration camp. She was an extremely wealthy woman with extensive business interests, now dormant due to Nazi occupation. Hermine detested the Germans and anything German, and her tell-tale flashing eyes when speaking on this subject convinced me she would be better as a friend than an enemy. Here was a very determined woman, albeit a very feminine one, who looked younger than her years. A woman of passions, was my conclusion. She also had every intention of learning English and insisted that the first lesson begin that very day – which was just as well, for Dick and I, being idle types, had not the faintest intention of trying to master Flemish. The speed with which she learned was nothing less than remarkable; another sign of the sheer determination of the woman.

We whiled away the evening playing cards in the dining room, with beer, wine and cigarettes on hand as one pleased.

As we sank deep into the luxurious feather mattress at the end of the day Dick commented: "Well, Russ, have you ever seen anything like this in your life? It's out of this world."

"I certainly haven't," I replied, "I just can't believe it. My idea of underground was secret passages, sleeping in barns and all kinds of subterfuge. Whereas in fact this is fantastic."

"This lot must be coming from the Black Market," he opined. "I have more drink and fags here than I had at home, and yet out in the streets people look hungry and drawn. Just what more could we want?"

"Who wants the war when we've got this?" I concluded, before dropping peacefully off to sleep.

Chapter Thirteen

For six weeks we stayed in Boomgard Straat, getting to know Hermine, her two children, father and mother – all of whom visited the house regularly, but did not live there – extremely well. Her English vocabulary improved daily and nothing happened to alter our first impression. She was a little ball of dynamite.

As before we had many visitors, as far as Dick and I were concerned far too many. All of these we gave nick-names for our own ease of identification. Hermine was known as Madame Mazonga, the dapper little chap who had brought us here was "The Gen Man", another regular visitor was "Mr. Withacar", being one of the few who always arrived in a car. These two appeared to be the main underground contacts – for most of our other visitors appeared to call for purely social reasons. Two men came regularly for a chat or game of cards. Albert, a friendly, middle-aged man of average build, owned the garage opposite Hermine's house, and Jack was a dry, quietly-spoken, grave individual from farther down the street who had relations in England. Jack would be in his sixties and was soon christened "Laughing Boy", for he never smiled. They were both excellent company and, in view of the fact that they could speak English, these evenings became something to which we looked forward, and night after night they would sneak home late, keeping to the shadows in order to beat the German-ordered curfew.

The highlight of our days, however, was the B.B.C. news which we received on a clandestine radio set which was cleverly secreted in a cupboard. To hear the impeccable English of the announcer, giving us the latest war news, made Dick and me feel so much nearer home, apart from keeping us abreast of the vital war news. The Belgians hung onto every word uttered. They were so desperate for relief and all whom we met simply lived for the day when the British Tommies would march into Antwerp singing "It's a Long Way to Tipperary" or "Pack up your Troubles in your Old Kit Bag", the songs they all knew. Even the school children sang them at school, much to the embarrassment of the teachers. It made one appreciate the impact the British troops had made during the 1914–18 War.

We did, however, meet the other types. One young chap, in particular, gave us a long drawn-out story of the dangerous part he played in underground activities, giving us the usual unreliable garbage about how soon he would have us back home. All the time he was speaking he waved a pistol around in gay desperado fashion and long before he had finished Dick and I were yawning wth boredom. He was obviously out to impress, but failing miserably – we could have told him something about guns and the right and wrong way to handle them. Thank goodness we never saw him again.

★ ★ ★

Every few days "Mr. Withacar" or "The Gen Man" paid us a visit and on every occasion promised we would be home soon, at times actually stating the date we would move, but each time, inexplicably, nothing happened. By the middle of the second week, however, "The Gen Man" brought along our identity cards and papers. My identity card described me as Albert von Meegan, a backersgast (baker's boy), hailing from Brussels and now working as a stoker in a nearby war factory. Dick was Albert Jan Van Meel, living at 223 St. Bernards Steinwick, Antwerpen 1 and was an aphataker (chemist) working in a chemical factory in Brussels. The cards were perfect, complete with photographs and stamped with the German eagle. Comparing them with Hermine Scheire's neither Dick nor I could fault them. Encouraging indeed!

One visit from "Mr. Withacar" had been most unsatisfactory for he brought forms with him which he required us to complete.

"But we have already answered questions as to our identity in the last house we stayed," I protested.

He looked at me rather sternly, "I am sorry but we have not received them and you must understand our position. We just cannot take the risk of Germans infiltrating the line. If this should happen we will all lose our lives. This information is essential to us."

It was always a powerful argument and one difficult to overcome.

"This again is exactly what we have been told previously," Dick broke in. "If we have to give this information everywhere we stay more people than ought are going to be aware of our existence."

"That is correct." He was getting a little annoyed. "However I must have the answers to these questions or we can proceed no further with your return to England. This will be the last time, I assure you."

"You are placing us in a difficult situation," answered Dick. "We are aware that some Belgians are selling the escaping fliers to the Germans for handsome rewards and the more forms we fill in the more likely they are to fall into the wrong hands."

"They are the traitorous Black Brigade," he said venomously, "who are responsible for that. A crime for which they will pay dearly when hostilities cease. Come boys, do as I bid. You must be convinced by now that we are not the Black Brigade or we should have sold you long ago."

I looked him straight in the face. "Regardless of the consequences this is positively the last time we shall answer any questions, for we are also convinced that by now you know our identity."

Squadron number, target, how we were shot down, time of take-off, time due to land, name, rank and number was all he got. Nothing very alarming, but I could not forget an intelligence officer telling us, "If I can get a man talking – no matter on what subject – I guarantee to extract some worth-while information from him sooner or later." As if reading our thoughts he concluded by saying, "Thank you boys, you will be flying out in two days' time. It is now finally organised. I appreciate you have heard it all before but you can take this as official. I will contact you tomorrow to give you a definite time and to tell you where you will be picked up. The only thing I can tell you at the moment is that it will be on a football field out in the country. Goodbye for now."

He shook hands and left.

I turned to Dick, "Could be a Lysander, that's the only aircraft that'll land on a soccer pitch."

"Well, he sounded genuine," Dick rejoined. "We'll keep our fingers crossed and hope for the best. I'd love to walk into the Mess at Kelstern as if nothing had happened."

"I'll second that, Richard," I concluded.

9 a.m. the following morning found us soundly asleep, dreaming of home, when the door of our bedroom was flung open and in dashed Hermine shouting, "Boys, boys, they cum. Zee English are cum! Along coast they cum. We free, we free!"

I heard Dick mutter an obscenity as I grunted and turned over sleepily. She was insistent.

"Cum, cum, quick," and without further ado she yanked the bedclothes off the pair of us till we finally sat up and took notice of the little fireball.

In a matter of minutes the three of us were gathered around the set and sure enough it was confirmed. The date was the 6th June, 1944.

"Dum, dum, dum, dah, dum, dum, dum, dah . . .", the victory sign in morse thumped out its stirring introduction to the overseas news broadcast. "Under the command of General Eisenhower the Allied Armies have made successful landings on the Northern Coast of France and have already achieved the element of surprise." One could detect the excitement in the announcer's voice. He gave more details and then proceeded to give a long list of instructions to the members of the underground movement in occupied territories.

"Damn, damn, and damn again," swore Dick. "That's buggered it up for us getting home for a bit."

He never spoke a truer word, but it was as well that Hermine didn't hear them. She couldn't, for she was dancing around the room with an imaginary partner, singing her head off.

Throughout that day it seemed that half the population of Antwerp paid us a visit. We were hugged, kissed, slapped on the back, hands shaken till we were well-nigh exhausted. So many toasts were drunk in any available liquid that food was out of the question. It made one feel good to be British, but it did get embarrassing at times, for both Dick and I felt that they were the real heroes – not us – but being the only representatives of the Allies around we came in for the lot.

The days went by and the war news was excellent, but Dick and I had suffered yet another disappointment. We had waited for an official to put in an appearance but had seen no-one, and the days were dragging, the darts board and bar billiards lying untouched. The evening card games had become a bore. We badly needed some movement and Hermine was not slow to see how we felt.

"Right boys, we go to cinema this afternoon," she stumblingly announced right out of the blue one day.

"The cinema," we chorused in amazement, for we had not set foot outside the front door since our arrival three weeks ago.

"The cinema," she replied with finality.

"We'd love to go for a change," said I, "but it's out of the question. If you get caught with us you're a dead woman and you know it."

"We go to cinema, have I to carry both you." She laughed at her own joke.

The three of us casually made our exit from the house, after lunch, and walked through the streets of Antwerp as if we owned the place, the relief of getting out overcoming any lingering doubts we may have felt regarding mixing with the population. The aerodrome nearby and the U-boats on the River Scheldt, plus a strong Wehrmacht contingent, meant that the city was teeming with troops, a fact which I now considered helped, rather than hindered, our situation.

Sirens began to wail their warning of an impending air raid, people melting off the streets quicker than snow in an oven, leaving us treading a lonely path on the pavements. The crump, crump in the distance heralded a dozen or so formations of American Flying Fortresses flying high, their long white condensation trails clearly marking their flight path. The booming of anti-aircraft guns became louder and louder and ominous white puffs intermingled with the leading formations. Shrapnel rained down, rattling on the roof slates and pinging on the cobbles, vicious jagged pieces of lethal metal. Whilst Dick and I looked at each other uneasily, anxious to take shelter, Hermine never faltered. With head bowed as if in a snowstorm she walked on, seemingly oblivious of the danger. Knowing that at times more people had been killed or wounded by shrapnel than by the bombs themselves, I grabbed her arm to pull her in to a doorway, but she shrugged me off as if trying to prove that no-one was going to stop this outing.

The thunderous bangs of the anti-aircraft guns seemed to suck in the glass of the shop windows, then out they would bellow to incredibly return to their original position.

"You're going to get us all killed," yelled Dick above the infernal rattling and banging. "Get under cover."

The brave little woman smiled, "We go cinema," she shouted, with me thinking it had been safer over Cologne in a Lanc. The bombers eventually passed over, carrying the flak elsewhere, and with considerable relief we completed our journey without further hindrance.

A mixed queue had assembled by the time we reached the small cinema and the three of us unconcernedly tagged on to the end as if going to the local flea-pit back home.

The film itself was difficult to follow, but the dialogue must have contained some humour, for each time a funny remark was made the German soldier sitting next to Dick dug him in the ribs and bellowed with laughter. Dick's answer to this was to nod and laugh with him. His expressive face could always raise me to a smile, but on this day he excelled himself, and each time I leaned forward I caught his eye, which was desperately trying to tell me about this silly devil sitting next to him. Dick's expression was so indescribably comical that I eventually developed an uncontrollable fit of the giggles. It did not help the situation overmuch when, for no apparent reason, up went the lights smack in the middle of the film and an overall-clad chap walked down the centre isle carrying an extension ladder over his shoulder. He placed the ladder against the wall, alongside the screen, and matter-of-factly proceeded to paste a huge bill on the wall advertising next week's programme. This bent me double and it was a timely interference when the more sobering propaganda-ridden newsreels appeared on the screen.

Hitler, of late, had been referring more and more to Allied airmen as murderers, and screaming all kinds of retribution. As luck would have it, the Germans had captured an entire Fortress crew, who in answer to his ravings, and with typical Yankee humour, had painted the words, "Murderers Incorporated", in large letters, across the backs of their leather flying jackets. The joke had backfired, and here they were, making the lead story for the newsreel men, offering proof of the accurate statement of the Fuehrer. One could not but admire the producers of these films, for the impression given was of victories on both Western and Eastern fronts, at a time when the enemy was suffering the biggest humiliation of the war with the Allied landings.

Two days later we repeated the exercise, to a different cinema, but this time on our return journey we received a shock. The tram on which we were travelling suddenly slowed and came to a halt in one of the less busy streets. Two soldiers, carrying rifles, entered the tram at one end and proceeded to herd the passengers off at the far end. On dismounting we found the street cut off by a line of troops, whilst at the front end of the tram stood a covered lorry, tail-board down, in front of which more troops milled. There were probably sixty of us sealed off with no room for escape. Two jack-booted officers and two Belgian police unceremoniously formed us into a line facing the tram, them proceeded to examine each individual's papers in turn. If satisfactory the people were allowed to re-enter the tram, if not they went in the lorry.

By this time Dick and I had drifted away from Hermine.

"Hope these papers are good," Dick muttered, "Unless they're after us . . ."

"Papiers." The officer was looking me straight in the eye and I could feel his eyes boring into me. With clammy hands I handed them over, conscious that I was trembling and hoping it didn't show. After what seemed an eternity he waved his hand towards the tram. Slowly and deliberately I walked to the vehicle, but my whole being wanted to run, and I took in long deep breaths to compensate for the oxygen I had lost whilst not breathing a few seconds earlier. In all, six people went into the lorry. Normality returned when all had been examined, as quickly as it had previously been interrupted.

Chapter Fourteen

"This is all very well, you know Russ, but where's it getting us?" Dick queried of me when we were alone and back in comparative safety at Hermine's home.

"Absolutely nowhere," I concurred. "What do you reckon? We haven't seen anyone in authority for a week. Days are growing into weeks and we are no nearer getting home than the day we landed."

Dick look hard at me.

"What about making our own way down towards the French coast and trying to meet up with the advancing troops?" he said.

"If that's what you want to do I'm with you," I answered, "but we discussed this the other night with Jack and as you know he pointed out the impracticalities of trying to get past the masses of German troops there will be at the front lines. Security will be hellish tight and don't forget we would have a fair way to travel to get there."

"I suppose you're right. What do you want to do?" he asked, "Stay here?"

"From choice I'd prefer to pull out and make our way down towards the Pyrenees as we would have done in the first place if we hadn't been picked up. At least," I answered, "we would be making some progress. At the moment we're static."

"On the other hand," mused Dick, "shouldn't we think ourselves lucky and simply stay put till the troops arrive, and put up with the boredom and frustration?"

After a long discussion that was precisely what we decided to do.

"Okay," I concluded, "we'll let commonsense decide and sit tight, and here's hoping they get their skates on."

It was a week later when the "Gen Man" next appeared accompanied by two Canadian aircrew members, "Ed" and "Doc", navigator and bomb-aimer respectively of a Halifax which had been hit twice by a night fighter before it blew up. Both had regained consciousness in mid-air, whilst floating down on their parachutes, and neither remembered clipping on their chutes nor bailing out. "Ed" had received a nasty gash on his leg which Hermine treated immediately as best she could. As Dick and I were in the process of receiving a hair cut from a barber, who had been brought in specially by Hermine, the new arrivals also came in for a "crop".

"Would one of you boys come with me?" asked the "Gen Man" almost immediately after entering the house. "I have four more aircrew boys at another house and I want you to ask them local questions. We are very, very busy at the moment, as you can imagine, and this makes the situation more dangerous for us. There are a lot of fliers around and frankly we cannot cope with them all."

It was agreed that Dick go.

"Find out what's happening if you get a chance Dick," I shouted before he departed.

After a long interesting natter with the Canadians I strolled into the back yard for some fresh air. The sound of aircraft, close by, attracted my attention, and there, coming in low over the rooftops, was a ME109, with wheels and flaps down, obviously coming in to land at a nearby aerodrome. It wobbled out of sight only to be followed by another one. For an hour I watched as JU88's, FW190's, ME109's and ME110's slowly crossed overhead on their landing approach.

It was such a strange feeling, watching enemy aircraft performing the identical movements I had watched our own planes making hundreds of times. In fact the only real difference was the markings, camouflage and huge antenna protruding from the noses of the twin-engined types.

The Luftwaffe were obviously expecting the main bomber stream to pass within striking distance of Antwerp that night. Defending such a large area of land was probably the biggest disadvantage they had. It entailed their having to move their night-fighter force regularly in an attempt to be in an attacking position early without having to fly long distances before finding the bombers.

Why should I have the impression they should be different from our own aircraft? Surely the crews would have the same problems as we. They would have to cope with the fog, thick cloud, icing up, navigating in atrocious conditions, plus any mechanical faults that may develop. On top of this they had to find their prey then pluck up their courage to finally make the attack, hoping they did not get hit first. Yes, in spite of the fact that I had always considered their job a doddle compared to ours, they would have lots of problems. Furthermore, as I had already seen on my travels, they were, like us, only teenagers.

I returned to the house thinking what a funny old world we lived in. If there was not a war on we might even be friends instead of trying to kill each other. During wartime such thoughts were unhealthy. They were the enemy and that was that, so I cast my thoughts aside and turned to less disturbing pursuits.

Dick unfortunately learned little to encourage us from the "Gen Man" during his outing. Apparently there had been so much activity since D-Day that the underground was in turmoil. The getting home of airmen seemingly had been put well down the list, other more pressing tasks understandably receiving priority. To complicate matters, "Mr. Withacar" had disappeared with the Gestapo on his tail.

Hermine was not happy with four of us in the house. She felt it was too dangerous and that advantage was being taken of her generosity. It also put a burden on the amount of work to be done.

"Tomorrow," she said to Dick and me, "Mother and Father cum children tea. I go see "Gen Man". Maid no cum. In other places can no tea. Oh, you no tell Engleesh good." The last sentence she said in desperation, shrugging her shoulders.

By now, however, we had become very familiar with her own brand of English and knew precisely what she meant.

"Tell you what," said Dick gallantly, "Russ and me will cook the tea. Tell us what we're having and it will be ready when you come back."

"Meats, can meats? Clandestine man bring for Engleeshmen. When I go are back."

"Cook them, cook them?" laughed Dick. "Have I never told you about the days when I was a chef? Stop worrying, tea will be ready for you."

As promised tea was ready and piping hot, the following day, when Hermine came home, both of us having worked all afternoon preparing it.

It was, however, a disaster. The meat was quite unchewable and the vegetables would have made a sound base for a soup and were served up as a kind of "mush", much to our amusement, but not so the old man's. He spent his time just glaring first at Dick, then at me, trying to make up his mind which one of us he should decapitate first. Unfortunately this was the last we saw of the elderly couple. I have often wondered why. Hermine reprimanded us and banned us from the kitchen henceforth, apart from washing the dishes.

"Doc and Ed" did not stay much longer, Hermine having made noises in the right places for their transfer elsewhere. She had however done well for "Ed's" leg, which was now much improved due to her constant attention. They had been great company for Dick and me and had seemed to relieve the boredom of our now self-inflicted stay inside the house. More to the point they had taken our minds off home for a while.

Normality having been restored to the household we reverted to the card games in the evening, darts and bar billiards during the day, not forgetting Hermine's English lesson, and generally being idle. It was during one session of games in the cellar, when Hermine asked us to move some heavy boxes under which lay a large wooden, heavily-padlocked chest. It must have measured all of 3 ft. by 2 ft. by 2 ft.

Both Dick and I stood back in amazement as she lifted the heavy lid, for there, neatly stacked level to the top, lay thousands of banknotes, secured in bundles by elastic bands.

"God almighty!" I blurted out. "Treasure trove. There's a fortune there."

Dick stood speechless for once, goggling at a sight we would never see again.

"My man and I work much well before war on fabrications. It was me imposs to go on. We again after war when my man . . ." her voice trailed off and her usual smiling face clouded over. We had rarely discussed her husband, for on each occasion the subject had raised its head she had changed the topic of conversation. Hermine never expected to see her husband again. And she didn't.

"Get it locked and covered up again. You shouldn't have shown us that," said Dick concerned, "we could easily steal it."

"You no steal money. Cum I smack bottom and sell you now Germans. I want show you."

"Well you shouldn't have. Lock it up and hide it somewhere

103

else." I meant it. I would have preferred her not to be so trusting.

Whilst it was quiet inside the house, outside was another matter, for air activity was increasing daily. The American Flying Fortresses and Liberators could be seen regularly by day in their huge high-flying formations, and during the night, the heavy drone of the Lancasters and Halifaxes filled the air. The news on the battle-fronts was still good. The Allies, having established themselves, were advancing in all but one sector, with surprising speed. It appeared to us that the opposition had not been as heavy as expected in some areas.

"At this speed they could be here in a few weeks' time," I commented excitedly one morning after hearing the news.

"We dance in straat and I much take my two Engleesh boys to first Tommies with so pain in my heart," laughed Hermine. "Oh it will be much much nice. You cum back in ceremonial uniform and the mine is ready sleeproom. Yes?"

"We'll come back and show you a night on the town," I promised.

Dick chipped in. "We'll do more than that. We will take you on a holiday. You deserve it. Boy what would I give to see those tanks rolling down Boomgard Straat."

Alas, it was not to be.

Chapter Fifteen

On the morning of Wednesday, 5th July, we had visitors, a man and three women. As with all callers we stayed upstairs whilst Hermine entertained them. The purpose of the visit of these strangers was to inform her that they were aware that she was hiding two airmen. They claimed they had no objections to this but as the underground was now in such a state, it was impossible for us to be got back home by normal means. However, one line had now reopened, and it would be possible to get Dick and me to England on Friday, along with a further two fliers, for they were the organisers of this line.

We shook hands all round with the four averagely dressed newcomers, on Madame's call to come downstairs. She explained to us what had transpired, as best she could, and asked our opinion. As none of them could speak English it was well-nigh impossible for us to make a realistic decision. Had "Mr. Withacar" or the "Gen Man" been present it might have been easier, but both now seemed to have disappeared into thin air.

Using Hermine as an interpreter we asked: "Can you guarantee Friday?"

"Definitely," was the reply.

"Why us? There must be a number of fliers about?"

"We only know of you and two others in the immediate vicinity and we know you have been here a while."

"We have had so many promises it is very difficult for us to accept you can arrange it when the rest of the underground movement cannot. How can you?"

"Because we have reopened what was a well-used line."

After further questioning we mutually agreed to risk it. More pleasantries were exchanged and they left.

"I not trust them," Hermine blurted out as she re-entered the luxurious lounge. "You judge like me. Looks alone not good," and so saying she donned her coat. "I be back soon," she said over her shoulder as she disappeared through the door.

It was an agitated Hermine who returned three hours later.

"Traitorous," she bluntly stated. "They am sold many men to Germans. No trust. Gestapo know you here."

Stunned by this news we could but listen.

"You must go. It is so improvist, but 6 a.m. tomorrow you go. I am so afflict that Gestapo know. Conceal all. Mr. "Gen Man" was known to Deutsch."

She spit out the last word as if it was mouldy cheese.

What belongings we had would have fitted in a jacket pocket, our escape kits and bits of parachute were all that remained. However, such things as razors, shaving soap, some drawings I had done, etc., were soon hidden away. A silent, depressing evening followed, with a tremulous Hermine unable to sit down for five minutes running.

For the first time she was scared and it showed. No longer did she glide about the house purposefully and sensually. It seemed as if her energy and vitality was slowly being sucked out of her. She tapped her teeth with her finger nails, crossed and uncrossed her shapely legs, fidgeted and fussed.

Not until six o'clock the following morning, when our new guide arrived, did the tears flow. Uncontrollable tears. Sat on the top step of 29 Boomgard Straat, her face buried in her lap, the small frame shuddered with each sob and no amount of talking and sympathising by Dick and me could make her uncurl. It was pitiable to behold.

"Christ, this is no good Russ. We'll stay. I'm buggered if I'm going to leave her in such a state."

"Come on, let's get her back inside. If anybody sees us they'll wonder what on earth's going on. You go," I waved to the guide. "We're staying."

"Stupid, stupid, stupid Engleeshmen," she managed somehow to get out. "One enough for Gestapo – not three."

"Then come with us," suggested Dick, desperate for a solution.

The guide, looking anxiously up and down the street, shouted, "You must hurry, hurry."

"Go. Go," screamed Hermine.

Reluctantly, and with a half-cowardly feeling, Dick and I walked slowly across the street, leaving a sobbing and pathetically frightened Hermine for fate to decide her destiny. It had been the hardest decision we had had to make thus far.

By foot and by tram, we made our way through Antwerp to the countryside beyond, where thankfully peace and quiet reigned. Only once did we have to show our passes and that was to a tired, yawning old soldier, who was more interested in sleep than in us. Our situation took on a different aspect as we walked along the cobbled roads, surrounded only by fields of waving corn. Eventually a long stone wall came into view and it was here we halted whilst the guide rang a small bell, suspended over a doorway, by a curled piece of metal.

In answer to the ring the door opened and to our surprise a smiling nun waved us in, closing the door behind us, and leaving the guide outside. We found ourselves in a large courtyard centred by a well-kept lawn. Alas the building, standing at the far end, had seen better days and the fact that it had sustained a direct hit from a shell or bomb did nothing to enhance its appearance. It was a forbidding building, even in the sunshine, but an ideal hiding place.

In a very dignified manner she led us across the courtyard, up three steps and into a long sparsely furnished room. Windows were non-existent or had been boarded up, the room being lit by three bulbs, down the centre of the ceiling, and in spite of the gorgeous weather it was cold and dank, carrying the smell only old buildings carry. Six bunk beds lined one wall and the nun motioned to two of them, the polished floor echoing to our footsteps as we crossed the room. A table tennis table, the ever-present dartboard and four chairs completed the furnishings, the four chairs being occupied by four pasty-faced individuals who had evidently not seen sunshine for some time.

Getting the four chaps to talk proved to be a Herculean task. In response to our smiles, shaking hands, questions and general conversation, the most we got out of any of them was a nod. We had just about reached the stage where we felt like kicking the chairs from under them when one at long last spoke, in good English.

Apparently two of them were Frenchmen on the run, the other two being German Army deserters, and it was one of the Germans who eventually succumbed. Once he got talking we couldn't stop him – not that we wanted to – for he turned out to be very interesting, having deserted, whilst on leave, from the Russian front. His story was one of little food, inadequate clothing in atrocious weather conditions, and brutality the like of which he never wanted to see again. He desired only one thing – the end of this senseless war. His stories of how Russian snipers, dressed all in white, would lie in the snow for hours without moving, even at the expense of frost-bitten faces and fingers, till they eventually got a German, were fascinating and it was not difficult for us to understand his reasons for deserting. He had experienced the type of war we knew precious little about.

Fortunately or unfortunately, as the case may be, Dick and I stayed only one night, the guide of the previous day calling early next morning to take us once again into the maelstrom of Antwerp. We would have much preferred to stay in the seclusion of the countryside but we were not making the decisions, and whilst the nuns and one German had made us welcome the other three occupants of the room certainly had not, having treated us like the intruders we were.

Our luck in travelling in and out of Antwerp could not hold forever and this one all but put paid to our escapade. The sirens wailed as we hit the outskirts of the city and soon police were ushering everyone into shelters, including Dick and me. Down in the packed, dimly-lit concrete room, we found ourselves sat on forms, cheek to cheek as it were, with the local populace. Conversation being the only possible pastime, the people sitting alongside naturally engaged the pair of us with a stream of meaningless Flemish. I fervently wished the ground would swallow us, but no such luck. We looked at the ceiling, the flaking walls, our shoes, anywhere but face the staring unbelieving eyes of our would-be conversationalists. Eventually Dick and I got our heads together and mumbled away to ourselves, treating the people in a most abnoxious manner, hoping they would pass us off as two ignoramuses.

To improve the situation, torch-carrying helmeted policemen began a tour of the shelter asking for papers. Our turn came all too soon. He was younger than the average and probably keen to impress his superiors – the worst possible kind. At his command we both opened our identity cards showing the photographs and official stamps, but he wasn't satisfied for he snapped a question at us. I looked at Dick bewildered, then, as one, we both touched our ears and lips, shaking heads at the same time to indicate we were deaf and dumb.

It was the corniest ruse in the book. There must have been three hundred R.A.F. lads wandering round Europe all acting deaf and dumb – yet it worked. He pulled a face, made a noise and moved on. The surprising thing about this near-miss was that we should both remember together what the intelligence officers had told us to do in such a situation.

"We can't keep getting away with it like this, Dick. Sooner or later we're going to get nobbled," I said when we finally and gratefully made our way onto the street again.

"My legs were like jelly. I couldn't believe it when he accepted us at face value," Dick answered. "I think I'd prefer travelling at night after curfew."

"Don't tell me your legs were like jelly. I was scared stiff. You're the biggest of us, I'm looking to you for a bit of encouragement," I grinned.

"Well you're looking the wrong way if you're looking for a hero, mate," the big lad laughed. "Better go look to Hermine, she's the one with guts."

"I know," becoming serious. "What a state we left her in."

Dick never answered, he was busy with his thoughts.

Number 6, Museum Straat lay in close proximity to the River Scheldt and, being a three-storey building, was sectioned into flats. One could not expect the opulence of Boomgard Straat, but our first-floor bedroom was more than adequate.

A reception party of four women had met us as we entered. Three of them would be in their late forties, the other an attractive twenty-year-old. Conversation had flowed reasonably well, though only one could speak a little English, and it was she who had led her "team".

The four had hung around us like wasps round a jam pot, after providing us with an enjoyable meal, and the laughs and giggles had soon developed. In my strict determination to stick to the truth, even at the expense of the reader disbelieving me, I can but report exactly what happened. The six of us had been stood in a group in the main living-room, where incidentally hung a huge picture of the Kaiser, when the "leader" had leaned forward, pushing her finger into Dick's nipple, which showed through his tight fitting shirt, exclaiming with a smile, "Wat is dat?" Without further ado Dick had pushed his finger into her nipple saying

"Same as dat." I thought they were all going to wet their pants, they had thought it was hilarious.

"Tell English swear words," she had said.

"No, no," we chorused. "Naughty."

"Cum, cum, tell," she had insisted.

"What a bleeding country this is," Dick said turning to me.

One by one we had covered the milder oaths of our nation but still they had not been to their satisfaction.

"I'll tell you what it is, Dick, they've heard them all before. The '14–18 lads left more than their songs here," and so saying we had launched in deliberately with every known Anglo-Saxon word or saying, each one bringing shrieks of laughter from the three older women.

A timely interruption in the form of an elderly man, introduced to us as Georges, had broken up the gathering by late afternoon.

"The trouble is," I said to Dick later in the seclusion of our bedroom, "they're all sex-starved. There's probably one man to every thirty women in Belgium. The men are in Germany in forced labour camps."

"Sex-starved or not, we're not getting tangled up. I've never come across anything like it. Lock that door," he suggested.

"Too late, I already have," I replied. "But there's one thing for sure, when the troops do get here they'll have the time of their lives. They won't be fit to go into Germany."

"Well it's a bit of a devil when we've actually to lock ourselves in. I aways thought it was the men who did the chasing," he laughed.

"Must have different rules over here," I said. "The last thing in their minds is us getting back to England. This is an added hazard which the intelligence people didn't tell us about. That's if it is a hazard. I could think of a few who would make pigs of themselves in this situation."

Julia Leutenant, the owner of the flat, and her son's young wife, kept the usual clean, tidy Flemish home, feeding us as best they could on their meagre rations. Conversing with the ladies was well-nigh impossible. Consequently, through no fault of theirs, common ground was never established during our five-day stay in the house. It was as well, therefore, that our second-day visitor, a thirty-odd-year-old lady by the name of Paula, spoke our language fluently. Paula Caveirne, of 176 Avenue de Belgique, was hiding two aircrew chaps at her own home and was evidently no newcomer to the underground activities. She brought along a goodly selection of English books, plus a number of records for us to play on an old gramophone.

"There's not much else I can bring you for now but you will not be here too long. Arrangements are being made for your return home on Friday, but I can't tell you any details. The guide who brought you here yesterday will call later today with more information."

A pleasant and friendly lady, of obvious good breeding, she spoke quietly and in a business-like way with little needless preamble. Paula was the efficient one and impressed Dick and myself probably more than anyone we had so far met.

"I don't have to tell you there is great danger in what we are doing," she went on. "So you must not go outside or get involved in any silly ideas of leaving on your own, for if you are caught we would be placed in a very difficult position." As if reading our thoughts: "Be patient a little longer and we will get you home."

"Tell me," asked Dick, "what's this picture of the old German Kaiser doing on the wall?"

"Simply because Madame Leutenant is a German. She came to live in Belgium after the First World War," she answered. "Don't worry, she is very much on the side of the Allies. In fact if you look in that cupboard you will find a map of the Western Front with the Allied advances marked on it. She listens to the B.B.C. and alters the map daily. She's like the rest of us. We're all so anxious to see the British march into Antwerp, they will receive an unbelievable welcome."

True to her word our tall blonde guide of two days previously appeared shortly after Paula left. He stayed a few minutes but brought with him the information we longed for. Friday midday we would be on our way home.

In jubilant mood Dick and I spent the next two days playing the records and reading books, content in the knowledge that something definite was happening. Apart from the ladies upstairs who came down for a game of cards each evening, Paula was our only other visitor. She never missed one day.

On coming downstairs from our bedroom for our evening session of cards the day before we were due to leave Madame Leutenant's home, Dick and I were surprised to find a roomful of people surrounding a table covered with party fare. The celebration was for Dick's twenty-first birthday, the date being Tuesday, July 11th.

The four ladies from the flats, a next-door neighbour, our guide, with two men unknown to us, Paula, and a dark-skinned girl opened the proceedings by wishing Dick a happy birthday and a safe journey home for the two of us. By the end of the evening everyone was drunk after what had been a successful party, our time having been spent dancing and singing, led by our dark-skinned guest who was, apparently, a Greek night-club singer.

We were not too drunk, however, to realise that getting to bed unmolested would be a tricky operation, but by a little guile and deception we both made our bedroom before "good-nights" were said, firmly locking the door.

It was an anxious couple who, the following day, awaited the arrival of the blonde one, but sure enough at midday there he was ready for the off. We sincerely thanked our hosts, offering them money as we did so, which as usual, was rejected.

The long wailing "All clear" was sounding the end to Antwerp's daily siren call as we stepped outside to follow the guide along the main road. It was good to be out again, in spite of the rain, which had been heavy at times during the morning and was by now forming tributaries in its headlong dash to oblivion via the road grates. We walked for some five minutes along quiet narrow cobbled streets, halting outside a confectioners' shop, whilst the blonde one crossed the street to engage a tall but stout man in conversation. We were waved across to join them as a car drove up to halt alongside the four of us.

Our guide bade us farewell and we climbed into the car, the large trilby-bedecked man sitting between Dick and me on the back seat. We alighted outside a factory-type building on the outskirts of the city, the driver and the large man leading us upstairs and into separate rooms. The driver of the car turned to me as we entered the room: "I just want a word with you on your last day in Belgium," he said in reasonable English. "Do you think the various people you have been staying with need money? You see , for feeding and clothing you boys they are entitled to 500 francs per week. We like to make sure they get this money to encourage them to take in more fliers. Really it's in answer to the Germans offering the population a bribe to hand over the fliers."

"We've offered them all money wherever we've stayed but it has been refused, so I haven't got the impression the people are in need of it, or alternatively their pride wouldn't let them take it," I answered.

The driver was a thick-set man. What he lost in height on his comrade, he gained by his physique. His steely-grey eyes smiled. "How long have you been here?"

"Seven weeks."

"Seven weeks," he repeated incredulously. "Hellfire, if they'd only get in touch with us as soon as they pick you up we would have you home in no time. We've tried everything to speed up this line. On an average it takes us nine days to get a man back. Where have you been staying? I'll see they get paid?"

"I'm sorry, I daren't tell you that. Is there no other way?" I said concernedly.

"Excellent. That's the answer I wanted. Let's join the other two," and so saying we crossed a small landing at the top of the stairs and entered the room beyond.

Sat on boxes in a circle the four of us nattered about the war, laughing and joking at the state in which Germany now found herself and guessing how long it would be before the final collapse. It could not be too soon for these two chaps.

"And then I'll visit England when it's all over," the stout man ended the conversation. "Come on, let's be on our way and get you two back home."

"What are the chances of us getting home now?" Dick asked of the man sat between us as we drove off.

"One hundred per cent," he answered. "But if anything unusual happens during this journey, keep your head. Say nothing: we'll do the talking. We have to cross the River Scheldt soon and the entrance to the bridge is guarded. Once past them we're okay."

In due course the car slid to a halt in front of some iron gates. The guard, carrying a bayoneted rifle, approached, only to withdraw at the sight of our driver's credentials, held out of his side window. Obligingly the gates opened allowing us to drive into what appeared to be a large courtyard.

"We must alight here and walk over the bridge," said the driver.

"Through the doorway and straight on," he whispered, waving us in the general direction.

On going through the doorway we saw no bridge, but the clattering of dozens of typewriters met our ears as we surveyed four neat rows of ladies sat at their machines, the far wall supporting a huge painting of Adolf Hitler.

The hard muzzle of a revolver dug into my back.

"German Military Intelligence. Empty your pockets." The

driver, holding the gun, was no longer smiling. In fact those steely-grey eyes had become positively sinister.

To say I was shaken rigid would be a gross understatement of fact – I was thoroughly shattered – angry, sorry and frightened all at one and the same time. As full realisation dawned, anger dominated. What a let-down. I had been so utterly convinced we were headed homewards and had even day-dreamed of how I would explain to my parents what had happened. Now all that was gone and God knows what lay in store. We had walked straight into Antwerp prison with the Gestapo as companions.

"Empty your pockets," repeated the larger with asperity.

Mechanically, as if in a dream, we placed what few items we possessed on a nearby table.

The typewriters had ceased to operate and every female eye in the room focussed on us. In his native guttural German the driver loudly made some comment to the typing pool which brought delirious laughter from them – our first taste of total humiliation.

Dejectly Dick and I stood facing the two responsible for our capture. For the first time in my life I desperately wanted to hurt somebody.

"Of course I suppose you know what will happen now?" sneered the stout man. "In possession of Belgian papers, dressed in civilian clothes and no other means of identification. You will be shot as spies at 8 a.m. tomorrow morning."

Silence. Utter and complete silence allowed his statement to filter through.

Chapter Sixteen

Dick Reeves and I lay in an untidy, tangled heap, on a dirty cell floor, having been unceremoniously propelled there, at great speed, by an over-enthusiastic push in the back delivered by the ugliest mountain of a man I had ever set eyes upon. His neck was the outstanding feature, for it resembled a bull's in every respect. The heavy iron door, with its glass peephole three-quarters of the way up, clanged shut.

"We've made a ball's of that little lot," I said as we regained our feet and attempted to dust ourselves down. Dick grimly nodded his agreement.

We had suffered the humiliation of stripping off in front of a doctor and three female orderlies, been made to touch our toes to enable a thorough search of our orifices to be made, given a complete medical and finally sat naked in a cold dark room for half-an-hour where side and front view photographs had been taken whilst we held our service numbers, chalked on a board, in front of us. It had been an embarrassing ordeal.

The large old prison was of spider's web design, the centre hexagon shape being formed by electrically controlled iron gates. As a particular gate slid open so it led into a self-contained prison with cells on either side of a wide floor space, surmounted by balconies containing further cells. Our cell was some fifteen feet long by 9 feet wide. Two tattered palliasses lay on the floor, a stool and a large lid-covered bucket completing the sparse furnishings.

"Well the bastards, somebody's shopped us there Dick," I said, angrily stating the obvious. I was blazing mad at the thought of being so easily caught and I paced backwards and forwards the length of the dingy cell.

"I'd love to know who's responsible for this, right now I could willingly strangle them. Who do you think it was?"

"I haven't the slightest bleeding idea, but it doesn't matter who it was now – it's too late. I just wish we had gone our own way when we had the chance. But we're in dead trouble now you know Russ. We can't prove a thing. We haven't even got our dog tags," he despondently replied. The usual laughing and joking lad was sprawled out on his palliasse and his morale was the lowest I had ever seen it.

"Do you think they'll shoot us?" he asked. During our adventures thus far there had been times when I had got low but Dick had never failed to pull me round with some antic or another. Now I felt it was my turn.

"Will they heck shoot us," I answered with all the confidence I could muster. "We're P.o.W.'s now and that's it. They're just trying to scare the living daylights out of us."

"I damn well hope you're right," Dick mumbled, not at all convinced. "Cause they're succeeding."

"They might have done a year ago but with the Allies knocking on their door now they'd be leaving themselves wide open. They daren't risk it. Don't forget there's quite a few people know we're here." I was desperately trying to convince myself as well as Dick.

"Damn, damn and damn again," he exclaimed, using his favourite expression when annoyed.

Beyond the cell door the clattering of buckets, swishing and sloshing of water, heavy boot-cladded footsteps and Man Mountain's thundered instructions could be heard incessantly as we tried to decide our fate.

After we had been left to meditate for a few hours our cell door was slung open – the gap that ought to have been left by the opening of the door being more than adequately filled by goliath himself.

"Raus, Raus," he boomed, waving to the door.

Dick and I, always willing to please, made the doorway in no time flat. He led us up the iron stairs, which lay at the end of the wing, and pushed us in separate balcony cells. My cell was crowded.

"Hi boy, join the clan."

The easy-on-the-ear American twang had come from one of ten Americans inhabiting the small cell, the first thing to catch my attention being the words "Murderers Incorporated" painted artistically on the backs of their leather flying jackets. The second was the obnoxious smell emitting from the bucket reposing in the corner, silent but vile.

"Oh no, not you buggers," I said smiling. "You'll not believe me when I tell you that three weeks ago I was in a cinema in Antwerp watching you lot on the newsreel."

"We believe you," one of them piped up. "Since we crash-landed we've been talked about, talked to, pushed and prodded, photographed from every God-damn angle and done everything but swing about in the trees for these sons-of-bitches."

The cell was identical to the first one, except that palliasses virtually filled the floor, leaving no walking room whatever, and there was a small barred window high up in the wall which I had failed to notice in the earlier cell.

"Say," said one of the Yanks as we shook hands all round, "who the hell are you anyways, and whadaya doin' dressed up like a dude?"

I spent ten minutes or so, sat on a palliasse, back against the wall, explaining what had been happening since coming down.

"Just one more thing, where the hell did you pick up an accent like that?" asked one when I had finished the tale.

"Well the fact is, they've put me in here with you lot to teach you the finer points of the English language so that you'll be able to enjoy the niceties of life when you get back home," I answered.

"Yeah we know, if we went back home with your lingo we'd be shot," the small, but broad-shouldered pilot of the crew mocked.

"Talking about shooting, they told me and my pal we would be shot tomorrow at eight," I said.

"Like I said when you so rudely disturbed us, join the clan." They told us the same thing three weeks ago and it's sure beginning to look that way. We oughta have been on our way behind barbed wire before now. They've moved one lot out whilst we've been in here," cut in the first speaker.

"You mean there's more of us in this place," I said astonished.

"There sure are. For a kick-off there's a couple of Canadians next door. I had a quick word with them when I put out our plates the other day," he answered.

"The big guy said he was called Doc. Sounded like a Canadian."

"Doc and Ed," I exclaimed. "They stayed in the same house as Dick and I for a while. It sounds like the Germans are roping in a lot of us. In a way I suppose it's encouraging, they'll never shoot us all."

Inwardly I was extremely relieved to hear his news, for I was now nearly convinced that the shooting was an empty threat. Snag was, I wasn't *sure*, and the German intelligence man's words would persistently creep to the fore in my mind despite my attempts to push them into the background.

"How are you spending your time, you must be bored stiff by now," I asked. The youngest of the crew, who had as yet not spoken, answered, "We're sick to the back teeth and it's a pleasant change to have some other company, even if it is a Limey, and I for one . . ."

He jumped up in the middle of his sentence and ran to the wall, "Got him," he jubilantly shouted as he squeezed a black, round-backed bug, with his thumb.

"That puts me two in front today."

A red blob of blood, like an ink blot from my school pen, stained the wall where he had made the killing, and on looking round the walls I saw literally hundreds of similar stains up to arm-length height decorating them.

"That's our blood you're looking at Russ," he laughed. "You can join in tomorrow, but don't kill any today. That's how we spend our time."

The dreaded 8 o'clock came and thankfully passed uneventfully, putting paid, I hoped, to their idle threat.

Five long, dreary, uncomfortable, stinking days I spent in this cess-pit, being awarded no fewer than 32 bug bites during my very first night's sleep in captivity. Never once did any of us step outside the atrociously smelly cell and the food served up once a day would have made the pigs sick. But by the third day I was eating it. Bug-baiting, talking, and short spells gazing down at the courtyard way below, allowed only by giving each other a 'leg-up' in turn, filled our days.

After the few weeks of luxury I had recently enjoyed it was quite a shattering experience and quickly made me realise how very lucky we really had been. Fortunately I had always found the Yanks easy to get along with and these chaps were no exception. However in such close confines arguments developed between the Fortress crew from time to time, and whenever Britain was criticised, justly or unjustly, I bristled and consequently became involved in petty, pointless, squabbles. Five days was more than enough. Mercifully, early on the morning of the sixth day of captivity, the staggering number of forty boys were assembled alongside the cells on the lower floor, and if ever in my life I had longed for a camera – this was surely the time.

Standing in a long, straggly line, as motley a mob as one could wish to see stretched half the length of the cell block. Our apparel varied from unkempt tramp-style to being positively garish. Pinstripe suits, mud-bedecked corduroys, some tied at the ankles, serge suits, sports jackets and flannels were all sported with pride, and working overalls were prominent. One chap wore shorts. Footwear ranged from cut-down flying boots through to the Dutch clog stage, ending with the snazziest pair of patent leather dance shoes. One member of our party, carrying a neatly rolled up umbrella hung over his arm in the best Mayfair style, his head adorned by an Anthony Eden hat and actually wearing spats, was a riot, particularly when he addressed everyone as 'Cobber' in his rich Australian twang.

It was probably relief at getting out of those stinking cells, combined with meeting the odd familiar face, that started the smiles which soon grew into open chuckles. But it was certainly Dick who finished it, for, never slow to take advantage of a funny situation, he proceeded to walk down the line inspecting them. "Haircut, fasten your tie-pin, slovenly son, slovenly, odd shoe laces," he commented keeping his face straight. It was enough to bring down the house, We were all laughing uproariously, tears streaming down some faces as we doubled up laughing.

Amazingly the dozen or so Luftwaffe automatic gun-carrying guards, who had obviously been sent to escort us to our next destination, actually saw the funny side of the situation and couldn't resist a chuckle or two, and I swear to this day that Goliath himself was last seen walking down the great wide corridor wearing an hitherto never-seen smirk on his face. The whole situation was hilarious.

We learned the boys had been brought into Antwerp Prison from all points of the compass, some from quite long distances, and four of our mob had even got to the Spanish border, having been captured on the very last lap to freedom.

Canadians, Aussies, Americans and British made up the group. Heavily guarded, the forty of us were transported by lorry to a prison in Brussels, during the course of which Dick managed to scribble a note on the inside of a cigarette packet reading "Traitors in Underground" signed "R.A.F." which we deposited through a floorboard crack of the wagon in which we travelled. At Brussels we were prompty placed in solitary confinement.

This cell did not have the luxury of a window, but it was clean and odourless, for which I was truly thankful. The most disturbing thing however were the scratches on the walls, obviously made by former occupants, for they covered three walls, all numbering the days that had been spent there by a particular person. The longest series of marks totalled no fewer than 121.

Surely men had not stayed so long on their own in this confined space – the marks must have been added to by following prisoners – and yet each series of scratches were totally different. How were they made? I had nothing on me to make a scratch, or had I? A button was the only thing I could think of. When, oh when would my parents be informed I was alive? What must they be thinking?

What about my mates at work? I bet they think I'm dead. They will never believe me when, and if, I get back. Ten to one we'll be interrogated here. I'm not looking forward to that. How on earth am I going to prove who I am? I wonder if the scratches have been deliberately put there by the Germans purely to demoralise me? My mind was in turmoil – and there was no-one with whom to discuss the situation. I fell into a restless sleep on the lumpy palliasse which served as my bed.

One day, two days, three days went by and I had spoken to no-one, and no-one had spoken to me. Even the guards who brought me a couple of meals a day said not a word. I wished at times that I could stop myself from thinking. It was difficult to answer all the imaginary questions I posed myself during an imaginary interrogation which I was more than ever convinced was coming.

The one consolation I had was a particular lecture given by one of our intelligence officers months before. He related the story of a 19-year-old Luftwaffe gunner, shot down near Scotland, and subsequently captured by a farmer and his wife armed with pitchforks. They contacted the local police who in turn got hold of the lecturer. On his instructions the unfortunate gunner was locked up in an outside toilet and given neither food nor water. He was left there until the following afternoon. No joke after the shock of having been shot down.

The intelligence officer eventually arrived at the farm full of apologies to the young airman. Making the excuse that he had only just been informed of his capture the officer proceeded to wine and dine the German in warm, comfortable surroundings, plying him with cigarettes whilst they chatted, and of course had not the slightest difficulty in extracting all the information he sought from the youngster.

The story partially convinced me that the scratchmarks were deliberately placed there – all part of the build-up prior to interrogation. But sleep was still the finest relief I could get. Intelligence officers were all very well but they were back in Britain – I was on my own.

It happened on the sixth day – before my first meal. The cell door opened as if by an unseen hand and two rifle-carrying guards stood outside.

I felt the blood draining from my face as I numbly and automatically walked into the passage. This was it. For the first time in six days my brain had gone into hibernation.

Dressed in dark blue trousers, grey jacket, with huge padded shoulders, which hung over my actual shoulders, open, and well and truly crumpled, shirt neck and filthy shoes, I found myself walking down a long never-ending corridor, flanked by my two guards, our footsteps echoing and re-echoing and thinking I had never seen such a highly polished floor in my life – for I was frightened of thinking of anything else.

After what seemed an eternity we halted and I was ushered into a huge, high-ceilinged room. Ensconced behind a large glass-like desk the immaculately dressed Luftwaffe officer's eyes never left mine as I slowly approached him.

Incredibly I had seen this man many times before, on the cinema screen back home, for he was exactly as portrayed in the films, with his high-peaked cap, jack boots which peeped through the aperture beneath the table top and, to cap it all, a monocle. Had the situation been different I would have laughed, but laughing was the last thing on my mind.

"Who are you?" His perfect English surprised me.

"2204613 Sergeant Russell Margerison sir," with a confidence which I certainly did not feel.

"Sergeant?" he queried, "Where is your uniform? What service?" He glared at me waiting for my answer.

"R.A.F. sir."

"Let me see your identities."

I wilted at that, why oh why, I thought, did we ever hand over our dog-tags to the underground.

"I have none sir, I surrendered them."

"No uniform, no dog-tags," he sneered. "You are a spy. Military men do not surrender their identities to anyone."

I felt two inches tall as he looked me over from head to foot and I was conscious of sweat in the palm of my hands.

The Luftwaffe man casually opened a drawer and withdrew a foolscap form, carefully placing it in front of me.

"In your case you had better fill in this form," and so saying he rolled a pen across the paper, rose and left the room saying, "You have five minutes."

Name, rank, number, being the first three questions, posed no problem, but the remaining seventeen or so questions were a different matter. Such things as Squadron name and number, Where Situated, Pilot's Name, C.O.'s Name, Aircraft Type, Bomb Load, Target, Date Shot Down, By Night Fighter or Flak, Radar Equipment Fitted to Aircraft, and so the questions went on.

I gazed and gazed at the paper in front of me, conscious of the eyes of the two guards boring into the back of my head. What should I do? What can I do? I can't answer these questions. What would they say in England? I would be Court Martialled. And yet if I did not answer them what was going to happen here in Brussels. My mind was in complete turmoil. I sucked the pen, looked around me for inspiration, but could find none. God, what should I do? I stared and gazed vacantly for the longest five minutes I ever remember at the three completed questions and found no difficulty whatever in providing myself with 1,000 good reasons as to why it would be perfectly in order for me to answer the remaining questions.

The door opened and with a purposeful gait the intelligence officer strode to the desk. His face appeared to turn a vivid purple as he surveyed my handiwork and then he exploded. He shouted, ranted and raved in his native tongue till the walls vibrated, a totally different person from the one of five minutes ago. The tirade seemed endless until, it seemed in sheer desperation, he withdrew his revolver from its holster and, whilst shouting unintelligibly, waved it under my nose.

I was petrified. All I could do was stand there and avoid his eyes, hoping the floor would open up and swallow me.

To my utter amazement and relief he resumed normality as quickly as he had exploded.

"Very well then," he said, "if you will not tell me then I will tell you." I could but marvel at his knowledge and his English pronunciation, as he proceeded to tell me exactly who I was and what I was, answering unhesitatingly every question on the sheet of paper one hundred per cent correct and even adding more information. I was dumbstruck.

Marching back to my cell with a feeling of elation, I could but wonder what kind of game we were playing. It was certainly above my head. There had been more going on behind the scenes than ever I had visualised.

Chapter Seventeen

Being reunited with Dick and the 38 other aircrew types, the very same day as our interrogation, was a gladdening occasion. It was obviously much easier to feel self assured when amongst friends. We chatted incessantly whilst on our way to the main railway station in Brussels, discovering that the majority of us had had a similar type of questioning, the exception being the few with us who had been captured within a day or so of having been shot down. The Germans had little information on them.

One wondered just what the Belgians were thinking as they stopped and stared at this group of young faces, many dressed in the most outrageous manner and heavily guarded on all sides. I believe they knew the score, for here and there a friendly wink or nod could be detected.

On arrival at the railway station we were seated on hard wooden seats in fours, two facing two, and across the passage sat two guards for each four. They were taking no chances.

Puffing and chuffing, the train, after a considerable delay, left the station only to come to a halt once out in the open. As far as we could ascertain, out of an extremely wide network of lines curving off in all directions, ours was the only one intact. Lines twisted in every imaginable shape, some rearing up to the sky like the tentacles of an octopus. Railway carriages, or parts of them, lay strewn over the whole area, in any position but the right one, whilst broken glass was everywhere. Ripped open trains, with their boilers exposed, lay on their sides or upside down. The rear end of one balanced precariously on some overhanging superstructure whilst its nose appeared to be well and truly buried in mother earth.

A complete state of chaos existed. Excited by the virtually unusable station we began pointing out to each other one or other incredible sight, only to be cut short by the guards all down the carriage.

"Sprechen verboten!" A silent journey lay ahead.

Whilst none of us was in the least of a hurry to get into Germany, the journey developed into a most frustrating one. Four miles forward, two back, stop, start, shunt into a siding, out of a siding. Progress was so painfully slow it was difficult to credit. Obviously we would be the least important traffic on the line. The Germans were moving troops and equipment up towards the coast to combat the invasion and whilst we were in sidings an occasional hospital train would pass going in our direction.

I was none too happy at being on a train at all. They had proved far too easy a target for aircraft. In particular the rocket-firing Typhoons, I knew, were capable of opening up trains as effectively as a tin-opener opened tins, and I preferred not to be around should such a thing happen.

We eventually arrived at Cologne, having passed through Aachen, and were required to change trains to continue to our unknown destination, though most of us had already guessed it would be Frankfurt, for there stood Dulag Luft, a name all aircrew were familiar with as the main interrogation centre for the Luftwaffe.

The sight of Cologne, or what had been Cologne, was indescribable. Huge mounds of bricks, girders, beams, masonry and all other materials which go to building a city spilled onto what used to be streets to such an extent it was quite impossible in many cases to know which was a street. Odd gable ends towered skywards looking as if one gust of wind would collapse them. Curtains and clothing fluttered forlornly from the rubble. Smashed trams leaned against the mounds, the lines completely buried.

Where on earth did the people of the city live? What about water, electricity, the essential services? How could they go on like this? Only a few short months ago, which now seemed like years, we had bombed this city, and here it was that I could still see the glow of the fires as we approached the English coast at Mablethorpe.

Unanswered questions raced through my head in quick succession. Surely we had not contributed to this wholesale devastation. Of course we had, there were seven or eight hundred four-engined bombers dropping their fearsome loads in just one raid. How many bodies were now lying under that lot? How many little helpless children? I wondered if any of our bombs actually killed any children?

The answer could only be yes.

The thought depressed me immensely. Well it was their own fault. They started it. They even fitted appliances to their bombs to make them scream down from their Stukas so as to terrorise the people of Poland, Holland, France, Belgium, Russia, etc. Why don't they just surrender and save themselves more of this punishment. They are obviously beaten.

This kind of thinking did nothing to ease my depression. I knew it was wrong and I knew I had done my bit to bring it about. It was with some relief that we steamed laboriously out of Cologne and away from the horrors of what was once a thriving city.

Our destination, as suspected, was Frankfurt, achieved no faster than our previous train ride, it being the following day when we arrived. We had passed through the graveyard of Bomber Command.

One lost count of the number of pieces of aircraft which littered the fields – tails, wings, turrets. Even a whole Halifax was spotted, virtually undamaged, as we slowly made our way through the countryside.

Dulag Luft was situated at Oberursel, near Frankfurt, and here we were unceremoniously stripped and our bodies searched. We each helped ourselves to a blue American electrically-heated suit and slippers from a great pile of these which formed a rising triangle in the corner of a room and from there marched to an outside compound which lay some two miles away.

These suits had a flap between the legs so as to enable the wearer to use the toilet. Unfortunately the method of fastening this in place was missing on my particular one, so it had no alternative but to dangle freely, leaving me embarrassingly denuded in exactly the wrong place. To add to my discomfort the slippers fell off at every step unless I held on to the short tapes which were attached to the slippers. Thus walking partly stooped, for maybe half a mile so clad, I left Dick, who was at the back of me, with no alternative but to say, "For Christ's sake Russ walk behind me, I'm cheesed off looking at your arse hole!"

To further the degradation the locals, now about in strength, began to stone us. The missiles whistled through our ranks with increasing velocity and a few screams and shouts evidenced the fact that some had found their target. The mood of the Germans was growing more intense as they shouted abuse, and had not the guards rushed the people, rifles across their chests, there is not the slightest doubt that I would not be writing this now.

It was the first time we had come across hatred and bitterness. At home we had been the glamour boys with people always prepared to go out of their way to help and please and this reception was a bitter pill to swallow. It wasn't difficult to understand, for Frankfurt had received more than its fair share of bombs during the last few years, but being stoned brought home to us the fact that we should have to tread very warily now we had arrived on German soil.

This compound turned out to be nothing more than a transit camp, holding probably some 150 personnel awaiting transport to a P.o.W. camp, all of whom had been interrogated. Good news for us for it meant that our questioning was over.

We were duly fed with a watery soup, Ersatz bread and Ersatz coffee. I had long since decided that I would never get used to the two latter items and I am still convinced that 40 per cent of the very dark brown bread consisted of cinders. One advantage was it never seemed to go mouldy no matter how stale it was (and I never remember trying it fresh) but then again I have never seen a mouldy cinder. The coffee really did not require an acquired taste, it preferably required no taste at all. It was forever vile.

Issued with R.A.F. greatcoat, hat, tunic, trousers, shirt, boots, socks, tooth-brush and tooth powder, the following day found us us speeding finally to our P.o.W. camp Stalag Luft VII at Bankau, in Upper Silesia. The nearest town of any size was a place called Kreuzburg. The journey was mainly in open country and consequently good progress was made, though we did pass through Dresden. Little damage appeared to have been done in Eastern Germany but that was soon to be altered by the controversial raid on Dresden when a fire storm was created, and appalling casualties inflicted. The only thing of consequence in the whole train ride was the giving of the Heil Hitler salute by railway personnel en route as we flashed past at maybe 50 m.p.h. I considered it totally idiotic that normal average workmen should respond to a train driver or guard in this manner.

"Where the hell have you guys been?" Gib, faced wreathed in smiles, was shouting above the noise of a few hundred other P.o.W.'s also trying to draw the attention of someone they knew, through the criss-crossed wire mesh which filled in the framework of the huge wooden gates. We were soon hugging each other and shaking hands.

For all Gib was the tough guy of the crew, he was really a sentimentalist at heart. It was perfectly obvious he had been at those gates for every intake of new prisoners, looking and waiting and hoping, but he would probably deny it if we had suggested such a thing. It was exactly the same when he missed an operation back on squadron through frost bite. The rest of us had arrived back at 3.30 a.m. from the raid and who should be sat in the Mess at that unearthly hour all on his own, but Gib. "Thought you guys were never coming," had been his only comment.

"When you've got fixed up with a hut come round to No. 12 and I'll give you the gen. Gotta lot to talk about. I'll have a drink ready."

The camp was nothing more than some one hundred wooden huts, a little longer but the same width as an average garage, the whole being surrounded by barbed wire. Below the compound was a larger area where big long wooden huts were in the process of being erected. This was obviously temporary accommodation only, and just as well, for they placed eight of us in a hut, with one straw palliasse each.

Fortunately the weather was hot, and the majority of the chaps were dressed only in underpants.

"Well what's been happening? What kept you? We get an intake about once a week. Hell I was about to give you up," Gib was doing the talking.

"Before we go into that Gib," I interjected, "what's happened to the rest of them. Do you know?"

He looked at me with strangely serious eyes. "Yes," he answered after a long silence. "Dave and Brick are both in an officers' camp not too far from here, but Frank and Max are dead."

"Oh no," escaped from Dick's lips.

"I knew it, I just knew it," and I told them for the first time how we had a row in the pub at Mablethorpe when both of them had said they would ride it down should anything happen.

"I wonder if they could have got out," Dick mused. "I really doubt it. They were both struggling with the control column. Frank might have, but not Max."

"We'll never know the answer to that one, but when they hit the ground Frank was still alive," said Gib.

128

The news staggered us.

"How on earth do you know that Gib?" asked Dick.

"'Cause I was captured early the following morning after we got the chop, but just before I fell into German hands a local told me that the one in a blue uniform was still alive when the Germans got to the aircraft but he was in such a hopeless condition they had to shoot him."

"You're sure they are both dead?" I asked, thinking that Max might have made it for he always wore his light American Khaki.

"Positive Russ," he continued. "The soldiers put me in a lorry and in the corner were the bodies of Frank and Max. One of the Germans was showing off Max's watch, another had Frank's lighter. It was a hell of a journey because, besides Max and Frank, there were about eight sacks, soggy, with blood oozing out of them, and when I asked who they were I was told Americans.

"They asked me if I knew the two on the floor but I just waved my hand and spent the rest of the trip staring outside."

We all fell silent. That was the end of that.

Dick broke the silence. "What's it like here?"

"I'm not crazy about it but it's bearable," Gib answered. "We're all moving to the camp below in a few weeks' time, which should improve things. I was amongst the first batch here. We get counted two or three times a day. Apart from that there's nothing else to do. We've plenty of food as we get a Red Cross parcel every week backed up by soup once a day and then possibly a few pig potatoes, sauer kraut, molasses, cheese or what have you. I'm with a bunch of Canadians in this hut, but it's the usual mixed bag. Plenty of Aussies knocking about. You guys will get a parcel tomorrow, oh and a card so you can write home.

"You get to send a card each week and a letter once a month. Don't trust any of the jerries, particularly the ferrets, they're dressed in white coats. They mainly speak some English but they're a slimy lot, talking to you as if wanting to make friends but really just fishing for information as to what's going on in camp.

"It's your turn now, fill me in with the latest," ended Gib.

It took us quite a while to relate our story and to give Gib the up-to-date news from the war fronts, assuring him the way things were going Christmas would see us back home.

The following day the whole intake were given numbers (mine was 379 L7) and as forecast we received a Red Cross parcel each (an English one on this occasion, but apparently American and

Canadian parcels were more common and popular) and a small postcard on which I promptly wrote in pencil:

"Dear Dad and Mum,

Fit and well, unwounded and unhurt. Frank and Max dead, rest O.K. Shot down Duisburg. Been on run Belgium. With Dick and Gib both fine. Will write regularly from now on.

All my love, see you soon,"

Russ.

I still have that card received in Blackburn at Christmas time, 1944. It reads:

Dear Dad and Mum,

Fit and well, unwounded and unhurt. Will write regularly from now on. All my love, see you soon.

Russ.

The rest had been censored with heavy black ink.

P.o.W. life is a life apart. I can think of nothing remotely like it. It is boring beyond description, it is humiliating and degrading in many ways, it is riddled with hardship and privation, it tries to the utmost one's patience, temper and character. It also brings out man's ingenuity.

The new camp in which we were soon installed was a hotel compared with the tiny huts. The large barrack blocks, split as they were into small rooms with twelve men per room, could be made quite comfortable. Double-tier bunks with loose wooden bed-boards lined the walls, whilst in the centre of the room stood a table and chairs. Each unit had at least one window. Washing facilities, housed at one end of the barracks, were primitive but adequate. The smell of new wood was anything but unpleasant. The whole camp, built in a square, was surrounded by barbed wire to a height of some 16 feet, the top 4 feet shooting inwards at a sharp angle. Towering above the wire stood 9 wooden structures, each surmounted by a cabin and a platform on which were mounted a machine gun and a searchlight. Inside the compound itself stood some 20 barrack blocks, plus a few outbuildings such as entertainment hall, showers, toilets etc. and finally 9 feet or so inside the barbed wire was the trip wire. This consisted of just one strand of wire nailed to the top of short posts running inside the whole camp 18 inches above the ground. The continually parading sentries and the ones in the towers were all under instructions to shoot anyone, for whatever reason, who crossed over the tripwire.

Under the Geneva Convention no-one over the rank of corporal was allowed to be put to work by his captors. Therefore, unfortunately, we aircrew never left the camp. Frankly it would have occupied us and given us more of a chance to do a spot of bargaining with our cigarettes and coffee – both well nigh impossible for the Germans to obtain – had we been allowed out on working parties. It left us with little else to do but to upset our guards at every available opportunity.

The favourite game played out successfully, daily, was at the count. We would stand in rows of four deep, before the Commandant and his officers, and the Ober Feldwebel (Sergeant Major) would begin his count, assisted by an "other rank". Before he had got to six the shuffling in the ranks would begin and spread like ripples on water, till he was totally confused. This would go on for four or five counts, in other words till we had had enough. Our occasional punishment would be to stand there in the hot sun till "soup up" at lunch time.

Should any work be given us in camp a complete hash of it would be made without further ado. Such as when a sectional shed was given to us to erect. The points of the gable ends were promply dug into the soft sand and we carried on from there. A bigger shambles was never made of a construction job. A lean on the completed structure was enough to collapse the lot, accompanied by hilarious laughter from the bystanders. It all occupied our time and theirs.

Slowly but surely the new camp became more and more organised. The election of a camp leader, an Australian by the name of Pete Thompson, deputy camp leader, Canadian John Waltky and a man of confidence, Canadian Dick Green, along with a committee, helped considerably towards this end. A man of confidence was a very necessary post in camp for he was the one to whom we could turn in case of personal problems or to discuss any escape ideas. We had been issued with only a mug and a large teaspoon, the mug being used for anything and everything, cooked potatoes, soup, drink, loose cheese, shaving and multifarious other requirements. Amongst a thousand or so men there is always someone with a specialised knowledge of any given subject, young as we were. An ex-tinsmith soon had the camp hard at it making dishes, plates, baking trays and containers from the great range of tins contained in our food parcels. The heavy spoon was used to tap down seams etc. His own products were incredibly well made and water-tight in spite of his lack of tools. The rest of us improved with time.

However nothing helped us along more than an intake of 96 old P.o.W.'s from Stalag 383, some of whom had been prisoners for four years. They brought into camp all kinds of gear which they had collected over the years. The morning after their arrival we realised just what "sprogs" we were at this P.o.W. game, when one of them, Jock McCann, looking much older than his years, came into our billet after count, and surprised us by saying:

"Close the door and put a guard on it." So saying he pulled a sheet of paper from out of his pocket and added:

"Here is the 9 o'clock news from the B.B.C."

We were stunned into silence as we held on to every word of the latest bulletin from London. It was quite incredible. On our arrival at Stalag Luft VII, we had been subjected to yet a further rigorous searching of our clothing and bodies. We could not and did not get a thimble into camp, and yet here the old P.o.W.'s had not only got a radio through but had got it working within hours of entering the compound. The only thing I ever learned of that achievement was that part of the radio came in inside a concertina.

The Old Boys, as I shall name them, soon taught us to make many things, including mud ovens for baking. But the most useful item of all was the famous blower. No less than a forge, it was made up from various sized tins mounted on a bed board, complete with enclosed fans and driven by means of a shoe-lace, geared up and operated by turning a wooden handle at a high rate of knots. The purpose was, of course, to boil a pan of water or whatever, as fast and as economically as possible. The blower did just that, and soon every little combine had their own blower, it becoming a common sight to see boys huddled over the contraption, turning as fast as they could to create the necessary draught, which in turn made even dust and bits of wood glow red.

A blower can be seen in the Imperial War Museum, London.

The snag to all this "Mechanisation" was the shortage of fuel, for whilst slivers from bed boards were the handiest fuel available, apart maybe from the cardboard of our food parcels, wood was at a premium, it being the most useful material with which to make almost anything, and so it came to pass that we all ended up sleeping on four boards. Four, maybe eight ins. wide, was considered painful but manageable, three was excruciating. The fuel situation simply meant that any combustible material carelessly left around disappeared as if by magic, particularly if it belonged to the Germans. A brush and shovel, for instance, would be pounced upon vulture-like and reduced to match-sticks in minutes. It did however provide us with a litter-free camp!

Generally speaking our guards, being rather older than the front-line troops, acted in a reasonable manner, most of them longing to get home to their wives and families at the earliest possible moment. There was, however, the odd exception, and one could never really trust any of them.

When air raid sirens sounded in camp everyone had to retire to their particular barrack and stay there till "all clear" screeched its prolonged note.

By chance the sirens wailed away one day an hour before "soup up" at lunch time. To avoid a long wait behind a queue, should we not be quick off the mark for our soup, we all crowded at our respective doors waiting to dash across the compound as soon as permissible. A distant "all clear" was heard, probably from Kreuzburg, but the camp siren remained silent. Unfortunately one anxious Canadian burst from his barrack, carrying his tin. Calm as you please, a guard carefully knelt on one knee, levelled his rifle and needlessly shot him in full view of everyone. He appeared to stop his run in mid-pace, hung there for an instant, then collapsed on the ground, where he rolled over two or three times. With the camp siren now blaring we arrived at his side as he gasped his last words. "Get that bastard for me."

The whole camp gathered and stared at the Nazi responsible, mumbling oaths and threats, whilst he resumed his parading back and forth outside the wire, untouchable.

The incident caused considerable tension and after a meeting of our Camp Leader and his committee it was decided that a state of non-co-operation should now exist. Meanwhile Pete Thompson and Dick Green demanded an immediate meeting with the Commandant. He defended the guard in question for his action, pointing out that the Canadian boy had broken the rules, but agreed the man would now have to be removed and promised that he would post him forthwith to the Russian Front, a punishment which all Germans dreaded. Whether or not he was sent East, I know not, but he disappeared from camp permanently the same day.

Somehow all this Russian Front business was inadequate from

133

our point of view. The camp mood seethed and when it came to the parade for counting no-one left their barracks until a whole contingent of troops moved into the compound, forcing us outside by pushing, shouting and cajoling, the count taking place hours late, much to the consternation of the Germans.

The result of all this upset was the increase of Goon-baiting at every possible opportunity and in every possible way, too numerous to mention here, apart from the ruse which gained star prize and is well worth relating.

Our two toilet blocks were identical wooden cabins, some 30 feet long by 18 feet wide. A large deep oblong hole covering practically the whole length of the building was divided into two, lengthways, at ground level only, by a 4 foot high partition, at either side of which rested long round heavy poles, like tree trunks, on which men sat, cheek to cheek as it were, discussing the latest rumours (always rife in P.o.W. camp) whilst going about their business over the stinking fly-ridden cess-pit.

It was only a few days after the shooting, with tempers still anything but normal, that a Ferret should happen on his walk-around to stroll down the corridor of one of the barracks. The usual cry of "Ferret lads" went up before he was within earshot.

"How's number four tunnel going on then," cracked one inmate, lying prostrate on his bed, knowing full well the Ferret's ears would be twitching.

"Number four tunnel, never heard of it, where the hell's that?" came the well rehearsed reply from another occupant of the room. "You know, the one in No 2 Toilet block, I've heard it's progressing well."

"Hope you're right, I'm sick of this bloody place, it's time we were out."

The conversation was timed to perfection, for only a few short weeks before two small tunnels had been uncovered during one of the regular searches made by the Germans, in which they would leave a barrack as if it had been hit by a whirl-wind.

The following morning on another beautifully hot day (we really were enjoying stupendous weather) a party of 12 men, dressed in black waterproofs from head to foot, complete with souwesters and wellingtons and carrying shovels and a ladder, entered the main gate ready to discover yet another tunnel. As the toilet blocks lay at the far end of the camp it entailed their walking across the large open area in the centre of the barrack blocks, thereby running the gauntlet of ridicule from every manjack in camp.

We crowded around the toilet in question as one by one the black-clad men, already pouring sweat, disappeared into the murky morass below, each one receiving his own special cheer. After possibly half an hour's digging had convinced the Jerries that no tunnel existed they emerged into daylight in the most smelly, indescribably filthy condition, each festooned with his own dangling gossamer webs. The cheers as they trudged despondently away went a long way towards alleviating our feelings. We felt we had got a little of our own back.

An awful lot of time was spent concocting all kinds of dishes so as to vary our eating and we had quite a range of food to go at. For instance an American parcel consisted of:-

1 Tin Spam 12 oz.

1 Tin Corned Beef 12 oz.

1 Tin Milk Liver Pâté 6 oz.

1 Tin Salmon 6 oz.

1 Tin Oleo Margarine 16 oz.

1 Tin Jam or Orange juice 6 oz.

1 Tin Dried (Klim) Milk 16 oz.

1 Packet Raisins or Prunes 16 oz.

1 Packet Kraft Cheese 8 oz.

1 Packet Biscuits 8 oz.

1 Packet Sugar 8 oz.

1 Tin Coffee 4 oz.

2 Bars Chocolate (D Bar) 8 oz.

2 Bars Soap.

100 Cigarettes.

Tin opener.

The German food issue was running at 1/12th block margarine every 5 days, 1/6th loaf per day, soup daily, 3 ozs meat per week, 3 ozs sugar per week, 1 lb potatoes per day (little pig potatoes), occasional molasses, round cheeses, cottage cheese, sauerkraut, jam (crushed turnip, saccharin with red colouring added) syrup, raw cabbage, erzatz coffee and powdered cheese. To sum up, with a parcel per week food was no problem, without the parcels we were in trouble.

We diced, cut, rolled, stewed, soaked, baked, separated, mixed and tried everything possible with varying results, and swore some of the recipes would be worth a try when we got back home. We lived day to day in a very boring world of dreams, nothing seemed real and one got a feeling that it wasn't really happening. We merely existed.

I sat alone on the barren, dusty ground, one day, my back resting against the gable end of our barrack block, gazing through and beyond the restrictive barbed wire at nothing in particular. The earth in front of me was as empty as the life I was forced to lead and the warm sun glinting on the machine gun's barrel, up in the look-out tower, served only to give an even more desert-like appearance to the scene. The guard looked as bored as I felt. It was a terrible anti-climax after such a full life and the excitement of the last 12 months. I was becoming more and more depressed and wondered how on earth the early P.o.W.'s had coped for so long behind the wire. I was not convinced that I could tolerate the situation indefinitely and foolish, unworkable escape schemes went through my head in quick succession. The arrival of the Old Boys had more than convinced me of the damage being done to one's mind for in our conversations it had been quite impossible to convince these men that the war would soon be over. Some of them had resigned themselves to being P.o.W.'s for ever.

Timely strains of the waltz, "Fascination," broke the deathly silence, and my train of thought, the violins rising and falling exquisitely in wonderful harmony.

It was the first music I had heard since capture and I hungrily hung on to every note hoping it would never end. The music was coming from a nearby barrack occupied by the Old Boys and as the record regrettably came to an end I called, "Play it again, please."

The unseen owner duly obliged and once again I basked in its magnificence. It was the most beautiful thing I had ever heard and it had the desired effect of cheering me out of my moroseness, giving me a needed feeling of optimism and a looking forward to better things to come.

Miraculously, within two weeks of the shooting, sports equipment of all kinds flowed into camp at a surprising rate and immediately was put to good use. The month of September must go down as a never-ending month of sport. Musical instruments also arrived, and these heralded the formation of an orchestra which was soon rehearsing regularly for shows which were later to be presented in the newly-built recreation hall.

Daily educational classes began to emerge and it was soon possible to study most of the major subjects under the expert supervision of trainee teachers.

County clubs and country clubs were formed and they devised all manner of ways to occupy one's time such as debates etc. Even cooking lessons could be had. A newspaper had originated which brought out 8 typewritten pages per week. Pinned to the notice board these sheets were avidly read, it being quite amazing the newsy snippets gathered from such a confined area. It even boasted a quite good cartoonist who soon became adept at mocking every error or every silly little extra regulation which the Germans brought in from time to time. For instance one of a thousand crazes which matured was the placing of a tiny wind-driven propellor onto the apex of the barrack roof. These did nothing but spin at a high speed when windy. The Germans banned them. The following week's cartoon portrayed a barrack block complete with its occupants, flying over the barbed wire, its little propellor buzzing round, being chased by two fist-waving guards shouting, "verboten, verboten."

There was really no shortage of material for a newspaper, as every man had a tale to tell of his own experiences and they were, of course, many and varied, some having had miraculous escapes which made good reading. Others had been in Germany years. One young chap, whose name eludes me, had parachuted into a tree, one very dark night, and had eventually got his feet onto a branch. Unable to see the ground and unaware of how high he was, the lad in question decided to light a cigarette before deciding on his best course of action. He fainted with the first draw, falling off the branch and becoming impaled on an old pointed tree stump which spiked him between the legs. Two and half years later, as a result of excellent doctoring and numerous operations, he arrived in P.o.W. camp fit and well.

Gib, having arrived in camp earlier than Dick and I, was billeted with a number of his countrymen, but we saw him regularly and had long chats with him and he and I spent hours throwing a baseball across the open parts of the compound. It is probably fair to say that deep, personal feelings were discussed more in P.o.W. camp than in any other environment in my experience and I always left those chats with Gib, not only confident he would survive, but in the knowledge that here I had a friend for life. I was correct.

October was heralded in by three consecutive days of rain, just as we had quite decided that it never rained in Upper Silesia. I congratulated myself for having had the good sense to send my boots (which had been well-worn when I was issued with them) for repair early in September. They had come back soled with one-inch wide wedge-shaped pieces of wood running across widthways. Virtually everything was made from wood, but I had never seen segmented wood soles before and I doubted their ability to withstand water even though they were extremely neatly done. I was to be proved very very wrong.

With nights drawing in, it became a necessity to provide ourselves with some light in the blocks and this was quickly dealt with by the introduction of our "night light". An empty salmon tin filled with German margarine (frankly about all it was fit for, that and squeaky hinges), melted till one could insert a shoe lace to act as wick and then allowed to solidify. The lid was left hinged to act as both shield from draughts and reflector. They worked well.

Stalag Luft VII was now becoming quite full of reluctant members. Not only did we have the regular flow of aircrew personnel, but the beginning of the month had seen the entry of all the glider pilots captured at Arnheim. They marched into camp still pale and dazed as a result of their ordeal. Advantageously, Medical Officer Captain Howatson and a C. of E. Padre also arrived in camp.

The story has often been told of the fight these chaps had put up against impossible odds. I can only say that I have never seen a body of men so shook up and nervous.

One of them, Sandy from Co. Durham, was billeted in our room. His stories of the action he saw made me feel glad I had been flying and not on the ground.

"And how did you finally get captured?" I asked him during one of our many chats.

"My pal and myself were crouched in a little dug-out near a large mansion-type house," Sandy recalled, "and German tanks were close by lobbing shells at us. It was as if the ground was never still, vibrating as each shell fell. We had a light Bren gun, as did the majority of us, but it was useless against tanks. It had become all but impossible to pop our heads above ground for heavy machine gun fire pinned us down. The noise was deafening. During the short lull my mate peeped over the top as I turned to get another magazine for the Bren. There was a peculiar thwack and I whipped round to see the cause. As true as I am here his head had completely split in two, just like an apple when cut down the centre. Without more ado I tied my hanky to the gun and waved it in the air still crouching in the hole. I'd had enough."

138

With such an influx of prisoners the stock of Red Cross parcels dwindled until it was a matter of waiting for a delivery. This meant at times we would be down to half a parcel a week, but no-one was going hungry, so it wasn't too vital.

The months of November and December slowly ebbed away with few highlights with which to break the monotony of life. So boring was it that I even began to look forward to a pending visit to the camp dentist, situated just on the other side of the wire. It did however mean walking through the main gates – rare treat indeed. It was not until three intended victims had gathered, accompanied by one of our own medics, that I had second thoughts.

"Listen lads," our young medic said, "this bastard detests the sight of us aircrew and if it is not essential for you to have treatment, skip it. He thinks he's God."

"What's the matter with you?" he asked nodding at me.

"I had the whole filling drop out of one of my back teeth whilst trying to chew a knacker-brock biscuit a few weeks ago. I'm getting more and more toothache with it, but after what you say I'd better give it a miss. I detest dentists at home, never mind here."

But on his inspection of the offending cavity he rightly advised me to have it dealt with, as he did with the other two.

"Well the drill is to walk into his surgery, come to attention, throw him one up and wait for his instructions. O.K. Let's go," he said.

I derived no pleasure whatever from my walk through those huge wooden gates and down the little uninhabited lane with its flat open views in all directions, for I could think of nothing but the forth-coming ordeal with dread.

When my turn eventually came to leave the cold, sparsely-furnished waiting room, and enter the chamber of his holiness, I did so with a false show of bravado which totally belied my abject terror.

"Good morning sir," I said, clicking my new-soled boots together and giving him one of the neatest salutes I ever mustered in my whole forces' career.

The little square-jawed, thick-set dentist glared through thick-lensed glasses. "Sit down," he snarled.

I hastily obeyed, over-anxious to please, and was conscious that I was visibly trembling. After a quick examination of my teeth, born from his job as a dentist rather than interest in the contents of my mouth, he reached up for his drill. The thing whirred into life like a distant motor bike starting up and was in my tooth without further ado. He seemed to be pushing me farther and farther into the chair, applying tremendous pressure, whilst the noisy vibrating weapon felt as if it was cutting chunks off my tooth. The nerve bared in seconds and electric type shocks reverberated through my system. Sweat ran down my forehead and I knew my knuckles would be bloodless as I tried to crush the arms of the chair with my fingers.

The drilling went on and on, till after what seemed hours he switched off and hung up the confounded thing. I was pale, shattered, annoyed and left frightened of dentists' drills for the next 20 years. It took him seconds to stuff the tiniest bit of filling in the bottom of the cavity, my tongue telling me that only the shell of the tooth remained. So much for that, I thought.

I obviously did not create the right impression on Dr. Jekyll with my initial entrance. One redeeming feature of the little excursion was that whilst in the waiting room I became engaged in conversation with the first German I had met who was utterly convinced that they had lost the war. A smart man of the age of 40 plus, he openly told me he was an intelligence man and when I commented that I had been astounded at the information they had given me in Brussels he brushed it off by saying that had the German Intelligence Service been as efficient as the British the story of the war would have been entirely different.

"You may not know it, but you have the finest Intelligence Service in the world," he had concluded.

A further highlight of these two months was a presentation of an extremely well-organised and presented stage show, held on two consecutive nights so as to enable the whole camp to see it, along with the senior German officers. Apart from a sketch entitled "The Rape of the Lighthouse Keepers' Daughter," which was disgusting, the show swung along at a fast pace, being thoroughly enjoyed by all.

The star of the show, a youngster impersonating a female singer, was nothing short of brilliant.

After the first performance the Germans banned the singing of "God Save The King", which brought an immediate response from Pete Thompson.

"Right chaps," he announced from the stage at the conclusion of the second performance. "Open all windows and doors. I want you to sing like you've never sung before. Two choruses of 'Land of Hope and Glory'." Never did men respond so willingly. The hall and surrounding countryside echoed and re-echoed with the stirring music, sung as loud as each individual could sing, by youths from no fewer than seven countries. It was a particularly moving spectacle.

It could only have been a few short days after the show at November's end that continuous far away rumblings of thunder sent the camp crazy and rocketed the rumour-mongering to unprecedented heights. Clearly and unmistakably the gunfire came from the Russian front and air activity increased accordingly.

"Katowice has fallen, they're only twenty-five miles from here. By the end of the week they'll be in camp."

"One of the guards has just told me he has got all his belongings packed and is deserting tonight. Don't say anything."

"That sharp-nosed ferret, you know, the one that's never away from our block, wants to know if he brings us a loaf of bread in every day will we find him a uniform so that he can go back to the West with us and surrender to the Allies."

"British troops have marched into Hamburg. Can't be long now. They're being pushed from both sides." "You'll never believe it but the Commandant has just arranged for a Fiesler Storch to fly him away at the last moment. The other officers are furious, what about them?"

And many, oh so many more baseless and pointless rumours were bandied about, whereas in point of fact nothing whatever changed apart from a basic reply by us, which quickly developed, to every German comment or request. "Joe is coming." It became the camp catch-phrase, for it was a well-known fact that the Jerries were positively scared of the Russians, a situation brought about by the horrific stories which the German front-line troops told whilst on leave. Their fear was genuine and warranted.

Early December brought snow and with it thoughts of Christmas. Considerable effort was put into decorating our room, even though by now it was overcrowded, and we decided to share our food for a Christmas dinner splash. Up to press Dick and myself had shared every little item. This called for a menu and I spent hours lettering and colouring them. The festive preparations were considerably marred when it was discovered that a quantity of "hooch" made from raisins, dried fruit, etc, etc, by a combine of chaps and hidden in the administrative block, had been acquired. There was no difficulty in recognising the guilty ones. They were staggering their way around camp completely and utterly pie-eyed.

An uproarious camp meeting followed and the guilty ones were severely reprimanded.

It was December 23rd before any mail arrived for our intake. 80% received mail in one form or another. I was one of the depressed unlucky ones and had to be content with reading Dick's letter from his mum which I did over and over again. The fact that I had never met the lady in question mattered not.

We made the most of Christmas, our feast being a huge success. We even had a Christmas cake, which had arrived in one of the parcels along with the mail.

The evening was spent mainly in bed to keep warm, singing carols and taking it in turn to brave the cold in order to make a brew for the lot of us. It could have been a sad time, but so much was going on, not to mention the dirty jokes, that one did not have time to become nostalgic.

Daily air raids had become the order of the day, carried out mainly by the Russians, interspersed with an occasional American raid. In a clear blue sky the Fortress formations made an impressive sight, their condensation trails leaving ever-expanding lines of white separating the sky into two halves. One could see the target marker leave the leading aircraft and curve its way down onto the unfortunate area about to be attacked. Our billets always lay too far away to feel any tremors, but the crump, crump of bombs as they struck home could be heard for miles around. However the raids only served to add to the incessant rolling thunder which became clearer and louder by the day.

All this activity had the effect of making the Germans difficult and jumpy. Parades lasted longer, billets were turned upside down more regularly as we stood outside shivering. Any excuse to upset our daily routine was used by the Jerries as if to say, "We are still in charge and that's how it is going to remain."

The constant searching of billets became embarrassing and we took to carrying as much food and cigarettes as possible on our persons. We had long since learned that cigarettes, coffee and chocolate were our main bartering items with the Germans and the searching, probing guards did not hesitate to steal these at any and every opportunity. This carrying of food annoyed them further and the order was given that in future all tins would be punctured. We could no longer store food. Something had to happen, and it did. Pandemonium broke out at the news, given to us by the Commandant early on the morning of January 19th, that we had one hour only to gather our belongings as the camp was to be evacuated.

Near panic broke out as we ransacked the stores, stuffing as much food, clothing, spare boots, cigarettes, anything we could lay our hands on that might be useful, into whatever containers were available.

At 5.30 a.m. on a cold, bleak, cheerless morning, 1,565 prisoners, including the camp leaders and committee, one medical officer and four orderlies, a C of E. Padre, two field kitchens complete with cookhouse staff, and the whole German unit, left a ravaged Stalag Luft VII headed to God knows where. We did not know our destination and, as it turned out, nor did the Germans.

Chapter Eighteen

Dick and myself had acquired a small Red Cross case each, the size of a large attaché case, complete with handle and webbing strap, in order to keep the unhinged lid in place. In these we had two-and-a-half days' marching rations consisting of half of a loaf each, bully beef, sausage, honey and cheese, plus a few unpunctured tins, a tin of Klim dried milk, a jar of coffee, a packet of tea, an empty tin and spoon and the inevitable tin-opener. We also had a spare pair of socks and our diaries, which we had religiously kept up to date.

It was indeed a pleasant change to be doing something positive and though we were obviously walking away from the advancing Russians our noses were firmly pointed Westwards. And Westwards was the way home.

The long column walked along what was no more than a country lane at quite a steady pace, many lads attempting to carry far too much in the way of large-sized packing cases. The constant swopping from shoulder to shoulder made it quite obvious that there was no way these cases would see journey's end. Extra clothing, in the way of trousers and greatcoats slung over arms, soon became a burden but a few more ingenious youths had hurriedly made sledges which slid over the thin covering of snow nicely.

Dressed in R.A.F. trousers, V-necked long-sleeved jumper, tunic, greatcoat and forage cap, I was perfectly comfortable and warm, apart from my hands, which soon became numb with cold, entailing a constant change of hand whilst the other nestled in my pocket. We soon reached the small township of Kreuzburg to find a different situation than we expected. The retreating German Army's vehicles slowly, but continuously, threaded their way through the narrow fume-ridden streets, whilst on foot a limited number of refugees, carrying their worldly belongings, spilled off the narrow pavement. Our arrival complicated things still further and it was some time before we negotiated our confused way through the town. The whole situation was very much to our liking and we began to sing and whistle when once again we reached open country. Our enjoyment however was short-lived. Snow started to fall and along with it came the icy wind. Cases of all shapes and sizes, clothing and other extraneous items soon joined the already littered roadside, others having found before us the impossibility of carrying much worthwhile when walking. Our old R.A.F. packs and webbing would have been invaluable, but no such luxuries were available. Surprisingly all military vehicles had disappeared, I could only assume on a different route.

We walked, with the snow becoming heavier and heavier and lying deeper and deeper on the unshielded roads, till 4 o'clock in the afternoon, covering a distance of twenty-eight kilometres. Our route had held little of interest, taking us, as it did, through Kreuzburg, Konstadt and Winterfeld. Commandeering a farm in the latter village the Germans began the laborious task of attempting to shepherd the whole 1,565 of us into three small barns. Long before a third of the contingent had entered through the arched wooden doors of our barn, men were falling over each other, for inside the barn banked-up bales of straw stretched to the high stone-slabbed roof on three sides, leaving little room for our large numbers.

The guards moved into the buildings, their raucous shouting and bawling drowning the prisoners' protests, driving, pushing and prodding the early entries to the uppermost heights in order to utilise every inch of space.

After an hour and a half's chaos the inky dark, freezing barn found itself filled. Quite unable to lie down, Dick and myself rested back to back, with our arms round our bended knees, fairly high up near the roof.

"Best thing to do here Dick," I said when we had finally got settled, "is to take off our boots and stick our feet and boots into as much loose straw as possible. They'll both be warm that way."

"I don't know Russ," the big lad answered, "I think I'll keep mine on. I know one thing, I'm hungry."

"And me, but we can't even open a tin here. I can't see you, let alone a tin-opener."

"We'll open a tin as soon as we start walking tomorrow, O.K.?"

"O.K."

"We could be in for a rough old spell in this situation. Where the heck's the food going to come from?" raising his voice so that I could hear above the babble of hundreds of similar conversations taking place throughout the barn.

"And this snow shows no sign of letting up. An electric fire would be handy," he ended chuckling.

Dick's sense of humour never deserted him.

There being little more to say we fell into silence, closing our eyes, but sleep was impossible. The freezing wind whipped under the cracks in the roof bringing along with it wisps of snow and no matter what position we got ourselves into those draughts succeeded in attacking particular parts of our bodies, which soon entailed vigorous massage to bring back to life the offending limb, neck or whatever. It also brought about the urgent need to relieve nature.

"Doesn't matter Dick, I'm going to have to go," I said, standing up.

"How the hell are you going to manage that?" he asked incredulously.

"No idea, but needs must."

The only thing I knew was the rough direction of the door. Two steps found my foot on someone's stomach, from which I nimbly hopped off putting the whole of my weight on him in the process. The howl of pain was replaced by the filthiest language drowned immediately by squeals and shouts as I literally slid down a few bodies, ending up on my back with my boot lodged in the side of a neck.

Regaining my feet, a push in the back sent me downwards in an uncontrollable roly poly giving some poor soul one almighty clout on my way. The cursing and bawling which accompanied my stumbling, falling progress, made me glad I was unrecognisable in the dark and the relief on finally reaching the door had to be experienced to be appreciated. The return climb, in an effort to find my little patch on the straw bale, was little better, it just took longer to lever oneself uphill by the aid of an unsuspecting arm or leg. What a nightmare.

The pattern was set, as evidenced by the continual shouted

abuse, as one after another, throughout the night, lads ran the gauntlet. The situation was ridiculous and unsolveable.

Dick and I eventually settled for a position which allowed us to curl up together, my feet rammed well into the straw, alongside my boots, equally well buried. We virtually got no sleep for we never got warm. It took us only an hour to discover that straw is the coldest, most inhospitable material one could attempt to sleep on, and being brittle there was certain to be at least one piece stuck in some painful part of the body.

Fine powdery snow covered parts of the two of us, icy jets of wind having decided where to build up the smooth narrow ridges, and it was something of a relief when at 4.0 a.m. our crashing, shouting, banging guards (they never could do anything quietly) announced in anything but gentlemanly terms that it was time to rise.

I had long since decided my feet did not belong to me and a greater effort than I imagined was necessary simply to stand up. Recovering my boots from the straw I found they had set solid. There was no way I could coax or even force them onto my feet. Half an hour I spent, beating the stiff leather objects against each other and stamping my feet in order to entice a little warm blood to flow into my extremities whilst being jostled, pushed and pulled, by a never-ending stream of humans who had had more sense than I and kept their boots firmly planted on their feet.

Outside, two small lights on the farmhouse wall silhouetted a long queue which jumped, jogged and thrashed its arms about, making its way to the far end of the expansive farmyard whilst driving snow challenged every effort to get warm. The smell of the soup which emitted from the soup kitchen was like nectar as painfully slowly I moved nearer to the food. Exactly one inch of thin, watery soup rewarded my efforts, poured into my two and a half inch diameter tin with a seeming reluctance by a young, fat, Liverpudlian cook.

It was however piping hot and had more effect on warming both my hands and my innards than anything I had hitherto tried.

It was 5.30 a.m. on Saturday before we once again began walking Westwards, accompanied still by the noise of the distant guns. Snow had built up overnight to a depth of three feet, having drifted in open spaces to a near impassable wall, and I wondered how on earth the contingent up front was faring. As Dick and myself were roughly in the middle of the column the snow had at least been trampled down to a more manageable level, but it was hard going, having to lift one's foot high up to clear mounds of the stuff with every step taken.

The extra pair of socks proved invaluable as gloves. Dangling loosely from my hands they kept out the difficult-to-deal-with cold winds, my hands becoming warmer and warmer as we struggled through the snow. They were however no more successful than our simple forage caps, for when unfolded, turned down and fastened under the chin, they gave ideal protection to the ears and provided a peak which helped to shield the eyes. Previously I had always thought that forage caps had been designed specifically to blow off one's head. Considerable thought had obviously been given to the design and we silently thanked them.

Between mouthfuls of our promised shared tin of cold meat Dick was saying:

"What do you reckon if it's another barn tonight, up at the top or down at the bottom? If we're at the top we get the wind through the roof, alternatively should we stay near the floor we'll get walked and rolled on all night."

"We haven't tried low down so let's give it a whirl Dick," I suggested, "and we'll be first in the soup queue don't forget."

"Right, let's work our way to the end of the column. Take it easy and let them pass."

"That won't be difficult. I don't altogether feel like breaking into a gallop."

We passed through a small village, typical of the area, a large farm, a small church, a school and a few houses, then nothing but open country, the roads at times being shielded by hedgerows not unlike England's.

"Did you notice that last sign-post Dick?" I asked. "It said Karlsruhe 7 kilometres. We'll walk through the village for about a kilometre and the next sign-post will read the same, Karksruhe 7 kilometres. What's happened to the kilometre through the village?"

"Yeah I know, I noticed it yesterday. It makes me feel the walk through the village has been wasted effort. It doesn't count," he answered with a laugh.

It took us five and a half hours hard slogging, battling against appalling weather conditions, to reach the haven of Karlsruhe (a distance of only 12 kilometres from Winterfeld) a deserted brickyard. At least here we found a cold water supply in the large open yard and were thus able to brew a welcome tin of tea and the brave could wash, provided one waited hours to get to the tap. Dick and I had to wait, being with the tail-enders, and we both agreed we would try the front next time.

Another inch of soup and a further shared tin of cold stew completed the day's intake of food, the rest of the day being spent resting and freezing on a concrete floor in a broken-down old building with only a partial roof for cover, which afforded little protection from the elements. Fortunately the snow had stopped falling. Darkness brought the really bitter coldness that penetrated every bone in one's body and I seemed almost rigid in one position, unable and well-nigh unwilling to move.

Surprisingly, by eight o'clock in the evening we were again on the move. The Commandant, who had so far given no information whatever, had informed Pete Thompson that it was imperative we crossed the River Oder before 10.00 hours on the Sunday. On being asked our destination he had simply shrugged his shoulders.

We had learned however, during our short stay in the brickyard, that Hitler had ordered that no P.o.W.'s must fall into Allied hands. All must be taken to central Germany, by whatever means at the disposal of the various Commandants. As far as we could see there was no other means than shank's pony.

The night march turned out to be the worst and the longest so far. Whilst it mercifully did not snow there was no escaping the strong bitter winds which continuously howled and whistled through our ranks. The moon, along with the starlit sky, made the white frost which soon formed on greatcoats and forage caps, glisten like tinsel. Hundreds of luminous bodies, crouched low, trying harder and harder to shrink into the confines of their coats, struggled and stumbled through the deep snow, hour after tiring hour. By the roadside, along with a miscellany of discarded belongings, dead horses appeared in increasing numbers and one wondered just how long ours would last. Their constant neighed protests suggested not long.

Up front Dick and I scoffed our last tin of food, sharing meticulously every morsel left therein. Weary, tired and desperately hungry, we finally reached the Oder at 5.30 a.m. Steel helmeted German troops milled about the bridge obviously ready to blow it when given the order. Where the troops came from, or indeed where they disappeared to when their work was completed, was a mystery; whilst marching we had not seen a soul, let alone troops.

Seven kilometres beyond the bridge, which had been dynamited within fifteen minutes of our crossing, we halted at Beurich, having covered a distance of 41 kilometres. Shattered, we once again found ourselves steered into a barn, the relief of escaping from the vicious, searching wind far outweighing the thought of yet another period of attempted rest under impossible conditions.

Being well to the front of the column allowed Dick and me to choose our position, six foot up on a ledge formed by the straw bales. It made little difference to the few hours' rest scheduled for us. Instead of walking on bodies, we provided the bodies to be walked upon and the three inch gap at the foot of the barn doors ensured total deep-freeze conditions during our period of immobility.

The vile language ought to have heated the air – a deep mood of resentment and annoyance was fast fermenting.

Roused at 2 p.m. on Monday the 22nd of January for our daily inch of soup we heard the crump, crump of exploding shells nearer than at any time previously and rumour had it that the Russians were shelling a village only six kilometres away.

The urgency of the Germans in attempting to form us up ready to march off was most noticeable and the lack of enthusiasm on the part of us prisoners was even more noticeable. The Germans were in no mood to stand any nonsense and rifles were brought to bear and fired over our heads. A few of the more obstinate types remained seated in the old barn only to find bullets ripping into the straw too close for comfort.

One can not and does not argue with a rifle.

By 4.30 p.m. a tired, hungry, foot-weary gaggle moved off once again in driving snow. Dilapidated, broken-down transport, from lorries to hand-carts, prams to flat wagons, narrowed the road, time and again, creating an aggravating stop-start situation, and when we slowly overhauled a long batch of refugees, attempting the impossibility of taking the kitchen sink with them, we had to filter past two abreast, which took an almighty long time. We were, in fact, witnessing the beginning of a chaos in Germany which was to grow and grow and eventually develop into an impossible man-gone-mad situation which has not been finally sorted out to this day.

There is no sight so pathetic as refugees with their young, crying children, and elderly ones struggling against blizzard conditions, falling from time to time in deep rutted snow and trying to carry great weighty bundles of their belongings to an unknown destination. Although they were Germans, and it was difficult for us to muster much sympathy for them at the time, one automatically knew that within days, many of these people would die and I found it hard to understand why all this was being allowed to go on. Why on earth didn't the Germans just surrender before it was too late?

Globules of ice hung from Dick's moustache, which he had proudly grown a few short months ago, like glass droplets on a chandelier. He was visibly growing wearier, the skin on his face having tightened, throwing into relief his high cheek bones. He looked as I felt, thoroughly worn out. Fortunately I could not see myself. Seeing a blue greatcoat by the roadside, spread out on a back cloth of white, we moved over to investigate for there was something different about this one. It was an old German Luftwaffe officer, face buried in the snow, his hat lying forlornly by his side. He was quite, quite dead and had been for some time for the corpse was already partially buried in the white killer.

"Leave him lads, nothing you can do." It was Father Berry's voice, our chaplain, who had joined us just prior to the march.

From Beurich, through the villages of Akzleuz and Sckonfield we trudged, eventually arriving at Jenkwitz, a distance of twenty-one kilometres. We had learned officially that the Germans had no destination in mind. Just how long could we go on walking aimlessly, and to us pointlessly, nowhere in particular and with so little food?

We youngsters tramped and shuffled our appalling way through unheard of village after village for a never-to-be forgotten eighteen days, eventually arriving at the township of Goldberg, which lies north east of Dresden, in a pathetic and desperate state. Our route had taken us through Kreuzburg, Konstadt, Winterfeld, Karlsruhe, Strehlen, Lagenzeslau, Schweidnitz, Falkenburg and Goldberg. In the worst eighteen days of my life I regret to write that I saw the so-called British spirit weaken. Some men acted like animals, stealing anything edible from friend and foe alike. If it meant someone being physically hurt in the process, so what? Hunger is the most difficult thing in the world with which to cope.

The worst day's march was on Sunday the 28th January, walking 25 kilometres from Pffaffendorf to Standorf. From the outset a blizzard raged, the like of which we had not experienced. Huge snow flakes whipped across the countryside parallel to the ground in such quantity as to give the effect of a solid white, impenetrable sheet, continuously speeding across our path. On numerous occasions it was a sheer impossibility to see another person. My boots froze solid on my feet, whilst the whole of my right-hand side held inches of snow, which, if shaken off, was replaced in seconds. As I write now it seems an untruth to say that I fell fast asleep, but I did just that, and, keeping on walking, drifted my own path across the blotted out road carrying on partway into what must have been a field, till finally, stumbling and falling – I awoke.

The carpet of snow was so deep I could barely see above it and it was with much difficulty that I battled my way back to the column, following the deep footsteps I myself had made. No-one had seen me wandering off – not even the guards. Either that, or they were past caring. Escaping at this point would have been easy, but escape where to? On my own I would not have lasted the day.

We were so tired and completely lacking food.

The march was now taking its toll and, on arrival at Schweidnitz, it was found that some men were quite incapable of further walking, arrangements being made by the Germans for these sick to be taken on ahead, by transport, when the blizzard subsided. I never did know what happened to these unfortunates.

It developed also that on arrival at a particular village the Germans no longer drove us into barns or elsewhere for they themselves, whilst having more food than we, had grown to detest this march and in my opinion were in an even worse state than we. Their average age of fifty, as opposed to our twenty years, put them at a tremendous physical disadvantage.

Provided they kept us in one area, such as a farm, they were content to let us fend for ourselves, provided we did not encroach into the farm house itself. This on occasion proved helpful. Dick and I made every effort to keep up front during the marching so that should an advantageous night's stay present itself, we should be first in.

As we wearily entered the now familiar farm-yard one night, a tiny light drew Dick and me like a magnet. Summoning what was left of our strength we broke into a run, reaching the small brick building first.

The opening of the door brought wafts of beautiful, but stinking, heavenly warm air surging around us – the first feel of warmth since leaving Bankau. The pig sty, in which we found ourselves, was fully inhabited by its natural occupants. The smell was totally immaterial.

It was warm, had an electric light, and more importantly possessed a tap which issued warm water. We had arrived at the Hilton Hotel!

Whilst we were joined by another pair of opportunists the four of us, quite amazingly, were left in peace for the night.

Simply taking off my clothes and washing under the warm tap created the most pleasant memory of the whole of my P.o.W. life. It was indescribably wonderful. I was delighted to discover that my wooden-soled boots, which I had so fortuitously had repaired, had unbelievably kept my feet not only snuff dry, but also free from blisters or suchlike. Dick, however, had developed a swelling of his right foot which promised to turn nasty and this received an extra bathing – the only thing he could do.

Actually lying with the pigs, our boots strung up by their laces along with our greatcoats and tunics, we spent the warmest, and by far the most comfortable, night of the whole march. We slept the sleep of the dead upon which the grunting, grumbling pigs had no effect whatever.

Our eyes had lit up the following morning at the unmistakable chuck chucking sound of nearby hens, obviously housed in an adjoining building. It took the four of us about thirty seconds to force an unseen entry into next door and get amongst our beautiful feathered friends. Throwing our greatcoats over them, swinging our boots, and literally trying to separate their heads from their bodies by pulling and tugging in the most amateurish frenzied manner, we soon turned the place into a mass of floating feathers and screeching birds. With the noise it was obvious we should soon be caught, so Dick and I beat a hasty retreat clutching two dead hens and one almost dead, along with ten eggs – a veritable feast!

Unable to do anything with our catch at present we joined the rest of the men, now assembled ready to move off, the hens tucked securely down our coats and the eggs in our cases. Whilst walking we drank four raw eggs but agreed to boil the remaining six, if possible at our next stop. We also gave away two of the hens – one to Gib – for we could not have coped with three ourselves, in fact we racked our brains on how we should deal with the one we still held.

A bucket was the best solution but, of course, the roadside cast-aways held no such receptacle and we rolled up at our next stopping place no nearer to a solution.

Finding ourselves in the bitterly cold, but lit, loft of a disused building along with about sixty other chaps and dreading another cold, miserable few hours, we were called up for soup almost immediately. Hanging back till the very last soul had departed down the ladder we hid the hen behind some loose brickwork near to our chosen spot for the night.

Hungry as hell, and clutching my meagre ration of hot soup, I ascended the perpendicular ladder wearily, but carefully, squeezing every last drop of pleasure from the thought of my few spoonsful of soup to come. My head had just reached a position where I could see into the loft when my tin caught on the top rung, tilted and spilled. Horrified and helpless I watched the life-saving liquid seep away between the mortar. I felt like screaming and crying like a petulant child – the injustice of it. At that moment I suddenly had the feeling that I could no longer go on. Slowly I made my way back to the soup kitchen knowing full well my story would not be believed.

"Sorry," I said convincingly to the servers, "you're not going to believe me but I've just spilled my soup and honestly I had not one drop of it. Can I have . . ."

"Bugger off, think we were born yesterday. The tales you lot tell us to get a bit more."

It was the fat Liverpudlian speaking in his customary coarse, brusque, bullying manner.

"There's one thing for sure," I shouted. "You're no thinnner now than when we set off on this bloody march. You lot are going short of nothing."

My temper was getting the better of me and I was overlooking the fact that for days now the cookhouse staff had been physically pulling the field kitchens and the cart carrying the Germans' belongings over almost impossible ground conditions – the horses predictably having died performing the same task.

"You'll get a bloody sight less next time you come up mate," he threatened, waving his ladle at me. "Piss off."

Telling him in unmentionable language what to do with himself, I trudged despondently back to the loft, inwardly fuming at my helplessness.

"This food job's an out and out racket," Dick was loudly proclaiming to all and sundry after hearing my story. "We'll sort this lot out when we've finished this march." As he was speaking he was also chewing – an action difficult to achieve on the march – for there was nothing to chew. On finishing speaking he pulled a large piece of gristle from his mouth and gave it to a nearby lad.

"What the hell are you doing?" I bawled at him. "I've had nothing to eat and here you are giving somebody else that gristle, you daft bugger."

Poor Dick was stunned, it was the very first time we had had a wrong word.

"It's only a piece of gristle and I've been chewing it for ages," he excused himself. "I didn't think . . ."

"That's just it, you didn't damn well think," I was blazing. "How would you feel if I gave food to somebody else?"

"Sorry Russ, I didn't realise." The big lad was genuinely hurt by my manner.

"Forget it, let's try and get some sleep," I answered, trying hard to control my temper.

"Before we do you may as well hear all the bad news. Some lousy bastard's whipped our chicken."

"Great, bloody great," I replied, closing my eyes and feeling more miserable than I had for a long long time.

Walking with glazed eyes – just walking aimlessly – we had carried on day after day coping as best we could with the lack of food and cold weather. And at night cuddling up together in an attempt to create warmth in our bodies.

Occasionally a mound of sugar beets would appear in a farmer's field, only to disappear under a pile of bodies as we made a mad scramble to aquire a few ourselves. Simply rubbed on our coats and devoured instantly along with bits of soil, the sugar beets were sweet, tasting mildly of turnip, but surprisingly did little to satisfy the pangs of hunger.

During the last few days a thaw had set in which turned the snow into ponds and rivulets, and the march into a paddle, rendering useless the sledges which soon joined the roadside débris and dead horses. Literally anything of value was now being traded for bread, our guards faring handsomely by the gain of propelling pencils, watches, cigarettes etc. We were in a desperate plight, and not only did the guards take advantage of the situation but they gloated over it, much to our annoyance. However the rumbling guns continued and we were only too aware that if we could stick it out our turn was coming, a point which was forcefully made daily to the Germans and which a few of them seemed slowly but surely to be grasping.

Dick's foot had fortunately improved considerably after a couple of days' limping, but I had got a chill on my kidneys which caused me great inconvenience, not the least when resting well up in a barn. I could not possibly disturb the boys every time I wished to relieve nature, for I was going every half hour.

My little tin was the best solution, for whilst I felt as though I was at bursting point, little water ensued. Unfortunately the following day's soup often went in the unwashed tin.

Maybe I would have been a little warmer had Dick and I developed the habit of a few boys and collected dry horse manure during the walking time, making a bed of it when the opportunity presented itself.

Only once during the march did a civilian offer us anything at all. A frail old lady came to the door of her outlying little cottage and, noting our state, disappeared, only to return with the familiar long large brown loaf tucked under her arm and a carving knife with which she began to saw off a thick slice. That was as far as she got. Youths shot across the road like a swarm of bees, brushing aside the startled guards. The old lady was knocked flying as the vultures pulled, tugged and tore at the bread. The column just kept on walking. Even the Germans did not stop to see what condition she was in. For the first time in my life I felt ashamed to be British. We were starving yes, but this was too much.

"Animals, bloody animals," Dick kept repeating. "I never thought I'd see the day."

On two successive occasions the Commandant had promised us transport at our next stopping point in order to get us to move, but each time he had let us down. At Prausnitz however he was given a positive ultimatum by a specially appointed committee. Not one step farther without transport were we going to take, regardless of what he did, and the M.O. made the point that if we did not move out quickly they would have to move us out in coffins.

As the appointed time for moving on drew near, every available German, armed with rifle, sub machine gun or revolver, appeared. They were determined to stir us into activity and the nearest group came in for the guttural rantings and ravings at which the Germans were expert, but no-one moved. On orders from their officers, some twenty guards stood in a line with rifles levelled at the P.o.W.'s whilst others physically pulled the men to their feet. Having got each man standing, the guards followed the same procedure with the next group, but the first batch of men, with considered deliberation, sat down again.

At this the Gemans went completely berserk and the lot of them, including the officers, joined in the mêlée. Bodies rolled over the place till once again the first batch were on their feet. But the second lot had sat down. The deafening, frightening, crack crack of rifle fire reverberated around the timber yard as bullets whistled and ricocheted over our heads. Still no-one moved, and whilst I was inwardly scared the episode helped to restore some of my lost faith, for we stubbornly sat it out.

Eventually, fuming with rage, the Commandant and his officers stalked off, leaving the guards unsure of themselves, knowing not what to do next, till they also sauntered away. We had won. It would have to be transport or nothing, and for the first time since leaving Bankau, a jubilant crowd of P.o.W.'s awaited their next move with interest.

Left to our own devices we lit little fires in order both to keep us warm and at least to make brews of warm water, and it was not until the following day that the Germans made their move.

They promised faithfully that a train would be waiting at Goldberg ready to take us to an established P.o.W. camp at Luckenwalde, if we would walk the necessary nine kilometres to get there. The committee were informed that road transport from our present position was impossible. Reluctantly agreeing we covered the last 9 kilometres on foot to find at Goldberg, as promised, the beautiful, heaven-sent sight of a train in all its glory, puffing steam up into the heavens, ready for the off.

They had not the slightest difficulty in getting us to climb into the roofed cattle-wagons until we realised, all too late, that these cultured Nazis had rammed sixty-four men into each truck.

We spent three nights and two days locked tight in these wagons with no food and no water. On the second day a few of the wagons were unlocked to allow a ten-minute stroll by the track. We, however, like the majority, were unlucky. This, in spite of the fact that for very long periods the train was at a standstill; that, or the usual mile forward and two shunted backwards. Intense frustration barely describes how we felt.

Lying down was impossible, so we arranged that half should sit and half should stand, and changed about periodically. Like stricken animals we stood or sat in the soon stinking truck. To keep up morale we spoke of food and its preparation, we spoke of home and its comforts, we spoke of restaurants, cafes and "Smokey Joe's" and the pies the old ladies used to make for us at Blyton. We had become stupidly obsessed with the subject.

By this time many of the boys had contracted dysentery, which entailed constantly holding one individual after another up to the open grills, which served as windows, with the results of their efforts mainly running down the inside walls and down the backs of lads unable to move out of the way. The results were anything but funny.

An occasional man would collapse but our shouting and banging to draw attention to our plight, when at stop, were completely ignored.

The nightmare journey amongst that filth ended 50 kilometres from Berlin and we tumbled out of those wagons just in time. Much longer and I, along with hundreds of others, would never have made it.

Never have I been so physically weak, never so desperately hungry, never so thin and never so bitter and angry. When our turn came they would pay for this.

Tired, stumbling, half bent and on the verge of collapse, we passed through the gates of Stammlager 111A, Luckenwalde, hardly noticing the fact that we had at long last reached a permanent P.o.W. camp.

Chapter Nineteen

News of our impending arrival had obviously reached the army P.o.W. camp for immediately we entered a contingent of Irish soldiers took charge.

They led, and helped, the long gaggle of men through a couple of wired-in compounds to where three beautifully steaming hot soup kitchens stood in an open clearing. Speedily everyone's can was filled to the brim – a novelty indeed – with thick barley soup which actually contained strands of meat. Only people who have experienced starvation could possibly appreciate the glorious, marvellous, wonderful, out-of-this-world feeling one gets from stuffing spoonsful of food into your mouth as fast as possible like a greedy dog bolting its biscuits. It was almost impossible to grasp that the whole tinful was mine, and to be given "seconds", on gobbling the first lot down, put the final touch to a memorable welcome to Luckenwalde.

One huge, wooden building, with three rows of roof-supporting posts running down its entire length, had been made ready to receive us by the spreading of a two-inch layer of straw over the wooden floor, passageways having been left clear at intervals. It was extremely well-lit by electricity ·· an hitherto unheard of luxury. The building was unheated and positively cold on entry but a veritable paradise compared to our varied accommodation of the past few weeks.

Issued with a blanket each, Dick and myself soon found string enough to lace ours together to form a double sleeping bag and, removing greatcoats, settled down for a much needed sleep.

For a couple of weeks the whole lot of us were in a sorry state, leaving our barrack only for the purpose of crossing to the nearby toilet, where we found great difficulty in performing what ought to have been the simple task of mounting the three steps leading into the latrines.

Once having stopped walking it was difficult trying to get going again. Occasionally a lad would stand, sway and collapse on the spot, completely blacking out. The number of dysentery sufferers increased and these were all kept in an area specifically designated for the sick.

According to the records of John J. Waltky, the deputy camp leader, a total of 1,493 prisoners completed the march. Of these, all suffered from extreme malnutrition, sixty-nine from dysentery, twenty from frostbite, twenty-three from septic foot, forty from diarrhoea, eight from bronchitis, twenty-five from muscular rheumatism and numerous other complaints. There were also one hundred and fifty men, who, as a result of weakness could not attend outside parades. They had to be counted in bed, bed being the floor.

Even the German doctors agreed that food was essential, but our ration of half a can of soup per day – though admittedly a larger ration than of late – persisted, brought round to us as we lay there. A limited amount of "seconds" were issued and that was how I came to disgrace myself.

On the fifth day at Luckenwalde I had been lucky enough to take my turn with extra soup, Dick being the next one in line. The following day the soldier dishing out the seconds asked whose turn it was and my hand automatically went up along with Dick's, I was so hungry and the thought of a second helping overruled all else. It was as I was finishing it off that one lad sitting directly across shouted—

"Hey you – you had your seconds yesterday."

"Did he hell," Dick immediately retaliated, jumping to my aid.

"Oh yes he did," chipped in his friend," I remember full well it ending at him".

"Come off . . ."

"It's no good Dick, forget it." And I put a restraining hand out.

"I'm sorry lads, you're right, what else can I say?"

With background mumblings and accusing nods being made in my direction I felt 2 inches tall, and the more I thought of what I had done, the worse I felt, till tears welled up in my eyes and uncontrollably overflowed. To think I had sunk to such a low level as to deprive a man of his extra soup – no not deprive, steal.

Steal from my comrades. My thoughts were totally in control, much to my humiliation.

"Come on Russ, bloody hell, blokes have been stealing from one another, we've been twisted out of food by people who we relied upon to give us a fair deal and some of them even knocked down an old woman – probably killed her – just for a bit of bread, and here you are upset at having seconds of soup." Dick was doing his utmost to console me and failing miserably.

"If I starve to death," I gulped, "I'll never do anything like that again. I don't care what happens. I feel so terribly ashamed. To think . . ."

I hesitated, unable to speak for the tears. "I should disgrace myself . . ." Unable to finish I rose and shuffled outside into the fresh air, my thoughts tearing me apart unmercifully.

I wondered what my dad would have thought of that incident had he been present. He was always a tough old customer, nothing or nobody seemed to get him down. Even when my mother, his mother and his son had died within the space of nine months he had weathered the situation well. Never at any time had he shown the slightest signs of emotion. In his army days during the first World War he was wounded three times. Had he not, I wondered, shown weakness some time or another? Somehow I doubted it. Oblivious of all and sundry around me I mooched around, trying all in my power to throw off the turmoil the incident had created within me, by thinking of anything at all, other than my present situation. I can but assure you, it took an awfully long time.

With the intervention of Swiss Red Cross officials who, thanks to the Geneva Convention, periodically visited P.o.W. camps, the food situation improved slightly over the next few weeks. They had openly rail-roaded the German officers in charge when a number of the dysentery sufferers had been paraded before them stripped to the waist, revealing their very pronounced rib cages. The sick were immediately placed on a noodle soup diet twice daily and the rest of us received a limited amount of potatoes and bread to bolster our soup ration. However the best pick-me-up of the lot came at the end of our second week – a Red Cross parcel per man. Not only did we eat well from this but it gave us cigarettes and coffee, the much-needed currency in all camps.

Luckenwalde was a very large camp, totally overcrowded. The place consisted of compound after compound, formed by upright posts and criss-crossed wire, split down the centre by quite a wide dusty track. It was a particularly scruffy camp as each compound bore little resemblance to its neighbour. Some had brick buildings scattered about, others sported wooden huts, some huge, some small. Many had nothing but great big canvas tents.

There was no uniformity about the camp whatever and when one considered it was inhabited by Serbians, Norwegians, Danes, Poles, Americans, Irish, Canadians, Australians, South Africans, Rhodesians, New Zealanders, French, Dutch, Belgians, Russians and ourselves, each with our own ideas of living and surviving, it's no wonder that a complete hotch-potch resulted.

The men of each nationality, fortunately, were separated, apart from all the Commonwealth personnel. It was soon obvious that the numerically strong French contingent ruled the camp and, much to our annoyance and amazement, appeared to wander in and out of camp at will, being on extremely, and to us unbelievably, friendly terms with the Germans.

The order that it was the duty of every P.o.W. to attempt escape apparently did not apply to the French, for they had all the opportunities they desired. All these comings and goings meant that they controlled the food being brought in daily, placing us in the unenviable position of having to barter with the French for anything at all, our only advantage being the Red Cross cigarettes and coffee – totally unobtainable in Germany. As parcels now began to flow into camp at regular intervals all kinds of possibilities presented themselves.

It became an essential, one way or another, to get down to the French compound, which lay way along the central wide road, and in pursuance of this object I managed to exchange my R.A.F. trousers for a pair of Polish corduroy riding pants, complete with leather chaps on the inside of the leg. These were warm but totally impracticable for P.o.W. life. A dozen stubborn buttons ran from ankle to knee height, which had to be fastened and unfastened daily. The calf was then covered by leather gaiters, held in place by buckle and strap. Whilst we slept fully dressed, to combat the chilly nights, it proved downright uncomfortable trying to sleep with the gaiters on and trouser legs buttoned up. However inconvenient they might have been, they were particularly effective in transforming me into a Frenchman, for many wore similar riding breeches, and the acquisition of a black beret by Dick completed the illusion. Dick was a marvel at "acquiring" our odd requirements.

It remained only a matter now of finding a method of getting out of our particular compound and mingling with the French, who sauntered backwards and forwards to and from their billets the length of the day. This was soon solved by loosening, under the cover of darkness, the wire on a small locked gate, which lay at the end of a long passageway of a building directly adjoining our own, a replica of the key for the door soon having been made by some industrious members of our community.

Armed with sixty cigarettes tucked down my shirt and with Dick acting as look-out, I made my attempt one afternoon, anxious to get as much bread as I could.

The timing had to be right, for guards patrolled this central roadway even though it was still inside the camp as a whole. There always came a point when the two patrolling guards momentarily had their backs to the gate, and it was at this time, having previously opened the wire enough to slip through, that Dick said "Now." Out I went like greased lightning and immediately adopted the casual strolling poise of the French before the guards had turned around.

It felt quite novel, strolling along with an affected couldn't-care-less attitude, glancing occasionally at my own comrades inside the wire, but my reception by the French, when I entered their barracks, was not of the best order – in fact I soon found myself in a heated argument. Quite a number of them spoke English and were considerably older than I.

"I suppose you're with the R.A.F. intake," one of a nearby group addressed me offhandedly.

"Yes, I am, I've come to see if you have any bread to spare," I replied.

Ignoring my question he asked, "Was you with the bombers?"

"Yes."

"Don't you think you have been overdoing the bombing of Germany?"

"Overdoing it?" I repeated incredulously. "We're trying to end this war. We didn't start this bombing lark."

"Do you realise the damage that's been done and the civilians that have been killed unnecessarily. They are not fighting troops you know."

"How long have you been in Germany? What about the number of civilians killed in England by German bombing when we didn't

163

have the planes to hit back?"

And so it developed into a ding-dong verbal battle, with me standing alone against Frenchmen who had been prisoners since 1940 and had been brainwashed ever since with daily German propaganda. Incredibly they did not even seem anxious to get back home, for when I asked them did they not want to get back to France, they simply shrugged their shoulders. I must confess to completely losing my temper at their attitude to the war.

I left the billet empty-handed – they could stick their bread. Fortunately I fared much better in the next building, totally avoiding controversial questions and sticking solely to the subject of how many cigarettes for a loaf of bread.

Arriving back at the loose wire with a feeling of elation I found Dick waiting, as arranged, to let me in.

"How did you get on Russ?" he queried anxiously when I was safely in the passageway.

"Just the job. I got two loaves for forty fags and that's ten less than the going rate." I smiled, highly delighted with myself.

Excursions down to the French quarters became a twice weekly outing thereafter, Dick and I taking it in turn. Unfortunately we were not on our own and visits became all too commonplace, particularly with the Americans who possessed far more cigarettes than we. Thus, predictably, the cost of bread rocketed and soon the French were asking eighty cigarettes per loaf.

Dick's diary reads for this period:

"It's like Petticoat Lane on a Sunday morning. Everyone is trading, the British and Yanks for bread, and the French and Serbs for blood."

And that adequately summed up the situation.

Bread was not our only requirement. Soap had become of paramount importance to some us. I deliberately say some of us, because far too many of the lads had conveniently never resumed the habit of washing and it had been noticeable of late the amount of scratching being done by more and more of our members.

"Thank God we have no fleas," Dick mentioned casually one day. The remark was overheard by a lad passing by.

"Just to suit me take your shirts off," he said, "and we'll see." Obligingly we did as requested.

"There you are, not a sign of a flea," Dick said after careful examination of the garments.

"Now turn back the seams and have another look."

Doing as bid we both looked in amazement, repelled at the long rows of lice, their translucent one-eighth of an inch long bodies with a prominent black line down the centre lying bumper to bumper under every single seam.

Our underclothes were in exactly the same state, literally lousy with the pests.

Up to that very moment we had been totally unaware of our unwanted guests, which suggested we had only recently been invaded. Having no spare clothes there was no alternative but to wear the offending garments, as it was far too cold to be without them. A vigorous but useless shaking had to suffice.

"As soon as we get some soap and it gets a little warmer we'll wash the lot and get rid of them," said I, confident I had the simple answer.

"You'll be lucky," the wise one pointed out. "You can wash till you're blue in the face. There's no shifting them with soap."

"How do we get rid of them then?" we chorused.

"You don't! The whole camp is full of them."

"Charming."

We P.o.W.'s settled down once again to make our blowers etc in order to heat soup and cook. Providing ourselves with boiling water was no longer a problem, as one ingenious youth had invented a highly successful immersion heater, utilising the barrack's supply of electricity. For safety's sake I had better not describe how this was achieved, but it was the simplest possible gadget, made as usual with tins, three pieces of wood and a length of cable. Whilst being highly dangerous the heater was capable of boiling a pan of water in the incredible time of nine seconds. Within two days every combine possessed one of these pieces of magic. The use of them at meal times thus resulted in a ridiculously heavy load being put on the electricity supply and the constant blowing of fuses. Fortunately for us the fuse box was of the automatic variety and it needed but a press on a large red button to get the supply operating again. A rota was drawn up and we took it in turn during the heavy periods to stand by the box, leaning on the button so that it never got a chance to spring out. Theoretically, I suppose the whole thing ought to have gone up in smoke, but it did not.

It was just as well we had at least one thing that eased our lot, for Luckenwalde was proving a difficult camp in more ways than one.

Our sleeping arrangements, with hundreds sleeping virtually shoulder to shoulder on thin straw, which scattered all over the place nightly, were, to state it simply, downright uncomfortable. One could be sure that settling down for the night was the time chosen for the lice to take their daily exercise, resulting in more twisting, turning, scratching and swearing than one would get on a bed of worms. Further, we had no table or chairs and nowhere whatever to store anything – just our bed space.

A two-minute walk, avoiding groups of men crouched over their blowers, was the time it took to cover our small compound. Since the march there had been no co-operation with the Germans whatever and even the white-coated ferrets no longer came along to chat. This situation only served to make the twice-a-day counts a difficult process – the guards making us stand in the cold for ages waiting for the officers and insisting on all kinds of little things being just so.

One did, however, have to accept that we had developed into a particularly slovenly lot – just on a par with the Yanks in the next compound.

The only men worthy of note in the whole camp were the Irish troops. They turned out each day as immaculately as it was possible for them to do, their lines being as straight as the guards at their best. The Irish billets, whilst fortunate in having bunks, were kept neat and tidy, as was the personal appearance of each man. I can only believe that it was all due to their army training and discipline. Whatever the reason they were indeed a credit to Old Mother Ireland.

Our relationship with the enemy sank even deeper into the mire when one night the sharp crack, crack of rifle fire woke us. Two Canadians had decided to make a rather foolish direct-type escape by climbing straight over the wire. One had got tangled up half-way over, the other actually made it to the ground outside, but once again the guards just shot them dead when it would have been far easier to arrest and punish them.

A visit to the camp by Max Schmelling, now a German paratrooper, but formerly the heavyweight boxer who was given a lesson he would never forget by Joe Louis, did nothing whatever for us, but the receiving once again after a long delay of the B.B.C. news did everything for us. It was brilliant news, with the Russians and the Allies apparently in a race to see who would be the first in Berlin.

It was as if hearing the news again had brought about a resurgence in aerial activity, for coincidentally that very day

Russian Yaks and Stormovicks crossed and criss-crossed the skies above us in large numbers, with numerous, and continual, puffs of flak bursting amongst them.

By April 1st '45 (All Fools Day), the very day, five long years before, I had commenced my apprenticeship in the printing trade (must be an omen there somewhere!) not only had the Red Cross parcel supply dried up but so also had our electricity supply, and water was down to a trickle. On the bright side we could easily once again hear the Russian artillery and this day to me will always signify the beginning of the end of our captivity. But not in the way I expected. As the days dragged on frustratingly, the intensity of the battles increased, whilst we sat helpless and virtually foodless in the middle. Our first taste of the shooting came one day whilst Dick and I were attempting to fill a pan with water in the so-called end kitchen. The familiar, but deadly, clackety-clacketing of cannon fire all but drowned the screaming, whining cannon shells as they rattled on and through the tin-roofed billets, followed by the roar of low flying aircraft. Huddled together under the sink, our water having found its way down the drain via the upturned pan, Dick looked at me.

"The last time we did this was in Belgium but it was a bed then."

"You're right kid," I answered with a sidelong glance.

"These aeroplanes are a bloody nuisance."

The B.B.C. news was telling us of a colossal advance by the Americans towards the River Elbe, north of Magdeburg, only 65 kilometres from camp, and the Russians were rumoured to be no more than 40 kilometres away. The Germans told us to prepare to move to Munich. Our leader told us to stay put. A confused situation was fast developing, but somehow a limited amount of Argentinian bulk food had arrived. Having shared out this type of food many times in the past we knew it could be at least a half-day's job.

Once it had finally been worked out by the powers-that-be just how much food a certain group would receive it was then up to that group to share it out individually – and what a performance that always developed into.

"Right lads, there's 24 of us to these rations. I suggest we share the corned beef first."

"No let's share the marg first."

"Don't be daft, it'll melt."

"O.K. who's going to cut it. Remember the one that cuts gets the

167

last choice."

"No, that's not fair. We'll draw straws as usual when it's cut."

"Right, give me the knife."

"Hold it – don't cut right away, just mark it to see how it pans out."

"I know, I know, I'll mark it five times this way, and three times this way. How's that. Are they equal?"

"No those two marks at the end aren't as wide as the others."

"O.K. I'll smooth them out and try again. There, that's as near as damn it."

"I don't see how that can work 'cause it slants at this end – it's not square."

"Well I'll slant my knife a bit each time, right? Shall I cut now?"

"Go on then, but take it easy, we don't want it squashing."

"Bags the bits left at the end."

"You've had it, we'll draw for that as well. Go and get some straws."

"Now no twisting. Turn your backs till I hide these straws under a blanket. Fair enough, start drawing."

"Just a minute. You drew first last time. Stand back and let somebody else have a go."

And after all that one ended up with a one-inch cube of corned beef, placed carefully in one's tin. This procedure was repeated with every item.

It requires little imagination on the part of the reader to decide how we fared with such things as a tin of rice pudding, or say Nestles milk.

Had it not been so deadly serious it would have been hilarious. It was also a study to see how different types of men handled their meagre rations, obtained after a full morning's bickering and arguing. The live-for-today type was always predictable, no nonsense, he would sit there after the drawn-out proceedings and scoff his bits and pieces in seconds. The more prudent type – no matter how little he got – always ate half and saved half till later, whilst the careful, cautious merchant saved the lot and never seemed to eat at all. This type always carried his bits of food with him wherever he went and it was not at all an uncommon sight to see lads carrying their tins into the latrines, for they wisely never let those precious bits out of their sight. It is quite staggering how men behave when they are really hungry.

Excitement was growing by the hour as the obvious day of

liberation neared. By April 15, it was impossible to look up without seeing aircraft of one sort or another. Shells had actually whined their way over our heads but none had exploded in the camp. All counts and parades had ceased and our guards were noticeably jittery – they had at long last realised the truth. An anti-tank gun was positioned in the field alongside the camp in full view of our compound, by 3 members of the S.S. , and in the late afternoon a message was read out from the officer in charge to the effect that should any firearms be produced by prisoners or should any disturbance of any kind develop, one hundred prisoners would be shot and the gun turned on the camp. The fools were still at it with their threats.

It was impossible to sort the truth from the hundreds of rumours being bandied about, but when the B.B.C. actually mentioned Luckenwalde itself, saying that a big battle was taking place and the Germans had lost 20,000 men in the area, the tension was just too much and the lads went wild, walking around the compound, shouting, singing and cheering every little rumour regardless of its authenticity. We were in a mood to believe anything.

Chapter Twenty

It was Saturday, April 21st, when dawn was but breaking over an extremely quiet camp, that we were abruptly awakened by a shouting, screaming youth.

"They've gone, they've gone. The bloody jerries have gone."

We stumbled and fell over one another in our haste to reach the door in order to verify for ourselves the truth of his statement. Never did such a huge camp come to life so quickly. Men teemed out of their various barracks by the hundreds – and then we just stood and gaped at the unique sight – no patrolling men with rifles, empty watch-towers and not an enemy uniform in sight. It was indeed true, after what had seemed an eternity we were completely unguarded. But the manned anti-tank gun was still in position – the last remaining obstacle to be overcome – or so we thought.

That day we ate what little food we possessed, ransacked the offices, where a number of us managed to retrieve our personal P.o.W. documents, organised ourselves into squads of 100 ready for evacuation, and received numerous requests from our Camp Leader to stay put, which reminded us the war was not yet over.

Our first view of the Russians came in dramatic fashion the following day when a jeep-type vehicle sped bumpily towards the anti-tank position, where the S.S. men frantically waved a white flag high in the air, attached to a rifle. Out stepped a long-coated khaki clad officer carrying a revolver. The Germans kneeled down and as casually as one might butter a slice of bread the officer grasped the hair of one and promptly shot him in the head. Polishing off the remaining two in similar fashion he studiously climbed back into the vehicle which disappeared whence it came, as quickly as it had appeared. The whole episode lasted but a few minutes and I could but think I had never seen anything so coolly and callously performed in my life.

Within a couple of hours, with all the camp congregated in groups, debating what the next move would be, we were officially relieved. Two armoured cars, one surmounted with movie camera and operators, slowly drove in front of a Red Star-adorned tank, its huge gun pointing menacingly skywards, which noisily clanked and rattled its way down the side of the wide roadway, crunching the flimsy posts and barbed wire effortlessly. In response to continual cheering from the inmates the square-headed, stubbly-bearded tank commander, smiling from ear to ear, waved to all and sundry, his woolly helmet ear flaps swaying from side to side as he looked one way then the other. The Russian newsreel men captured the whole ecstatic scene and received an encore when the tank returned on the opposite side.

The excitement of the moment did not, however, blind us to the fact that the outside wire was left intact, and awakening the following morning to find more forage-capped Russian guards round the perimeter of the camp than the Germans had had posted was a devastating experience. We were still P.o.W.'s.

Russian P.o.W.'s had been faring badly in Germany and we had rarely seen them about the camp, but we did not realise how badly till we saw two four-wheeled flat handcarts, pulled by Russian soldiers, pass our now open compound. Bodies, little more than skeletons, were built up pyramid fashion on the carts, thin arms and legs swaying grotesquely as they passed over every pot hole and, following behind, a straggly, pathetic group of survivors stumbled and shuffled along, the stronger supporting the weaker. The Russians had been starved of food and we all bowed our heads in respect till the primitive cortège disappeared from view, the only sound being the whirr of the newsreel cameras.

"No wonder the Nazis are frightened stiff of this lot Gib," I addressed our Canadian rear-gunner, who was stood by my side scowling.

"Gee, will the goons suffer for this lot, I'd sure hate to be in their shoes. Boy they're goin' to get massacred," Gib answered feelingly. "I never realised this was going on here."

It was indeed a sobering thought, that men had been dying through lack of food within a few hundred yards of us, whilst we had been haggling with all and sundry regarding the number of cigarettes we should pay for a loaf.

Amazingly the fitter ones were immediately absorbed into the ranks of the Red Army, a move which completely astounded us.

Within days of these P.o.W.'s leaving camp, two high-ranking Russian officers approached the British and American camp leaders. Up to press they had grudgingly recognised the Americans and British as Allies, but had virtually ignored the dozens of other nationalities. They requested, and it was a request they expected would be accepted, that all Allied personnel join them in battle again the Common Enemy. We would, of course, be issued with Red Army uniforms.

Much to their annoyance, this request was turned down flat, which did not altogether put us in the Russians' good books. It was clearly pointed out to them, by our leaders, that even if we should want to fight – which we didn't – legally we could not do so, for the Allies, having signed the Geneva Convention, were bound by the rule which clearly stated that no P.o.W. could fight again on that soil until a period of twelve months had elapsed from the day of his release. During the short meeting, which quickly became quite heated, it was also mentioned that had the Russians themselves signed the document, they would not have taken dead comrades from our camp, for they too would have been receiving Red Cross parcels.

It all made no difference to the attitude of the Russians – we were in the dog-house!

As food was, once again, non-existent, however, they promised front-line rations for the Allies only. As for the rest of the camp – too bad.

A complete lack of organisation and a general lack of interest in the whole situation grew worse by the day. The promised rations never arrived. The French and Poles had been officially informed they were leaving camp – they didn't. R.A.F. personnel were told we would be moving to the German officers' ex-quarters – we didn't. Under no circumstances would anyone else be allowed into the grossly overcrowded camp; foreign workers streamed in by the hundreds, both men and women, directed there by the Russians. It was categorically stated that the whole camp would have to be evacuated as 8,000 enemy troops had broken out of an encirclement by Russian troops – we weren't.

It was true, however, that violent fighting had again flared up in the area. Artillery fire was incessant as both sides pounded away and air activity had once again increased with, we were delighted to see, more American Thunderbolts and twin – boom Lightnings in evidence. Fortunately only the odd stray shell exploded in the vicinity of the camp, none actually falling on us. It was in fact Germany's last fling.

In camp the mood was one of sheer frustration. We were thoroughly sick of the Germans and the treatment we had received. Desperately hungry, and frantically anxious to be on our way home, we now experienced more indecisive decisions by the Russian commanders. Try as we did there was no way either we, or the Yanks, could organise a situation which daily grew worse with the continual influx of people of every nationality. One had to remember the Russians had a war to fight and that, of course, was of paramount importance. We came way down the list of priorities, being nothing more than an encumbrance. To us, all this mattered not – we were starving and something had to be done and quick.

The Russians came up with the answer – organise foraging parties, consisting of 12 men in each, and they would supply us hand-drawn carts, but we would have to go with Russian guards. We agreed – anything to get food. It was fixed for the following morning, Wednesday April 25.

For the first time, the Russians remained true to their word, the four-wheeled, rubber-tyred carts being received early morning. In pouring rain the 10 parties of us left camp, Dick and myself having made certain we would be in on the act this time. I can make no apologies to the reader for what followed and I can but hope that he or she understands the impossible situation in which we had found ourselves. Morally it was unjustifiable.

Having one thing, and one thing only on our minds – to steal as much food as could be reasonably piled on the carts – we split into individual units, each unit being accompanied by four guards. We moved along with such single-minded purposefulness that the fact that we were out of camp with no barbed wire in sight virtually went unnoticed.

Reaching the outskirts of Luckenwalde we settled on a short row of three houses, four men to each house, to begin our plundering. The door of our chosen house was locked, but three hefty kicks was enough to leave it swinging on its hinges. In a largish room, at the back of the house, two women and one child looked up in shocked, startled amazement, which quickly turned to abject terror as we four rough-clad youths and a Russian guard strolled determinedly

173

into the room. Within seconds the house was in uproar. Dick walked to the oven over which one of the ladies was frying their mid-day meal, took the pan from her hand and poured the contents on the floor at her feet. I had found a shopping bag and was busily engaged in filling it with two plates, two knives and forks, two mugs, salt and pepper, etc etc from the already laid table, completely oblivious of the hysterical child crying loudly into the other lady's lap.

"Any Eir? Any Kartoffel?" one of the lads was shouting, using the odd German word we had picked up.

The women did not answer, they couldn't, for they were petrified. It was as if all our pent-up feelings of the march, the train journey and our present conditions were being vented on this one house.

Every cupboard was ransacked and what little food they possessed deposited onto the table. The other rooms came in for similar treatment just in case some food had been hidden away, and, with all three occupants terrified and in tears, the house all but wrecked, we left as quickly as we had entered, leaving not one crumb under the roof.

Our next port of call was a small farm where we fared much better. Immediately on entering the farm yard we came across three elderly men working under a lean-to roof. A horse was hanging suspended from a couple of beams feet upwards, its feet having been tied together. Steam rose from the newly-killed animal and its skin lay in a heap on the floor. I walked over to one of the frightened men, took his long-bladed knife and carved four half-inch thick slices off the rump of the still-warm beast, unpleasant and distasteful though I found it. We would have taken the whole horse could we have managed it. As before, the kitchen was ransacked and quite a good haul of potatoes and vegetables were pillaged. It was as we were about to leave that the stupid hens made themselves known. Expecting such a situation to develop, the farmers had hidden them in the cellar, and it was not long before dead hen after dead hen was flung up the cellar steps, followed by a bucket full of eggs. Powerless to stop us, the old farmers and their womenfolk just looked on despondently, knowing full well that this was just the start of things to come. At least we had not physically injured anyone.

It took us but an hour to load the cart to capacity and our arrival back at camp with food, glorious food, was greeted with cheers from the starving P.o.W.'s.

We had, however, not been the most successful of the foraging parties. One group, on examining a deserted train in the sidings at Luckenwalde, had found to their amazement thousands of untouched American Red Cross parcels, something the locals had obviously missed, and something which our departed German Guards must have been aware of. A shuttle service soon had the whole lot safely in camp.

Against this background Dick and I set about preparing the meal of our lives – the one we had been promising ourselves weekly for the last nine months. And although desperately hungry we prepared it with the care of the head waiter at London's Savoy Hotel. Having been done slowly, patiently, and lovingly in the frypan over an open fire, the meat, covered with just the right amount of soft, lightly browned chopped onions, was scrumptiously tender, whilst the clean soft orange coloured carrots lying alongside eye-free white potatoes, the butter melting in little rivulets over them, were exquisite. We ate it as slowly as we had cooked it, savouring every mouthful with sheer ecstasy. And the joy of eating from actual plates, with actual knives and forks, all laid out in the very best style on a white floral tablecloth (even if it was on the floor) remains with me to this day. Pancake mix provided us with an ideal sweet, liberally spread with marmalade and sprinkled with shavings of "D" bar chocolate. Cheese and those thick round crumbly breakfast-type crackers, washed down with Sun Filled orange juice, completed the glorious, heavenly, delightful meal, the envy of all who stood round watching and laughing – they could afford to – their bellies were also full.

The fact that neither Dick nor I ate one more morsel for a full three days – both of us being racked by violent stomach pains – would not deter us from doing precisely the same thing again, for it provided one of our outstanding and everlasting memories.

So many Red Cross parcels did we and the Yanks have that we supplied the whole camp with one each, apart from the French that is, who received one parcel between four, it being strongly taken into consideration how they had screwed every possible cigarette out of us in exchange for one measely ersatz loaf. It was our turn now and it can be rather a nice feeling.

During those three foodless days when our tummies ruled our habits, the B.B.C. news told us that a link-up by the Americans and Russians at Magdeburg was imminent. It also spoke of the magnificent reception being given back in England to the lucky home-coming P.o.W.'s whose camps had been overrun by the Allies, but added considerable concern for many still unrelieved as they had it that some were near to starvation. The Russians informed us that the Germans still had four Divisions in the area, two panzer and two infantry, but they had few tanks left and little equipment. It was strongly rumoured that a peace conference was scheduled to take place.

Our daily foraging parties brought back the news of mass rapes being perpetrated by the Russians, and the frightened women of Luckenwalde were pleading for English or Yanks to sleep with them in exchange for protection. Four French tried it – they were shot dead within the day. The Russians were doling out unmercifully the same treatment as their own womenfolk had experienced back in Russia from the German troops.

An American war correspondent came into camp during this period, much to our surprise and delight, to inform us that the powers that be appreciated our position and lorries would be arriving to evacuate us. Precisely the news we wished to hear.

As usual, no lorries arrived and as the days went by the position in camp became impossible. The only vehicles we saw were Russian, endlessly moving westwards throughout both day and night. The tremendous Red steamroller on the move.

We were frustrated and desperate to get out of camp, whilst the ravished German women were equally desperate to get into the camp, mingling with hordes of people from every part of the globe, anxiously seeking any kind of refuge available – anywhere away from the Russian onslaught.

On Friday, May 4th, Dick, myself and four colleagues decided the time had come to leave under our own steam and accordingly we formulated a simple plan. Whilst we were very heavily guarded by the Russians they were in fact noticeably lax, and the guards would often congregate together for long chats, leaving stretches of the outer wire unmanned. We would wait during the night for such a situation then nip through a hole which one of our group had noticed existed, run across the nearby field where the anti-tank gun still stood, along with the bodies, and so into a small copse. From there we would set off across country towards Magdeburg and the Americans.

No sooner had we laid our plans than great cheers rent the air from our section of the huge camp. Two American lorries had driven straight into our compound and had become engulfed with elated cheering youngsters. What a moment! At long last the Yanks had arrived. It took quite a while for things to settle down enough to allow the drivers and their mates time to explain the situation.

The news was brilliant.

Apparently they were the forerunners of a convoy which would be coming the following day in order to evacuate all American and British personnel. We would be taken across the Elbe and flown home to England, as simple as that.

They also, incidentally, informed us that they believed Hitler was dead. In fact he was. He died on April 30. Peculiarly, when this fantastically marvellous news had seeped through our ranks the mood of the compound significantly changed.

A strange quietness developed as each individual busied himself with his own private personal thoughts. How would they find their parents, their near relations, their friends. But most of all the long-standing P.o.W. married men wondered about their wives. Conversations in the past, by the younger end particularly, invariably ended with discussions on sex and about the great times they had had back in England with both the married and the unmarried women, without giving a thought to the unfortunates who had been in Germany for years. One sensed that these chaps, though delighted beyond words to be going home, were doing so with considerable apprehension. However, for such as Dick and me pure excitement kept us talking and scratching till the wee small hours eventually caught up with us.

Up early on the Saturday, washed, breakfasted and waiting, we soon organised ourselves into groups of fifty, Dick and myself finding ourselves in the second party to leave. Couldn't be better. By 12.30 nothing had been seen or heard of the convoy. At 2 o'clock Pete Thompson posted up a notice reading:

"Convoy on its way."

Cheers, cheers and more cheers reverberated through the whole camp. Eventually, after what seemed a week, 4 lorries and 6 jeeps arrived loaded with food!

We did not need food, we had more than enough. The officer in charge of the fleet of vehicles announced that the evacuation lorries would come tomorrow. we would be taken to Hildesheim and flown home from there. He seemed distinctly surprised when we all turned our backs on him and shuffled dispiritedly away, mumbling about broken promises. No-one seemed to understand just how anxious we were to see the end of the barbed wire.

Sunday: The notice board read: "Convoy definitely left Elbe Bridgehead at 6.0 a.m. en route to Luckenwalde."

The inmates were all but frantic, all eyes looking in the direction from whence the previous lorries had come. 12.30 p.m. No news. The suspense was unbearable. When will the damn convoy arrive? Amid sighs of relief some twenty-five lorries, their large white stars gleaming like jewels in a crown, rolled up accompanied by a jeep. The captain in charge wasted no time.

"We are taking the Americans out with this first convoy," he announced through a hailer, "but before I hear the moans from you British I must tell you that sixty-four vehicles are close behind and they will come in immediately we leave, O.K.?"

"O.K." we shouted, delighted by his direct approach.

Within the hour the promised trucks were lined up outside the camp gates.

Then it happened.

It began with three unexpected rifle shots coming from outside the camp and ended, inexplicably, with the reluctant, depressed Americans, who we thought by now would be well on their way, trudging back into camp, mouthing oaths which if written would surely never be published. Everybody was asking the same question, "What the hell's going on now?" without receiving an answer. It transpired that the Russian Commandant had stopped all evacuation on two counts.

Firstly, he had not received any movement orders and, secondly, the Russians themselves would deal with the evacuation and we would be returned to England via Russia. Panic broke out as the news spread and the lads would have cheerfully strangled every Russian in sight. Meetings took place with the Americans, our leaders and the Russians, but the latter were adamant.

No evacuation. We were completely deflated and disillusioned. What a let down at the very last minute.

"That's it. Tonight we go Dick if we've to wait all bloody night for the opportunity," I said angrily.

"You're on, I'll tell the others," he readily agreed.

"Bugger them, we'll make our own way."

Gentle rain was falling as the six of us gathered in the darkness of the early hours by the doorway of the latrine block, a vantage position near the hole in the wire, from where could be seen a considerable length of the boundary fence by merely peering round the corner of the building. The searchlight sweeping laconically across the camp was in fact an advantage, for it allowed us to see exactly where and what the guards were doing, and as they patrolled we waited and waited and waited. It was a foregone conclusion that eventually they would gather together for a cigarette and a natter – but where and when? They could not have judged it better when finally they got together well away from the break in the wire in which we were interested.

Outwardly clean but lice-ridden, all attempts at washing the pests from our clothes having failed miserably, it took little skill, but a certain amount of nerve, for us one by one to make the silent dash, scramble through the hole and cautiously, but quickly, head for the haven the few trees presented.

The fear of a sudden crack of a rifle was very real, as bent double and moving as fast as this position would allow we crossed the small field. We all made it without incident.

We were free!

Chapter Twenty-One

Once out of camp there was no way we could possibly be missed. The Russians never troubled to take a count, and so we set off in good heart, delighted to be at least making some progress towards home, across the fields for a while in the rough direction of Magdeburg some fifty or sixty miles away. Unfortunately when we eventually found a road, which incidentally led to Juteburg, it was packed solid with refugees, even though it was still dark, and we immediately discovered what ought to have been obvious to us from the outset – we were now just another six people ambling forlornly along amongst the thousands that were on the move westwards.

On reaching Juteburg we decided not to stand on ceremony and headed for the first house that appealed to us, brushing ignorantly through the moving human masses. Nor did we trouble to knock. Somehow we had to make it clear to everyone we came across that we were making the decisions and that we were not just another group of foreign workers. We realised it was pig-headed, but if we were to get back to England quickly this was the way to do it. Straight into the house we barged to find an already looted, ransacked, shambles occupied by two Frenchmen, two Frenchwomen, one Serb and the family of the house, consisting of mother and two children – all with no food and scared stiff at our entry.

It was obviously as chaotic outside camp as it had been inside. We each chose where we would sleep without any consultation whatever with the occupants, and placed our coats and little cases in that particular spot, making it obvious that's where we were sleeping by pointing and telling them to leave well alone.

They could not understand English but they got the message. Two of our members then went foraging for food, returning with bread and eggs and bacon, stolen from goodness knows where. There was enough for the lot of us so we all ate – lucky for them.

We were quite taken aback the following day, having walked for three hours on a beautiful Spring morning which had taken us through gorgeous avenues of apple blossom in which birds had twittered and sung merrily, both in blatant contrast to the pitiable state of the country, when we called at an outlying farm. As we entered, the farmer immediately recognised the language, vigorously shook our hands in turn and, beaming all over his face, called his wife to meet us.

The reception was precisely what we had not expected and when he plied us with milk and bread we just couldn't believe it. Unbeknown to us the war in Europe had officially ended the previous day and, staggeringly, overnight we had become the Germans' friends. It was as if all that had happened over the past five years had suddenly been forgotten and it was the Russians who were the naughty boys – not us, nor them. It was just too much to swallow and in an attempt to draw him out one of our party asked him was he a Nazi. Looking disgusted he said vehemently, "Nicht Nat, Gut Deutsch."

We soon discovered that they were all good Germans, not Nazis, and it became a standing joke with us, prompting Dick to remark.

"Four hundred and twenty-one million, three thousand and forty-two Nazis in Germany, all giving the Heil Hitler salute up to yesterday and here we are near Berlin and we can't find a bloody one of them. They're now all good Germans. Marvellous."

The farmer had told us to head for Elster on the banks of the Elbe as he thought the Americans were across the river at that point. He was wrong. The Russians were firmly in control and after great communication difficulties, they insisted we made for Wittenberg and into the Lager from where we would be evacuated. As Dick's foot was again beginning to swell he permanently borrowed a Slav's cycle and we eventually found ourselves in a small country cottage.

Five Dutch Jews from a concentration camp had made it their resting place and quite frankly we decided it would be their last resting place. They were so pitifully thin and haggard that they found great difficulty in even crossing the room. All of them appeared to be impregnated with some horrible substance which gave off an evil, obnoxious smell. It was impossible to ascertain their ages for they were no more than living skeletons, desperately in need of help, but therein lay the snag, everybody we saw desperately required help, apart from the troops.

Intending to steal food, the six of us visited a few of the farms in the area but found incredibly, once again, stealing unnecessary. Whilst the farmers themselves had only a limited amount of food, once they realised we were British they were only too willing to share what they had. Suddenly we had become the local heroes and such a turnabout in attitudes we found quite inexplicable.

Whatever the reason, it solved any food problems we might have had and saved us from using any bullying tactics, and on this occasion we collected enough food not only to provide a meal for ourselves but to enable us to leave a few days' supply with the Dutchmen. I hope they made it but I very much doubted it.

We were taking quite a roundabout route to Wittenberg, having left the more major road on our fruitless visit to Elster, and in fact Wittenberg itself did not lie in a direct line to Magdeburg. Luckenwalde, Wittenberg and Magdeburg actually formed an inverted triangle with Wittenberg forming the point at the bottom. All of this greatly extended our journey, but it also made it far more pleasant, as the lesser used country lanes were virtually free of the pathetic streams of refugees – a depressing sight to any eyes.

Our trek was voluntarily held up for a couple of hours when quite by chance grounded aircraft came into view. The aerodrome was completely deserted of personnel but dozens of Luftwaffe aircraft stood in their dispersal points.

Could we but have transferred those planes to England, then and there, we would have had a ready-made museum. We found it quite fascinating climbing in and out of M.E.109's, 110's, H.E.111's, J.U.88's, F.W.190's and the Dorniers, comparing them with our own aircraft and wondering just what mischief they had been up to. I suppose at the time the most remarkable thing to us was how very similar to our own they really were, though why we should expect them to be different I don't quite know. It was here that we first saw the deadly upward-firing 30mm cannon mounted in the M.E.110 night fighters – an alarming sight to all of us. If we had but known many lives could have been saved by having the bomb-aimer permanently looking underneath our Lancs.

A large delightfully attractive house, idyllically situated on the banks of a narrow, but fast-flowing river, with no other houses in sight, drew us like a magnet as the perfect spot to lunch – even if we ourselves had no food.

It was as beautiful inside as it was out and appeared unoccupied. A huge chandelier decorated the thick-carpeted hallway and a wide highly polished stairway curled its elegant way to the bedrooms. The large, tastefully furnished and decorated lounge held two glass showcases full of a variety of solid silver trophies of every shape and size, but the most noticeable object was the huge framed portrait of an S.S. officer, dressed in full regalia, which covered most of the wall space over the old, but attractive fireplace.

"Hey, do you know there's two women upstairs?" one of the lads who had been investigating the rest of the house queried.

"Have they got anything to eat?" I asked.

"I haven't a clue. They're so frightened I doubt if they can speak. They're just sat there trembling."

We were busily engaged examining the silver and conjuring up all kinds of evil thoughts such as, "I wonder how much this would bring in England," when with a crash and a thud in walked three rifle-carrying Mongolians.

It wasn't the first time we had seen these small, slit-eyed members of the Red Army and we had so far managed to give them a wide berth. With long moustaches sometimes drooping below the chin-line, wearing peculiar pointed hats with the ear muff section turned up they were beyond doubt the most sinister-looking troops one could wish to meet – and we had yet to see one smile.

They just glared at us questioningly. We were already aware that these types never wasted time. They shot first and asked questions afterwards.

It was, fortunately, the smallest of our party who made the first move. Apparently, we later learned, they were particularly allergic to large men.

"Hello, hello," he said, walking towards them, hand outstretched and his face wreathed in a false smile. Receiving no response from the expressionless faces his proffered hand fell limply by his side.

"We're English, British flyers," he stumbled.

I held my arms out in imitation of an aircraft and waggled them about from side to side, saying,

"Buzz, buzz buzz."

"English," Dick said and broke into the first two lines of "God Save the King."

"British flyers," repeated one of our party slowly and deliberately, and wetting his finger tried hard to trace a Union Jack on the wall.

Eventually, after we had tried everything we could think of in our attempts to explain who we were they held a short mumbled conversation, turned away and climbed the stairs, the noise of their heavy boots resounding hollowly in the large hallway.

"Let's get out of here quick," one of the lads suggested.

"No, if we do it will look suspicious, let's brazen it out," another said.

"They might come looking for us."

After a short discussion we reluctantly decided to stay put. With great difficulty we tried hard to close our ears and ignore the periodical screams which rent the air from upstairs, our imagination running riot. We fumbled with the silver uninterestedly and rummaged unseeingly through the drawers till the clump of boots coming downstairs and the slamming of the door denoted their exit.

"Thank God for that," exclaimed Dick, expressing the relief of all of us.

We allowed five minutes to elapse before venturing upstairs, then wished we hadn't.

Lying on the bed naked, eyes open, one woman was dead. The other, dress torn and hair dishevelled, was curled up in a corner as if trying to hide in the brickwork. She was sobbing pitiably, her shoulders moving up and down with each sob, and her unseen face bowed towards the wall.

"Oh no, what do we do now?" asked one helplessly.

"What the hell can we do," I replied angrily, emphasising the word can. As one we turned to the door without further conversation and walked downstairs and straight through the front door, relieved to breathe in the sweet fresh air, all thoughts of food and silverware completely gone.

It took us one more day to reach Wittenberg on Friday May 11th – but this time we did it the easy way. A country gentleman, dressed in his Sunday best and seated in a small one-man buggy pulled by a horse, was sedately making his way up a long curving drive, flanked on each side by acres of grassland, seemingly oblivious of the continuous stream of unfortunates passing by his gate. Coming to the conclusion that he was probably the local Burgomeister we decided to investigate. At the top of the drive nestled a delightfully secluded house with the resting horse tethered outside.

The gentleman in question hesitantly came out to meet us.

"You a Nazi?" we enquired menacingly.

"Nicht Not . . ." his hands held up in front of him. As he was answering the horse was being unhitched from the buggy.

"Yeah, yeah, we know, good German."

"Yah, yah," he said, smiling sheepishly.

A four-wheeled cart, seats either side, but with wide shafts obviously intended for two horses, came into view, pulled by three of our group.

"Then you won't mind lending us your horse and cart, will you?" Speechless, and afraid to do a thing, he just stood and gaped as we struggled and improvised by means of a rope to hitch the horse between the wide shafts. The makeshift transport provided us with a bumpy, drunken passage, the shafts constantly slapping the horse's side as we travelled, but at least we were seated. Further, we had painted, whilst at the Burgomeister's, two large, but rough, Union Jacks which we had fastened on either side of the cart in an attempt to differentiate us from the masses. This move in fact proved pointless, for not one Russian recognised our national flag.

During the ride we picked up an American Ranger, dressed in full uniform and wearing leather leggings similar to my own, which turned out to be our best move since leaving Luckenwalde. A few hours later we rolled into the square of quite a large ex-Wehrmacht camp, situated on the outskirts of Wittenberg, in fine style and condition. Not so the horse, its sides were red raw. Immediately we unfastened the ropes and freed it from the shafts the beast reared up on its hind legs, thrashed its front legs wildly in the air, gave a long protesting neigh and whinnied (which clearly said "bugger you lot") and as soon as the horse's feet touched the ground it shot off like a bat out of hell, scattering foreign workers left, right and centre. Our last sighting was a cloud of dust disappearing through the camp gates. The whole scene was reminiscent of a Disney cartoon where the legs of the caricature are spinning whilst in mid-air and as soon as they meet the ground they hurtle away in the distance, at no less than 250 m.p.h.

As usual, the square and long wooden huts were packed to suffocation with humanity. There was no escaping them. It was as if the whole world was on the move.

"We can't stay amongst this lot," Dick was saying to all within earshot.

"There's no chance of us being evacuated from here."

"Let's see if we can find the Ruskies," I suggested.

"You never know."

"Fat lot of good that will do," replied one of the group.

"If our success so far with the Russians is anything to go by we'll be sleeping in the middle of this courtyard."

Ray, the American, butted in,

"I'll chance my arm with them. At least I'm in uniform, you guys stay here till I come back."

"Well, I suppose it's true lads. He carries more authority than we do."

"We could be anybody," I said when he had gone. "Let's give him a chance."

A good half hour went by and we were beginning to wonder what was happening when from out of the crowd Ray emerged, beaming openly.

"Hey fellas, this way, follow me."

To our utter amazement he led us across the square and into a long low building, along an empty, spotlessly clean, corridor and flung open a door.

"Two of us in here and five in that room across the corridor. They're just making us something to eat."

"You what?" we asked incredulously.

"The Russians are making us something to eat," he smiled mischievously. I went into the room for two with Ray, and what a room. The building had previously been used as a hospital and this was a private little dormitory containing two sprung-beds, complete with clean linen and blankets, a table and four chairs, two of them upholstered easy chairs, and the window looking out on the courtyard had fold-back shutters and a small office type opening window.

"Come on Ray," I chuckled, "how on earth did you arrange this, we've never managed to get through to them yet?"

"I omitted to mention Russ," he answered, "Mom and Pop were Polish. I speak it fluently and the Russians understand me."

"Three cheers for your Mom and Pop then, that's all I've got to say. This is terrific."

For the next four days we lived a life of luxury. Our food was brought to us regularly by a young, friendly, round-faced Russian girl and immediately we had finished the dirty dishes were removed. We were visited by high-ranking officers and offered trips out in their jeep-type vehicles which we gladly accepted. We requested a radio, typewriter and other odds and ends and got them. Nothing was too much trouble, but our first thought – that of getting home – appeared to be the Russians' last thought. Our every request to be allowed to cross the River Elbe was politely turned down with a brief "Nyet."

Dick and I spent one afternoon in a Russian armoured car visiting a town named Zerbst I believe, a place I have never heard mentioned before nor since, but Zerbst will forever be to me the perfect example of the idiocy and futility of war.

I know not how it happened, but the town had been utterly razed to the ground – not even a gable end stood upright and one could only view it from the main road which sloped gently downwards and then bypassed the place. Walking its streets was an impossibility, and the sickly stench of dead bodies so permeated the whole area that it was necessary to cover one's nose and mouth. Not a single thing moved, we never even saw a cat or dog. Zerbst was a ghost town and not only Dick and myself, but I am convinced our driver as well, were only too glad to leave this unblessed cemetery. Why we even visited the spot baffles me unless in some obscure way it was an attempt to show us what had been achieved by shell and bomb.

It was late in the afternoon on the third day at Wittenberg that, much to our astonishment, a queue of inmates began to form in the courtyard, the head of which began at our little opening window.

On making enquiries it was discovered that rumour in camp had it that we seven were British and American liaison officers, here for the sole purpose of arranging the evacuation of all the foreign workers back to their homeland. With us having been so friendly with the Russians and having received V.I.P. treatment it was not difficult to see how the false rumour had spread.

We, for our part, were more than a little fed up at our own lack of progress and, youth being what it is, there was only one thing for it – play along. A rubber stamp, sheets of paper, scissors and pens were all willingly supplied by the conquerors who, I believe, realised what we were up to, and within an hour, by which time the queue had grown alarmingly and stretched all around the courtyard, our office was ready for business.

An excited mumbling and jostling by the front members of the queue greeted the opening of the window.

Ray was seated directly in front of the window and conducted his brief interviews in Polish, regardless of their nationality. One of our group was typing madly whilst two others busied themselves with scissors cutting up small, official-looking permits. I rubber stamped them and Dick scrawled a signature in flamboyant style across the lot. Delighted, the recipients left the office by their hundreds waving their bits of useless paper for all to see.

They read in English:—

"Shoot this bugger, he's a Nazi."

It was fortuitous, and totally unexpected, when early the following morning the Russians sent round a lorry before breakfast to transport us to Magdeburg, and I still wonder if they knew something we didn't. Armed with a letter giving us permission to cross the Elbe, which had been provided by a major of the Red Army, no less, we evisaged no problems in at long last putting East Germany behind us. We were wrong!

Billeted on the very banks of the river which to us had now become the river of freedom, in a severely bombed three-storeyed house, we found ourselves overlooking the Roosevelt Stalin Bridge which had been erected alongside the huge concrete bridge normally used, but now its ruined centre sections dangled precariously in the swirling waters. But we found ourselves in the same old situation – just a small group amongst thousands of people milling about with the one single-minded aim, to cross the river.

The front-line troops in this area were all Mongolians, apart from rather more than a smattering of Russian Army women, all armed with short-barrelled, round-magazined automatics. One minute's walk – in which the smell of corpses and the constant crack of rifles were the main feature – brought us face to face with the numerous guards on the bridge itself and, having previously on our excursions from Wittenberg learned something of how to handle the Mongols, we employed the same tactics.

All smiles, Ray opened up with his Polish whilst the rest of us slapped the troops on their backs in the friendliest of manners and soon, as had been the case only a few days earlier, had them taking shots at the pots on the telegraph poles – a pastime they thoroughly enjoyed and one which appeared to be condoned by their officers. When we considered the time right, there was no use pushing it in our anxiety to walk across the bridge, we produced the vital letter – and not a soul on that bridge could read it. Not only could they not read the letter, they could not understand Ray's Polish either and finally, having no alternative, we left the bridge in search of Red officers. We ought never to have troubled ourselves, for we found no-one in the length and breadth of Magdeburg who could read the letter.

"Maybe it's the same kind of note we dished out at Wittenberg," Dick suggested despondently.

"Yeah and maybe they're all illiterate," suggested another of the group.

"No matter what we do we're baulked every time we try to cross the Elbe." Cheesed.off and sick to the back teeth we made our way back to our billet where there was barely room for us to lie down, the place was so crowded.

Sat on the grass by the river's edge the next morning Dick and I pondered our position.

"Just how do we get across this bloody river?" Dick said, more as a statement than a question.

"These Russians take some weighing up – one day they're all friendly and helpful and the next they don't want to know. What's wrong with us just walking over that bridge. Blast, we can see the Americans at the other side." I looked at him quizzically without answering.

"You're thinking the same as me aren't you?" he said, in answer to my silence.

"Yes, I am."

"Well come on then, let's try it."

We walked more cheerfully some way down the bank, stripped down to our vest and underpants and, leaving our clothes and cases on the grass, waded into the cold water.

Being a fair swimmer I was confident of my ability to make it with ease but before we were anywhere near the middle the strong current was carrying us downstream alarmingly. Out of the corner of my eye I could see Dick was struggling with something and at one stage he disappeared under the water. The something was a puffed up body which bobbed horribly downstream in front of me.

The sucking and pulling current near the middle was more than we had bargained for and, fast getting into difficulties, we turned around. More than relieved to get back into calmer water we waded out, dejectedly, way downstream, gasping, and facing an unpleasant mile or so walk, scantily dressed and freezing cold, in order to retrieve our clothes and cases.

"Where have you devils been? You look like drowned rats?" queried an army chap who had been in the billet for two weeks, on our return.

"Well we didn't fancy waiting till the Ruskies made up their minds what to do with us so we tried swimming across," I replied shivering. He looked staggered.

"You silly buggers. Don't you know they're shooting anybody who tries to cross. What do you think all the shooting is? They have guards posted all along the banks."

"Now you tell us," Dick said.

"Anyway we never saw a soul. Not alive that is."

"If you look out of the window, every now and again, you'll see another body floating past," he retorted.

It was so. Over that next six days we quite decided that Magdeburg in 1945 was not the best of places to be. Looting, raping and shooting were rife with, it seemed, nobody attempting to control the situation. One rarely saw a local woman on the streets and the sight of another body strewn across the pavement was commonplace. We ourselves felt insecure and soon realised we were walking on thin ice whenever the Mongols were about, and though the war was over I always considered my few days there to be the most dangerous I have ever known. Life was so cheap it was impossible to comprehend, and incredibly the bodies were just left where they had fallen. I came to the conclusion that the aftermath of war was far more difficult to cope with than war itself.

From our personal point of view Sunday, May 20th, ended the nonsense. I know not who organised or arranged it, nor did I care, but the sound of a Yank's voice below our window shouting,

"Hey fellas do yah not wanna go home?" was enough to send me into near-hysterics, for he was standing by an empty American Dodge lorry. I don't remember my feet touching the stairs, but I remember shouting at the top of my voice,

"Come on Dick they're here!"

The American sergeant just asked,

"Nationality?"

"British."

"Get in."

It was as simple as that, no red tape, nothing. The wagon was full in no time and whilst many unlucky ones argued their case for being given priority the driver let in the clutch and off we sped, swinging onto the bridge and across it before we had time to collect our thoughts.

190

Chapter Twenty-Two

At long last freedom was ours and a more jubilant, joking, singing group of lads never rode along that road to Hildesheim. The feeling was one of tremendous relief and tingling excitement. It was as well we did not know that at that time Gib and the other ex-P.o.W. Canadians were on the high seas homeward bound – so much time had we lost by our, arguably foolhardy, decision to make it on our own. I'm glad we didn't know. I would not have wanted the moment of release marring.

What a joy it was to be greeted by friendly Americans and to hear nothing but English spoken – the language barrier had been our biggest single handicap throughout. And to shower under incessant hot water using soap that actually produced a lather, whilst our lice-ridden clothes were burning outside, was a delight beyond description. A thorough spraying with D.D.T. powder, an issue of new American uniforms and a delicious meal – even if the cooks still tried, without success, to serve the sweet on the same plate as my main meal – rounded off a day to remember.

Our best night's sleep since God knows when got off to a great start with the words, uttered by an officer,

"We'll fly you guys to Brussels tomorrow."

That was better than any lullaby to our receptive minds.

By lunchtime the following day we were circling Brussels aerodrome in a Dakota, viewing a scene unparalleled before or since. Literally hundreds of the old faithfuls – Lancasters – filled every available space. Some still, some taxiing, some taking off, some landing, but all engaged in a mass exodus of happy, thrilled and overjoyed ex-P.o.W.'s.

A repeat performance of hot shower, sprayed from head to foot with D.D.T. powder, new clothes – R.A.F. uniform this time – and a meal brought us to late afternoon when we were allowed to wander around Brussels at will. A Red Cross shop opened at the edge of the 'drome specifically for P.o.W.'s was stocked from floor to ceiling with cartons of cigarettes, for which there was no charge, and the assistants' sole job was to stuff our cases or whatever, with as many as they would hold.

A small souvenir shop next door did a roaring trade selling cut-price bric-a-brac and with the few Belgian Francs with which we had been issued I purchased a miniature pair of Dutch Clogs on which were painted R.A.F. wings and the slogan "Vive la R.A.F."

Without any preliminaries whatever, the following morning 26 of us boarded one of the Lancs which stood in all their majesty nose to tail all round the perimeter track, but not before I had contacted the ever so young-looking mid-upper gunner to request I be allowed to fly home in the turret, a request with which he obligingly agreed. Memories, oh so many memories, came flooding back as I nimbly climbed into the familiar upturned fish bowl. Everything was exactly the same, the smell, the oil, the sun glistening on the perspex canopy. Fantastic. This wasn't the silly barbed wire stuff and nonsense, this was something that really mattered, something I knew I could never possibly forget if I lived to be a hundred.

As Brussels fell away below us we flew directly over a burnt-out Lanc which tragically only a few days earlier had crashed, killing all 26 ex-P.o.W.'s and crew. Years spent behind barbed wire and then to be killed on the very last lap home must have been a heart-breaking experience for their loved ones, anxiously awaiting their home-coming.

Second sense told me what I would see when I rotated the turret forward and sure enough I was correct – Dick, beaming from ear to ear, had his head stuck up in the astro-dome and I waggled the guns at him in exhilaration. So ended our last Lancaster flight, putting down at Cosford, near Wolverhampton, before lunch.

The welcome we boys received (no not boys any longer for surely now we were men) was out of this world. The Lanc halted in front of a huge hangar across the front of which mammoth letters read, "Welcome Home."

Funnelled through small gaps, W.A.A.F.'s armed with D.D.T. sprays cheerfully gave us one in the hair, one up each trouser leg, one down our shirt front, and with a laugh, one for good luck, down our trousers, before moving into the hangar. The whole building was filled with cloth-covered tables and chairs. Hundreds of men sat there dining and almost as many women bustled about meeting their every requirement.

"Another cup of tea love?"

"Have another cake?"

It was all just too much and everywhere one looked men could be seen openly crying or discreetly blowing their noses.

"Before you leave this hangar," the notice read, "please spare a thought for those who have not returned and if you have any information regarding any of the listed names please let us know."

Along the length and breadth of the hangar walls large boards contained neatly painted lists of names and ranks of airmen, hundreds upon hundreds of them. So many it was impossible to read them all. It was a sombre sight. I could not help but think,

"There, but for the grace of God, go I."

In our own leisurely time we strolled through a series of buildings to find the most sophisticated, highly organised manoeuvre operating that it was ever my pleasure to behold. To think that thousands of men per day went through the same routine without any panic or fuss left one gasping, and I dearly wish today's generation could have witnessed the well-oiled machinery at work. Indeed it was proof that when Britain sets its mind to do something well it is unsurpassable.

Bearing in mind that it was approximately two o'clock in the afternoon, we first had a choice of five differently worded telegrams we could send. All one had to do was tick the required wording and provide name and address to which it had to be sent. My parents received that telegram the same day. It read:–

"Fit and well, be home tomorrow. Russ."

Next, we were fitted with uniforms, any necessary alterations being made by seamstresses, and fully kitted out exactly as when we first joined up. The whole lot, except the tunic, went into a kit-bag which was left in a room allotted for that purpose. The tunic was taken to the next department in the chain, where a label was pinned to it giving exact details of what was required to be stitched thereon. Mine for instance needed Sergeant's stripes plus crown (for due to aircrew's automatic promotion I was now a Flight Sergeant), and an Air Gunner's brevet.

I was issued with a six weeks' leave pass and ration cards, duly stamped and authorised. I was paid £50 from my accumulated pay and given a travel warrant to Blackburn, the earliest train time and any necessary changes to be made to reach my destination being provided without enquiry. We returned to collect kit and completed tunic, thence to a shower and to dispense with the clothing we wore. By five o'clock I was clean (in fact I was shining after so many showers and changes of clothes) correctly dressed in full uniform and sat on my made-up bed complete with brilliantly white sheets and of all things, neatly folded coloured pyjamas, in a beautifully clean and brightly lit billet. The whole procedure had been pleasantly satisfying and incredibly easy.

Transport awaited us the next morning at any time we desired to leave camp (and the majority of us chose a ridiculously unearthly hour) in order to take us to the nearest railway station, where special trains had been laid on. The only thing which marred our almost immediate departure was a goodly number of unfortunate, pitiable mothers, enquiring after their lost sons, though it was barely daylight. They obviously spent every day at the station patrolling the platforms making the same enquiry from the returning ex-P.o.W.'s. It would have given me great pleasure to have been able to give just one mother the news she was waiting to hear, but alas, I could not.

By an incredible 7.45 a.m. on May 23, 1945, just three days after our crossing of the Elbe, my train hissed and screeched to a halt at Blackburn. Overjoyed and excited and feeling that I wanted to shout the good news to everyone, I silently joined the queue on Blackburn Boulevard waiting for the 8 o'clock bus which would take me home – sweet home. Just one more to board the Ribble bus and it was my turn. The conductor barred the way.

"Sorry full up."

"Just a minute," I heard someone on the bus call, "he's just come back from Germany." I have no idea who it was but it did the trick.

"Come on lad, ged on," the conductor said smiling.

He never knew how good it was to hear his strong Lancashire accent – horrible to most people, but to me that morning, it was music.

I turned into the cul-de-sac carrying my kit-bag and, facing me, stretched from one bedroom window right across the circle to the adjacent bedroom window of the semis, huge letters read,

"Welcome home Russell."

Why I did not go round the house and enter the kitchen as usual I don't know, but I knocked on the front door. My hard-bitten Dad, his hair surrounding his bald pate now driven white, opened it, gulped and turned his back on me, walking away as he did so. I never saw those tears which I knew were streaming down his face.

There were still six months to go to my 21st birthday.

Report in the *Northern Daily Telegraph*, Blackburn, in May 1944.

A Sequel:

Just a Muddy Track

I returned to Antwerp, Belgium, at the beginning of July 2003 with my wife Bette, some fifty-nine years after watching my Lancaster bomber Y LM 513 crash in an almighty explosion. On that occasion I had been floating down on a pitch-black night at the end of my unseen parachute, hoping fervently that none of our crew was still in the plane.

From 2001, three Belgian researchers, Luc Cox, Francis Huijbrechts and Wim Govaerts, had been trying to persuade us to go over for the purpose of retracing my steps in the underground with the Belgian resistance. Finally we made the visit and found that their very thorough and meticulous investigations had uncovered the whole story, not only pinpointing where we five surviving crew members had fallen to earth but also tracing our steps before capture by the Germans.

On our first morning in Antwerp we received a phone call from a Mrs Arlette Van Dun, expressing her wish to meet me. At our meeting that evening, Arlette produced an old diary of her father's of which she had been totally unaware until his death. He had helped nine aircrew evade capture and received a citation after the war from the R.A.F. My name and address appeared on the fourth page. He had apparently been one of our night guides on a rather hairy cycle ride that Dick Reeves, our wireless operator, and I had undertaken. The one, in fact, on which I had catapulted straight over the handlebars of my bike, crashing into the gateway of an SS-inhabited house because I had completely forgotten that on these cycles one had to back-peddle to apply the brakes and I had tried to free-wheel past the house for the sake of silence.

Our next visit was to the outskirts of Hoogstraten, approximately thirty-four kilometres from Antwerp, to meet Theresia Snoeys who had hidden our Canadian navigator, David Weepers, for a few weeks at great peril to herself. (Death was the punishment for helping allied flyers.) The 83-year-old's welcome, as in the case of all the people we met, was ecstatic, and out came letters and photographs relevant to the time. What we had not expected was the presence of a journalist and photographer, resulting in a large photograph and write-up the following day in the *Gazet Van Antwerpen* newspaper.

Mrs Snoeys had received a citation from the Canadian Government which read:

> On behalf of the Canadian Government and indeed, all Canadians, I wish to express our profound gratitude to you for your act of bravery in assisting David James Weepers, a Flying Officer, following the crash of his Lancaster in Belgium in 1944.
>
> The men and women who served our country during the war are greatly admired as are individuals such as yourself who risked your own safety to help Mr Weepers when he needed it most.
>
> For your contribution to peace and freedom, we offer our heartfelt thanks.
>
> Yours sincerely and respectfully,
> George Baker, P.C., M.P.

Mrs Snoeys was very proud of that letter from Canada but even more proud of the photograph of David that she had kept in pride of place since war's end. She would not let us go without presenting us with two bottles of port.

At our next stop I was greeted by farmer Christ Vermeiren and his wife. I knew that we had arrived at the crash site of our Lancaster, for a television crew was setting up its camera. We walked along a muddy track by the side of their farm to be told that a full wing had landed at the back of the house and a petrol tank from the plane had fallen nearby exploding violently. The blast of the explosion blew off the whole side of the roof and left the other side intact apart from a running crack down the side of the wall, still unrepaired to this day. The fuselage came to rest at the end of the track in a cornfield about one hundred yards from the farm.

As we walked towards the site the television camera was in front filming our every move, while Christ explained that the bodies of Max Dowden and Frank Moody were thrown clear with Frank still alive – just. The Germans, having a garrison nearby, had soon arrived on the scene and refused the local priest permission to read the last rites over them. They shot Frank in a mercy killing, he being impossible to save. On asking Luc how Christ could be so sure of these events he, to my absolute amazement, informed me that Christ was one of the children asleep in the farm at the time of the crash.

I managed to hold back the tears, but only just, as I placed two small wooden crosses at the spot where Luc and Francis had dug up bullets and parts of our aircraft. The inevitable interview followed, a video of which we were presented with later in the week.

Apparently there had been so many aircraft crashes in the vicinity (over two hundred planes crashed in the Hoogstraten area during World War Two) that the children at the farm had slept in the cellar and the parents downstairs. This saved the lives of the family.

Christ picked two large punnets of strawberries from a nearby patch and gave them to Bette and me.

We learned also from Luc and Francis that Gilbert McElroy, our rear gunner, had landed close to the crash site and had sensibly headed for the nearby church. Unfortunately the Germans captured him before he reached it. Had he made it he would probably have remained free for some time for the local priest was known to have underground connections and would have hidden him. As it was, he was put into the back of a lorry with Max's and Frank's bodies.

The beautiful tall church tower and town hall of Hoogstraten were our next amazing port of call. We were to have an audience with the mayor, Arnold Van Aperen. Unlike people in Britain, generally the Belgians remember all too well the happenings of the war and want these incidents never to be forgotten. The walls of the town hall, severely marked by bullets and shells, serve as a permanent reminder. The Germans had used the church tower as an observation post for their artillery. They blew the whole thing up on leaving and it crashed on to the town hall, destroying the upper half of it. All of the buildings were restored to their former glory after the war.

I was given pride of place in the mayor's parlour, sitting opposite the mayor at a huge highly polished ornate table, with cameras clicking again as drinks were poured. With Bette to my right, we discussed my experiences and the war in general, with Francis acting as interpreter. The mayor smilingly thanked me and all allied forces for the part we played in their liberation as I stressed the wonderful help we had received from the Belgian people. After half an hour and more drinks, the mayor's deputy produced a large leather-bound visitors' book, a page of which had been specially prepared to commemorate our visit to Hoogstraten, with Bette's name and mine and details of our visit printed at the top. I wrote a lengthy friendly thank you to the people of the area in my best calligraphy hand-writing and everyone present signed the page.

Arnold Van Aperen, who had been mayor for thirty-two years, promised to forward me a copy. He presented Bette with a framed pen drawing of the town hall and me with a history of the area as we bade our farewells.

The most remarkable of the researchers' discoveries unfolded when we drew up at an isolated series of farm buildings and Luc asked me if I recognised the place. We were beside an archway with closed doors and could not see beyond them. After considerable thought I said, "If the archway doors lead to an open courtyard and on the right-hand-side are stables with a hayloft and two small wooden doors, yes." And sure enough, to my utter amazement I found myself standing in what had been an old farmhouse yard with the hayloft to the right: the very place where I had slept fifty-nine years ago, the night after I had been shot down. The farmer had picked me up, still in uniform and wearing flying boots, and had signalled me to hide under the logs of his horse-drawn cart. I had stayed at the farm for twelve hours before moving on. How Luc and Francis ever found the place, God only knows, but they had certainly done their homework.

The buildings and surrounding land are now owned by Mr and Mrs Martin (Ties) Ridder, very wealthy Dutch people who immediately made us feel at home and allowed us the freedom of this now totally renovated luxurious property. Everyone present was surprised when, on entering the lounge, I asked whether there had been a doorway in the far corner, for furniture now stood there. "Yes," came the reply. "We bricked it up." We were in what had been the old kitchen where the farmer's wife had given me a large bowl of milky porridge (my favourite food at the time). But one spoonful had been as far as I got: the aftermath of being shot down had set in.

I climbed into the loft to find it as I remembered it, complete with hay. Quite incredible. We ended this day with our guides taking us to the exact field into which I had parachuted. It was just as I describe it in this book. What I hadn't known was that Arthur Brickenden, our bomb aimer, was kept in hiding for a few days at a nearby farmhouse.

The only disappointment came the following morning in Antwerp when we found 29 Boomgard Straat where Dick Reeves and I had lain hidden for six weeks. It was completely empty and neglected and it had been so for the past eight years according to the landlord of the pub opposite. No trace of Hermine Scheire's family could be found. Here we had been hiding when on 6 June 1944 we heard on the clandestine radio that the allies had landed.

We had no problem, however, in finding the large, gloomy, ancient prison in which Dick and I had literally been thrown by the Germans after they had stuck revolvers in our sides, saying, "Empty your pockets. German Military Intelligence." It looks as menacing now as it did then. I would have loved to have gone inside and tried to find my own cell but with the prison in daily use that was out of the question.

As all military cemeteries, the large one on the outskirts of Antwerp was very well cared for but the number of aircrew graves is a strong reminder of the futility of war. Many hundreds of youngsters with an average age of twenty or twenty-one from all over the Commonwealth are buried in this peaceful setting and many of the youngsters of today could do worse than spend an hour quietly walking around and reading the impossibly long list of bygone boys' names.

Max and Frank, our comrades in the crew, lie buried almost alongside each other and a tear fell not just from me but also from my wife, for Frank Moody had been her boyfriend in wartime. We put a flowering plant on both graves and once again the cameras recorded the poignant moment. Flowers, incidentally, had been placed on the war graves up to 1942 but the Germans did not approve of the practice and had stopped it.

Our next stop was Wit Hofken, a country house, where the present owners allowed me to wander around as I wished, for here Marcel Vermeulen had kept us hidden in what was then an almost empty building. I stood in the bedroom where Dick and I had been rudely awakened on our first morning by the rat-tat-tatting of machine gun fire. We had both rolled under the bed in quick time only to hear the clop-clopping of someone coming up the uncarpeted stairs. It was, however, not the Germans but Emilie Vermeulen telling us to "cum" as breakfast was ready. Feeling shamefaced, we had peeped through the shutters of the bedroom window only to see that we were hiding on the very edge of a German firing range.

Marcel and Emilie helped many evaders and luckily survived the war. We were fortunate in meeting Marcel's son, Robert, who lived nearby, and spent a memorable two hours with him, discussing his father's wartime activities and looking at dozens of old photographs. Robert showed us appreciation letters for Marcel's bravery from both Britain and the US, signed respectively by Mr Churchill and General Eisenhower.

At every house we visited we were plied with food and drink and met with the utmost friendship and cordiality. Robert's home was no exception. We left with photographs, eggs, a bottle of Bière Brut, a large box of chocolate biscuits and an invitation to visit whenever we wished. I sincerely thank all the Belgians for their kindness but frankly I expected no less from these sociable and amiable people.

Now, back home, I feel that I have fulfilled a need that has been nagging me for years, possibly only understood by those who were part of this wartime situation. I shall always remain indebted to Luc, Francis and Wim.

Index of Names

Albert, 94
Alkemade, Nicholas, 43

Baker, George, 198
Berry, Father, 151
Bishop, Flt. Sgt. D.Y., 61
Blackmore, P/O D. M, 65
Brickenden, Arthur ('Brick'), 21*
Brown, Sgt, N. D., 44*
Bulger, Flt. Sgt. J. P., 27, 55

Canham, Sqd Ldr, 65
Caveirne, Paula, 110-11
Churchill, Winston, 202
Clark, F/O N. A.W., 55
Cosgrove, 40, 44, 59-60
Cox, Luc, 197-202
Crawford, Flt. Sgt., 1

'Doc', 101, 103, 117
Dowden, 1st Lt Max, 19*

'Ed', 101, 103, 117
Eisenhower, General, 96, 202

'Gen Man', the, 93, 101-2, 105-6
Georges, 110
Gigger, Flt. Sgt. D. J., 27, 55
Govaerts, Wim, 197, 202
Gray, Sqd. Ldr, 56, 57
Green, Dick, 131, 133

Greene, Flt. Sgt. W. J., 59

Haig, Sqd.Commander, D. D.,
44, 46
Hawson, Sgt. Bill, 16
Hitler, 98, 149, 150
Hodgkins, Sgt. F. O., 27, 55
Howatson, Capt., 138
Huijbrechts, Francis, 197-202

Jack, 93, 100
Jamieson, Flt. Sgt., R. D.W., 55

'Laughing Boy', 93
Leutenant, Julia, 110
Leverett, Cyril ('Lev'), 9*
Louis, Joe, 166

Margerison, Bette, 197-202
McCann, Jock, 132
McElroy, Gilbert ('Gib'), 9*
McMaster, F/O I. E., 40, 55
Middlebrook. Martin, 55
Middlemiss, Flt. Lt, 61
Mims, W/O C.L., 65
Moody, Frank, 11*

Nicholls, F/O T. M., 44, 55
Nuffield, Lord, 59

Owen, W/O J. D., 55

'Porky', 38, 60

Ray, 186, 188, 189
Reeves, Richard ('Dick'), 9*
Ridder, Mr and Mrs Martin, 200
Roscoe, P/O, 28, 30

'Sandy', 138
Sawyer, Sgt., 8
Scheire, Hermine, 91-4, 96-107, 201
Schmelling, Max, 166
Snoeys, Theresia, 198

'Taffy', 9*
Thompson, Pete, 131, 133, 140, 149, 177

Van Aperen, Arnold, 199-200

Van Dun, Arlette, 197
Vermeiren, Christ, 198-9
Vermeulin, Emilie, 81-2, 85-7, 202
Vermeulin, Marcel, 81-2, 85-7, 202
Vermeulin, Robert, 202

Wade, Fred, 9*
Waltky, John, 131, 160
Weepers, Dave, 19*
'Withacar', Mr, 93-5, 102, 105

* The only page numbers given for members of the crew are the initial pages on which biographical information appears.

The various ranks are not necessarily those held at the end of the war.

Index of Places

Aachen, 49, 125
Akzleug, 151
Antwerp, 82, 85, 88, 94, 96, 101, 107-8, 112, 117, 119, 197, 201
Aulnoye, 59

Bankau, 127, 152, 157
Berlin, 26, 40-41, 43, 55, 158
Besançon, 63
Beurich, 150-1
Binbrook, 26, 66
Blackburn, 194
Blyton, 11, 13-16, 157
Bovington, 52, 54
Brecht, 82
Bridlington 6,
Bristol Channel, 2-3
Brussels, 119-20, 124, 140, 191-2

Charleroi, 49
Cologne, 59, 97, 125
Constance, Lake, 63-4
Cosford, 192

Dieppe, 51
Doncaster, 19, 21
Dresden, 127, 151
Duisburg, 65, 66, 130
Dulag Luft, 125-6
Düsseldorf, 61

Elbe, River, 167, 177-8, 181, 187-8, 194
Elster, 181-2
Essen, 40, 55, 61

Falkenburg, 151
Frankfurt, 29, 34, 39-40, 55, 125-7
Friedrichshafen, 61-2

Goldberg, 151, 157

Hamburg, 141
'Happy Valley' (the Ruhr), 42
Hildesheim, 177, 191
Hoogstraten, 198-201

Jenkwitz, 151
Juteburg, 180

Karlsruhe, 61, 148, 151
Katowice, 141
Kelstern, 25-7, 29, 31, 45, 54, 58, 60, 65
Kirmington, 17
Konstadt, 145, 151
Kreuzburg, 127, 133, 144-5, 151

Lagenzeslau, 151
Lindholme, 19-20, 23
Little Chalfont, 53

London,
        St John's Wood, 5
Louth, 44, 47, 58
Luckenwalde, 157-61, 165, 169,
173, 175-6, 178, 182, 185
Ludford Magna, 26, 56
Mablethorpe, 25, 37, 56, 125,
128
Magdeburg, 167, 175-6, 180,
182, 188, 189-90
Maintenon, 61
Manchester, 15
Meir, 71, 83
Munich, 167

Nuremburg, 48, 50, 55-56

Oberusel, 126
Oder, River, 149

Padgate, 4
Pffaffendorf, 151
Porthcawl, 3
Parusnitz, 156

Ruhr, the, 42, 59, 65

Scheldt, River, 97, 109
Schweidnitz, 151
Sckonfield, 151
'Selsey Bill', 51
Sheppey, Isle of, 23
Silverstone, 52
Stalag 383, 132
Stalag Luft VII, 127, 132, 138,
143
Stammlager 111A, 158
Standorf, 151
Stormy Down, 1-4, 10, 52
Strechlen, 151
Stuttgart, 26, 50, 55

Whitchurch, 7-12
Winterfeld, 145, 148, 151

Wit-Hofken, 82, 202
Wittenberg, 181-2, 184-5, 187-9
Wolverhampton, 192

Zerbst, 187

Index of Planes

Avro Anson, 1, 2, 8, 36, 52

Dakota, 191
Dornier, 182

Flying Fortress, 46, 62, 97-8,
104, 142
Fiesler Storch, 141
FW190, 101, 182

Halifax, 11, 14, 19, 20, 22-3,
49-50, 101, 104
Halifax Mark 3, 36
HE111, 123

JU88, 34, 38, 43, 60, 101, 182

Lancaster, 11, 15-17, 19, 23-4,
26-7, 30-2, 35-7, 40-3, 45,
48-49, 52-3, 59-60, 64-68, 104,
182, 191-2, 197
Liberator, 104
Lightning, 173
Lysander, 80, 95

Martinet, 2, 3
ME 109, 47, 79, 101, 182
ME 110, 47-8, 101, 182

Spitfire, 14
Stormovick, 167
Stuka, 126

Thunderbolt, 173

Whitley, 8, 9, 11

Yak, 167

The author at Max Dowden's graveside near Antwerp, 2003.

Appendix

FRED WADE (pilot) – died a few years ago in his native Wales.

CYRIL LEVERETT (navigator) – died in 1983.

MAX DOWDEN (pilot) – buried on the outskirts of Antwerp.

FRANK MOODY (engineer) – buried on the outskirts of Antwerp. He and Max Dowden lie next but one to each other.

DAVE WEEPERS (navigator) – died shortly after the war's end, in Canada.

ARTHUR BRICKENDEN (bomb aimer) – died some thirty years ago in Canada.

RICHARD REEVES (wireless operator) – died a few years ago in Truro, Cornwall.

GILBERT McELROY (rear gunner) – fighting fit in Ottawa, Canada. We keep in regular contact and tell lies to each other. (In 1977, as a direct result of Martin Middlebrook's book, *The Nuremburg Raid*, Dick Reeves, Gib McElroy, Cyril Leverett and I enjoyed an out-of-this-world reunion after not having seen each other for thirty-two years.)

HERMINE SCHEIRE (Belgian underground) – married an English soldier but died within a few years of the war's end.

MARCEL VERMEULEN AND EMILIE (Belgian underground) – married each other and died some years ago. I met his son on my visit to Belgium.

PAULA CAVEIRNE (Belgian underground) – I have been unable to trace Paula.

JULIE LEUTENANT (Belgian underground) – believed to have been killed in an American air raid.